Thoughts of the Soul

Elizabeth Slingsby

A Self Help & Inner Awareness Book

2016
Copyright © 2016 Elizabeth Slingsby
All Rights Reserved
Title ID: 6749796
ISBN-13: 978-1540659057

Introduction

I do not take full credit for the wisdom you will find between these pages, for I did not intentionally set out to put it down on paper. It was rather a case of it getting hold of my attention, and then refusing to let go.

The original format was quite different, but that is another story, and it was only when I eventually sat down to write the book in its present form, I realised my soul had been suggesting that I write it for thirty years or more. I had simply not been listening fully as it spoke to me.

When you are searching for clarity around where you wish your Soul Path to take you, there deep within is the simple and yet profound wisdom that knows without doubt what course of action will produce the outcome your soul is seeking.

The value and power of the insights in the book lies in its simplicity and ability to re-open your connection to your soul and its profound wisdom.

It is the natural wisdom of the Universe, which is always within and around you, but which can temporarily elude you in times of stress and confusion. The insights here will remind you of the simple truths that underpin your different life experiences

For most of your time here on earth, you may tend to forget that your physical body is effectively a car you are travelling in, and that your soul is really the driver. In short, you may spend large amounts of your time relegating your soul to a passenger seat. This is like trying to drive a car with one hand tied behind your back.

So, you can go through this life with one hand tied behind your back; or you can accept that you are stronger and wiser at the level of your soul, than you are at the level of your physical or mental aspects which you connect with on a daily basis.

I have to confess to being as guilty as anyone else, of forgetting on occasion that I have this wisdom within me, and adopting the 'one hand tied behind my back' method of dealing with issues that arise in my life, before remembering that help is there if I will only open myself up to it.

Within these pages is an opportunity to consider what your Soul might be saying to you if you were to stop and listen. I believe (from my limited human perspective of course!) that the purpose in drawing my attention to this wisdom was to make it available to those of you who have reached a particular stage on the path of your soul through this life.

I believe this is the stage where you are ready to start the process of remembering that you are more than the 'vehicle', and allowing the 'driver' to take over when things get too difficult for you to manage 'with one hand tied behind your back'.

The complete book is comprised of five smaller books each of which offer insight relevant to various aspects of this life and to the path of life itself that we are walking with our soul.

I offer my grateful thanks to those who helped me to bring this book to completion.

Thank you to my husband Jack for his patience during the seemingly endless time I have spent at my computer, often into the early hours; and all those friends who believed in me sometimes more than I believed in myself. Their support has been invaluable in so many ways.

Finally my heartfelt thanks to Kate Williams who in the process of creating a completely new website for me has also designed the new 2017 cover for the book.

Contents

Contents

Contents

Contents

Contents

Book One
Concerning the Path of life

The thoughts expressed here concern the stages of your Soul path through life from birth to a state of awareness. This awareness can be achieved in early life or take a whole lifetime, and so the first thoughts I share with you here relate to to some major issues and goals you may seek guidance on as you encounter them in the course of your life.

Concerning The Path of Life - Chapter One

I am your Soul

I am your soul; the deeper aspect of your consciousness; and I have come to earth to follow my path through your life. Although you may not be aware of this I am your essence, a vital and relevant part of your present identity. I am your universal connection with all that is, and a quiet but powerful sense within you that you are more than your human physical condition would lead you to believe.

When you use the expression "soulful" it may not be a direct reference to me. You might simply be referring to something you perceive as profound and otherwise difficult to describe. Eyes are often described as "soulful" and as "the windows of the soul". The reason for this is that most of the feeling and true expression shown in your face and through your eyes reflects my presence within you.

You can smile with your mouth, but if the smile does not reach your eyes it will appear false, almost a grimace. You may say that eyes light up, but they have no physical means of becoming illuminated, so what does this expression really mean? It means a smile that reaches the eyes reflects the presence of your soul – spirit – essence – the divine life force within you, or whatever else you may wish to call me. You are thus describing that within you, or someone else, which makes you so much more than your physical body.

Even those who say they do not believe in the concept of a soul often use this word "soul" to try and describe my intangible essence, which they sense but are unable to come to terms with or explain. I am not present only in your physicality, for I am eternal and so much more than this life you are living here and now. I am an intrinsic part of you and will experience and share with you as you live this life, your joy, sadness, and all of the other emotions you experience. When you need reassurance and strength it is time to reach down into the quiet depths of your being, for that is where you will find me.

If you fear there are experiences which can destroy me you may let go of that fear. The expression "soul-destroying" simply relates to those times when your faith, confidence and hope become dimmed; for I cannot be destroyed by human experiences.

I am a part of the eternal plan and at the allotted time I will move on to another stage of my journey and perhaps change form, but I will not, unlike your physical body, be destroyed or cease to exist. Having experienced this life to its end, my energy and soul consciousness and your human consciousness will return home together. There we will take whatever healing is needed, and rest a little before continuing the journey.

The wonder of this soul path experience is that once my path through this life is completed, and your physical form is no longer able to sustain **our** consciousness and

our experiences, the veil that presently lies between your human memory and my soul memory will be drawn back. All will again become clear and we will merge and become as one.

Then in time (as you would understand time) I will plan the next stage of my soul path journey; with the benefit of your life experiences and with the aspect of my soul consciousness that you have become. I can tell you that you would do yourself a greater kindness if you were to cherish me and keep your connection with me open, rather than to dismiss me because someone you consider to be more knowledgeable insists that I do not exist.

Nor will you benefit from allowing our connection to lessen, simply because the way you live is focussed away from me and on the material world. For when this happens communication between us fades, and I must wait until your experiences bring you back to awareness of me, when we will be able to commune once again. The veil drawn at birth between your human consciousness and my soul memory is a normal and natural part of being human. Nevertheless, at times of need you can draw back that veil, in order to seek the guidance and support appropriate for you to complete my path, (your soul path) through this life and its many experiences.

When you first seek me out you may find I am elusive as a visual image, for I am more about feeling than seeing, about energy rather than form, as are so many other intangible aspects of your life. Human beings often use the expression "seeing is believing" for this is the nature of being human; namely to need physical, visual and tangible proof that a thing exists. When seeking me be aware that there are more ways of seeing than with your physical vision.

If you wish to visualise me you may find it helpful to imagine you are looking at a model of planet earth, and that you are able to open the top of this globe and see inside. When you do this you will encounter a dazzling white light shining from within, spreading wider and wider as it escapes outward to fill the universe. This light glowing from the centre of the globe is like the spiritual light which radiates from the centre of your being. This is the light which brings you to life and carries you onward.

As you visualise this image you may also become aware of the explosion of energy with which the light escapes from within the globe. It is a light so radiantly bright that it illuminates everything around it. This is my light which nothing can prevent from rising upward out of the shadows within, to bring me into your awareness and to help make you stronger and wiser when the time is right.

You will at times sense this light even before your conscious search for me begins. Before you can clearly identify it, you will feel its healing power as it flows through and around you. As you continue to observe it, enjoy its warm caress pouring through you, making you feel stronger, calmer, and more at peace with your world. Imagine the light growing until it shines from you like a beacon and surrounds you with the protective embrace of your soul.

This power to be – to give – to love – to forgive – to

guide, and to be an example to others of what they can achieve, is woven through every fibre of your being. All you need to do is acknowledge its presence and guidance in your life; for when you and I are as one you will have the strength and the wisdom of many.

Look for this light in the eyes of those you communicate with, and know that when it is dimmed through fear or anger, their own soul connection is in need of healing.

Each human being needs to instigate the quest which takes them on the journey to find their own soul connection. Only when they have taken that first step of having the intention to do so, can another help them to heal and strengthen their soul awareness.

Remember this: I have brought you here and will take the essence of you on through eternity, so listen now in the silence to what I say to you, for I will always lift you to your highest potential.

Concerning The Path of Life - Chapter Two

Somewhere in the Ancient Past

From a human perspective it is sometimes difficult to fully understand the concept of time. However, in knowing that my consciousness within you reaches back through the mists of what you would call the past, you may begin to view time   from a different perspective. You can see it in a purely mathematical and linear way, past followed by present followed by future, and it will seem straightforward and uncomplicated.

If you consider it from the wider perspective of your various life experiences, you will know that you experience different periods of time in varying ways, and they can seem to be longer or shorter depending on which human experience you are having. If what you see as a specific time frame can seem to contract or expand, perhaps the past present and future are not as rigidly placed as you might believe. If this is so, you may begin to sense that time is not as linear as logic and rationale would suggest. Still, from a human perspective it may feel less complicated to view time in a linear way, as past followed by present leading to future.

When you use the expression "ancient past" you will usually be referring to a time that existed long before you were born. I should remind you here that human beings who have lived in that ancient past were also my partners and vehicles for different stages of my journey, and so we are all connected.

Somewhere in the ancient past I began my journey through creation. The beginning of this life we are living here and now was simply the starting point of a further stage in that journey. Many of the souls following their paths here today will have lived in a time before this life, a time that goes back through eternity and into the ancient past. We have gained new experiences in each of those lives, and my soul experiences are held within me at the "soul" level of your being. It is this ongoing journey of your soul that you may begin to perceive as what you might call "past lives".

You may see the past as something which is gone forever and irretrievable, but the past is never gone. It is part of the present and will be part of the future. The ancient past from those lives before this life is a part of the fabric of **our** ongoing existence, and it is held deep within me as part of **our** present and **our** future.

When you look at the past you can recall and have regrets, keep in mind that each significant event or occurrence in your life (and sometimes an event or occurrence you consider to be insignificant) has a purpose. As a human being you have free will to decide whether it will have a positive or negative place in this life and its experiences.

Consider also the part of my past you will be unable to recall, the past I bring with me into this life I share with you. This is my ancient past, and locked inside it are the lessons I have learned and experiences that can help us both with this current stage of the soul path journey. When you focus more fully on this, you may find stirring inside of you knowledge that cannot be explained within the framework of the life you are living here and now. If this is your experience, you are starting to turn the key that will open the door to knowledge locked inside you at my deepest level.

You will know there are structures which have stood through many centuries of earth time. There are the pyramids in Egypt, many ancient temples, and the enormous standing stones which can be found dotted around the planet. Stonehenge in the South of England and the gigantic stone statues on the Polynesian Easter Island are also examples of this type of structure. There they stand solitary and undisturbed, observing the centuries of time passing by and yet remaining within each of those centuries.

Now imagine you are solitary and undisturbed, walking alongside such giant stones that have stood for so many centuries. Then imagine the stones are no longer there and you see only trees, grass, and sky. This gives you a feeling of peace and stillness, even though the scene offers nothing to indicate where you are or what point in the past or the future you have arrived at.

Now look to your right where you see a stream, and walk along the bank of that stream. Think of the stream as a time line and look ahead to the future where you see a tiny figure in the distance. Then turn and look backward to the past where you also see someone walking toward you. You are now becoming aware that past and future are all part of the same journey and cannot be separated. The person ahead sees you as being in the past and the person behind sees you as being in the future. If you turned to walk in the opposite direction it would seem that the person who was previously ahead would now be in the past and the person who was behind would now be in the future.

The time line is endless and without beginning; the ancient past is simply a part of the eternal circle of that time line, and the present is a speck even less than a grain of sand in a desert. To be able see this life and the nature of time from such a perspective is a precious ability to have.

If you visualise the structures I have mentioned, which were constructed in the ancient past, it may almost seem as if you are gazing into a portal through the mists of time, and directly into that time so very long ago. However, what you are looking at is still in existence on earth today in its original form, even if it is showing signs of material ageing. This is the past brought forward into the present, and it will no doubt still be standing in the future. For what is now the future becomes the present within a moment, and the past within the moment after that one.

As these structures were created in a time you see as the ancient past long before your present life, you may feel a sense of detachment when looking at them. For others who observe them it may be that they evoke a sense of connection somewhere deep within their being. Although you may remain untouched by some of these images I have mentioned; there will be others from the ancient past with which you may feel an inexplicable sense of familiarity or connection. These will be from the path of my ancient past, and those experiences will be stored in your deeper soul consciousness, affecting your every thought and decision even without you being aware that this is happening.

While these structures are considered ancient treasures, your own ancient treasures are my ancient past experiences and my memories of them. Perhaps it is time for you to become an Archaeologist and to dig deeper to where your ancient treasures of wisdom are buried within me. when you make this decision to explore my past life memories you can choose to carry the experiences you have recalled from my ancient past as a burden in the form of unidentified unease. Alternatively you can acknowledge the value of those experiences, and learn to identify with your deepest instincts what it may be wise to avoid this time around. If you make the second of these choices, you will empower yourself to bring to the forefront of your mind (when they can be useful to you) the previous decisions that were life enhancing. If you do so it may feel this is something from within your everyday consciousness that you simply 'know' for no apparent reason. However, if the sense of it is strong enough you will probably make use of it, and find you are able to draw real value from my ancient past, as well as the past within our current life experience.

Learn to trust the wisdom I impart to you. Listen to your heart and to your intuition, for this is your soul speaking to you. I am now stirring our memories of ancient past, to guide and support you on this path of the soul we walk together.

Concerning The Path of Life - Chapter three

Into the World of Sleep

When this path we walk together is ended, I will "return home" and will be wiser for having completed this stage of my journey. This is a journey for which I am truly grateful, for you will have carried me through every step of the way from the moment of your birth to your very last breath. Your deeper consciousness will have absorbed and learned from each and every one of your life experiences and it will become another aspect of me, so we will make that journey "home" together as one.

When I made the decision to enter a new life as a human being, I knew that I must fall into a sleep that would temporarily veil my soul memory from your consciousness. This helped you to start this life as all new born infants do, with complete innocence and an open mind. By the time of your birth I was awake again and I became a part of who you are here and now in this life. However, my soul memory would remain beyond your human awareness, and so for you this seemed to be the beginning of your journey as that new born infant, and this is how it appeared to be for those whose lives you entered.

Similarly, when you are awake you may believe it is your only "real" state of consciousness. While resting your physical body and waking mind in sleep, it can seem as if you are in a truly unconscious state. However, if you look in a dictionary for the definition of this word "unconscious" you will probably find words like lifeless, and unaware, and these descriptions would be misleading. Sleep is not a time of inactivity. It is simply another state of consciousness where a different kind of activity is taking place. You would be right in thinking it is a time to rest and repair both physically and mentally, but (contrary to some of those dictionary definitions) this is a time for us that is overflowing with life and filled with awareness. It is a time of connectedness between your human consciousness and my soul consciousness; and a time for the layers of your mind to expand and explore.

During this life you will fall into many periods of sleep, and at these times you will be more in touch with the deeper levels of your being and we will be more closely connected.   Within these hours of sleep you will undertake journeys into the different regions of your consciousness, and you will be able to access the universal knowledge held in me.

These are sleep states where you leave the world of science, technology and the material behind you, and the portals of time and space are opened to you. Here in this sleeping state when the different dimensions become accessible, the expanded levels of your consciousness are able to guide you.

This is where the veil drawn over your soul-memory at birth is temporarily lifted, revealing my store of memories and knowledge. Here you can reach out to me and remember your connection with the universe. Your sleep experiences may sometimes be so vivid that you feel they cross the boundary between sleeping and waking, still being present when you do awake. They may feel powerful and remain with you for as long as they are needed, whether it is a day a year or even the rest of this life.

Those sleep experiences which remain strongly in your waking memory and stay there for extended periods of time, are not the simple mechanics of your brain dealing with the issues of the day. They are your connection with the truly powerful aspect of your being. Here in sleep you travel to a level of your consciousness where the barriers of human logic and rationale (so powerfully at work in your waking life) are removed, and we can travel together. This is when you can share with me and experience more fully, the universal aspect of our journey through time and space. This is a journey where different dimensions are opened to both of us when the barriers of your waking mind are taking their rest.

If you wish to visualise this realm of sleep it may be helpful to think of the relaxed and drowsy feeling which overtakes you when you are about to fall asleep. It could be described as being wrapped in a soft blanket of soothing energy, or perhaps having a veil drawn across your consciousness, so that you begin to gently lose your connection with the everyday world around you.

Picture that veil and draw it to one side with your hand, and you will find yourself looking into the world of sleep. Watch the veil gently dissolve into nothingness, and as it does so it reveals a doorway filled by a warm golden light. You walk through the doorway to find yourself surrounded by a library of more books than you could ever imagine. As you gaze at these books you become aware that here you will find the wisdom of the ages, and the answers to all of your questions.

This is when you begin to realise that all of this wisdom, knowledge and guidance, is here waiting for you to access it each time you sweep aside the veil and slip into a state of sleep. The drowsiness will be gone, and you will find yourself in a beautiful world of light, colour and movement, a world where the universal level of your consciousness begins to stretch and then to awaken. Here you will discover a fullness of experience that your everyday consciousness is unaware of.

Consider those memories from your sleep experiences (what you might call dreams) when you bring them back with you to your waking state. If you compare them to the experiences of your every day consciousness you will no doubt feel it is a place which can seem "larger than life". This is because from this sleep level of your being you can visit other worlds and other dimensions, where all of the wisdom of the universe is available, and you can if you truly wish to; find all of the answers to all of your questions.

You may believe your conscious mind has been dormant at every level while you slept, because you are unable to recall at will what has taken place during that sleeping state. However, your recall will be there as needed, only at the right time and in the right situation. It will however be strengthened, when you acknowledge that this other level of your life experience is taking place while you sleep.

So if you seek answers take your questions into sleep with you, and offer them to me here in these deeper levels of your being where your connection with the universe is open. I am here waiting for you to offer your questions to me so that I can answer them or to help you find those answers somewhere in space and time.

If you begin to contemplate your sleeping hours in the way I have described, you will find when next you slip into the state of sleep the veil will be so much easier to sweep aside, and the door to those wonderful dimensions will be so much more widely held open for you.

Concerning The Path of Life - Chapter Four

Freedom From Denial

I have said that at the time of your birth my memories from previous lives were taken into safekeeping by the universe, and there is good reason for this. If I were to come into this life of yours (or any of the other human lives I have taken part in) with those memories freely available to both of us, there would be little for me to learn from your human experiences.

You could perhaps compare this to entering a classroom to attend a lesson with the answer book in your hand. No thinking or working out would be necessary, the purpose of the lesson would have been disposed of. There would in short, have been no need to attend for the lesson at all. You could simply refer to the book containing all of the knowledge you needed.

Still, while you would have the knowledge from information you have accessed, you would not have had the experience of gaining that knowledge. It therefore follows that I also would not have had the experience, for you are my key to the experiences which become a part of my journey, and which expand me again and again.

It is for this reason I have come here, to be a part of you and to live within the human condition as your soul. I do this in order to fulfil a further stage in the journey of my soul path. For the duration of this life this path is also your soul path. The physical, mental and emotional aspects of you help me to continue my journey and to expand my experiences. Whilst we journey together I am your spiritual aspect, and you are my physical aspect.

Functioning only from the perspective of the human condition is limiting; for you are in a situation which does not allow you to access with ease the experience, wisdom and strength I have already gained in previous lives. You will see I do not say these valuable resources cannot be accessed, only that it would require a greater effort and focus on your part to do so, but this is exactly as it should be. This means that for most of the time you can only work on the basis of what you have experienced since the day of your birth into this current life. It is almost but not quite, as though each human life (to use an expression of the modern age) is a 'stand-alone unit', as it functions in its own right.

When the connection between us is strong, you as a human being are able to function in harmonious partnership with the experiences of my previous lives. You may find this difficult to understand; because you will usually be unaware this is happening until the experience for which we have attended the lesson has been gained.

You could perhaps describe it as the pieces of a puzzle coming together to complete the picture. This lack of awareness I speak of will cause you to be in denial of your universal nature and of me. Such unawareness will also cause you to find yourself in denial about certain issues you encounter in this life, and these are issues that

I am also experiencing through you.

If you are unable to understand something in this life or you find it painful to look at, you may close your mind to it and retreat into a state of denial. This can cause you to suffer a form of blindness to beauty and universal truth, for you are in denial of my presence as an essential part of you. This means you will also be in denial of the souls of other human beings. It is a challenge of my soul path that your inability to call upon those previous memories and experiences will bring you into this state of denial of your place in creation, and the magnificent and eternal nature of our combined being.

When this denial is present in your everyday consciousness be assured that it will limit how you view the universe and your place in it, and will cause you to encounter a greater degree of difficulty on this path of the soul that we walk together.

It is a paradox of this life that whilst this state of denial appears to be counter-productive in the process of learning and progress on our soul path, it is just another part of the soul path experience. It is more a practical exercise in remembering and retrieving from me those memories "from the deep", and using them as a tool to handle the challenges of this current life. As a result of facing these challenges and overcoming them you are then able to see the beauty within and around you.

In times gone by (measured in human terms) it was seen as madness to dispute that the earth was flat, and so rather than be seen as mad, many human beings accepted the belief held by those with the loudest and most powerful voices. This limited perception of the planet was upheld for quite some time, until some brave soul was able to help its human counterpart see that there was in fact another dimension to this beautiful planet we live on.

It is sometimes necessary to turn and face what you do not understand, and have confidence that you and everything around you may after all have other dimensions. These dimensions are additional to those you can experience with your five human senses, and I can tell you they will not cease to exist just because you deny them.

When the time is right awareness will start to grow within you in respect of your true nature and purpose in life. As this awareness is triggered my deep memories will start to become useful to you. At first this may occur unconsciously, but as the connection between us grows stronger you will start to knowingly, and then naturally, retrieve my deeper memories and find freedom from denial. This is when you will begin to replace difficulty with understanding and have less need in your life for denial of any kind.

Even when this awareness comes only toward the end of your human life it is still valid to your consciousness and mine; for as I have said, when this life is ended we will leave this physical body so that it may be returned into the earth. Then we will be as one and our journey will continue.

In order to recognise this principle of denial more clearly

it may help you to look into a mirror at your own image. If you then turn away from the mirror, and raise your hand as if to put up a barrier between yourself and the image in the mirror, you will soon realise that in taking this stance of pushing it away you are not changing anything. You may not be looking at it in the mirror, but the image is still there.

For instance if you heard a knock at your door and opened it to see a friend standing there and then closed it again, you would be unable to see your friend but he or she would still be standing there. From the human perspective you cannot see through the barrier of the door, just as you cannot see the essence of who you are and of the whole of creation, when viewed from behind the three dimensional barrier of logic and rationale.

Now look again at your image in the mirror and see a brilliant white light shining out from the centre of your being. You may find you recognise the image of yourself but not this light shining from within. It is not a part of yourself that you have been aware of, and so it may feel your eyes are playing tricks, for you are in denial of what you see. Turn away and close your eyes, and realise that the light still burns strongly within you.

 This is my eternal flame; the flame of your soul. It is not unusual or unreal; it is your power, your strength, and the essence of your eternal nature. To deny this light would be to deny your own existence.

When you are able turn quietly inward, reach into my light, and hold out your hand in acceptance, you will no longer be in a state of denial. You will be ready to walk out of the darkness and into the light.

Concerning The Path of Life - Chapter Five

Weariness of the Soul

When you wish to see what time it is, you will usually look at the face of a clock. While you see the time on its face you will know that the clock also has an inner mechanism, and this must be properly maintained if it is to continue to fulfil its function, which is to show you what the time of day or night is.

In looking at the outward aspect or face of yourself and denying my existence as the inner mechanism within your being, you are failing to be guided and supported as you would be if you allowed me to participate more fully in your experience of this life. Whenever you are in denial of your spirituality you are unable to use your inner mechanism, namely the strength of the universe always available through your connection to me. To continue in this state of denial will eventually drain your energy and cause you to experience a deep sense of weariness. You could compare this effect to a time when the clock has not been rewound and it stops working altogether.

This is a weariness you might feel when carrying a heavy burden and rejecting an offer to share the weight. For to do so is like attempting to carry the burden with one hand tied behind your back. You will be aware that the burden I describe here is symbolic of any challenge or difficulty you encounter in this life, and I also am aware that there will be certain times in your life when these words will have greater meaning for you than at others. For instance you may experience such a feeling after a hard day's work, a battle of wills or an emotionally traumatic experience.

When your body is tired, your mind does not work well. If your mind is tired you have no will to use your body, and if your emotions are over taxed you may also feel a lack of energy. All of these can be remedied with rest and loving care, for yourself and for others who may suffer from these kinds of fatigue. But, there will also be times when you are unable to find words to describe the weariness you experience, for it is a feeling that gives you a sense of your life energy almost draining away. When you are burdened with a weariness for which you know there is no physical or clinical source, it is time to reflect on my presence within you; a time to consider the possibility that I am fading into the darkest corners of your being from lack of use in your life. In other words you may find that we are both suffering from weariness of the soul.

For this weariness there is no remedy that you can eat or drink. You could stay in bed for the rest of this life and you would not be refreshed or revitalised. You may look at the sun and moon, the stars in the heavens, a new born child, or the miracles of nature in spring each year. If you are feeling a weariness that I am experiencing because of your increasing disconnection from my presence within you, the weight of it does not lift so easily. You may feel as though someone has placed a heavy weight upon your heart, and a film across your eyes which dims the brightness of whatever beauty you may behold. Or you may feel unable to share in the joy and laughter of others, lacking the emotional energy to feel joyful or optimistic.

When you believe you are just this lone individual standing in a sea of humanity, whose efforts can reach no further than the limits of your logical mind and physical body however hard you try to surpass them, you will reach those human limits and go no further, and the weariness may engulf you.

In order to heal such weariness, you need to enlist the greatest source of help in existence, the source of creation deep within that I am connected to at all times. You will need to turn around from your denial and acknowledge that you (and all others) are more than you can possibly perceive when you look only from a human viewpoint.

So step back from how this weariness would feel as a personal experience. Reflect for a moment whether you have on your path through this life, encountered at least one other human being in whose company you began to feel as though your energy was diminishing. Their eyes would have lacked sparkle and their shoulders and the lines of their face would have somehow had an appearance of following a downward curve. Although you may not have been able to see it with your physical eye, there may have been a sense of "greyness" about such individuals, as though their vital life force was depleted; and all of this without any condition physical or otherwise to explain it. This is when you are seeing weariness that goes beyond the physical and reaches down into the depths of human understanding. It is not the feeling one would get from a hard day's work for it is deeper and more overwhelming, although it does produce the same level of exhaustion that results from heavy physical toil.

Now take your focus to your own heart centre and picture a light shining inside of you, as though it is glowing gently within a darkened room. Go to the window of that room and open the curtains to allow in the daylight. As that daylight floods into the room, watch the light grow and become brighter as the inner light and the daylight are merged. I am this inner light awaiting connection with the outer daylight of your everyday awareness. As you begin to acknowledge me I will grow and shine more brightly, pouring my strength through every layer of your being. You will feel my brilliance dissolving the weariness and helping you to glow with vitality and enthusiasm for life. This source of energy is here whenever you need it. My power and brilliance are activated by your simple act of acknowledgement of and reaching toward my presence within you and asking for help.

The cure for such a malaise will be found in the quiet and undisturbed time with me you may often deny yourself in today's busy world. However, if you consider the state of weariness I have described, you will be acutely aware that you do not wish, nor do you need to succumb to this weariness of the soul.

Remember always that we are as one. When you halt the battle between body and soul we can work in harmony with each other, and you will release yourself from all of the signs of this weariness I have described. This is when you will once again become light and cheerful, bright and filled with vitality.

Allow yourself some tranquil and undisturbed time with me and with the creative forces of the universe, and find the courage to see this other dimension that is your soul. You will then find that I become refreshed and vibrant once again, and the weariness will also fall away from you. This is when our work can continue.

Concerning The Path of Life - Chapter Six

Healed by Your Act of Relaxation

If you wish to recover from the weariness I have spoken of it is essential you find the space and time for relaxation and peacefulness in your life.

Universal awareness requires you to accept much that you will find difficult to understand when viewed from a human perspective. But, in resisting this level of awareness you are continuing to fight the natural laws and the natural flow of life.

Nevertheless, somewhere along the path there will be a fading of the veil placed over your memory when you awoke from that sleep of the soul, and we were born into this life. When this fading starts to occur it is the first sign that you are beginning to release your state of denial. There is no secret to finding this release, for everyone has the key. This key can be described in a single word and that word is "relaxation". I cannot overstate the importance of complete relaxation, and its effect in helping you to achieve this empowering release.

You will no doubt be aware that there is a need to find time and space for relaxation within the structure of your life; but, you may not be aware how sluggish and stagnant your energies become when you remain in a state of tension for too long. This sluggish and stagnant condition within your energy system is what happens when you ignore your deeper needs, and neglect to take time out in order to experience a good level of relaxation.

If you do not relax fully on a regular basis, you will be unable to release the old stale energies of fear, pain, anger, frustration, resentment and many others of that nature. These will inevitably have accumulated in your system while you were dealing with the issues that have arisen in your life. Failing to release these negative energies will cause them to become embedded in you, and the need for you to consciously relax will grow more important even vital for your wellbeing.

The process of relaxation will help in the release of those stale energies, thereby creating space for new revitalising energies the universe is waiting to pour into you as a physical being, and into me as your soul.

Know that you will need to grant permission for the release of those unhealthy energies and acceptance into your being of new revitalising energies. Furthermore you will need to do so with a sense of deep conviction, not as an automatic exercise which simply appears to do what is needed. In short there is a need to be genuine and sincere.

When such relaxation and release take place you instinctively and naturally strengthen the connection between us. In allowing yourself to relax completely you are starting to give your permission for this transaction to be completed. So, if you really want to live your life joyfully and to its full capacity, and to make room for the fresh energies which will enable you to do so, remember the key is to relax completely.

As the doorway opened by this relaxation empowers you to naturally release negativity from your system, you are able to move toward new understanding of our place in creation, and the eternal nature of our being as we walk this soul path together. This is when we can see our way forward as one, when the dark clouds of negativity have been dissolved by the power of your relaxation, and cleared away by the release which ensues; for this is when the process of re-learning shines new daylight into the dark corners of your being and into my soul essence.

If you have truly perfected the art of relaxation the process of release will occur effortlessly. The re-learning of your universal aspect and re-connection with all that is will begin in earnest. You will start to feel more alive and your energy will increase; for when you have learned the importance of such relaxation, your experience of life will shift from darkness and monotone to lightness and colour.

I would ask you to visualise the following process which illustrates the essence of how relaxation can be of help to you. Begin by taking your focus to your shoulders and neck, and allow any tension to gently dissolve. This is a tension you will have been holding there far more than you realise or would care to admit. You will probably have held it for so long that you have become unaware of it and have come to perceive it as a natural part of how you feel. If you find the tension difficult to release from your neck, picture an ice cube melting under a hot sun and imagine your tension is flowing in the same way as the ice becomes water and flows.

Now imagine you are looking at an unlit candle sitting on a candle stick, and see that the room around you is growing darker with no other means of lighting. The candle is cold stiff and rigid and has no usefulness in its present form. Now you notice that while the candle was being created it accumulated several pieces of debris which are now solidified within the wax. You can see they are no use to the candle, and will only detract from its attractiveness to those who watch it burning. Light the candle and you see that the warmth of flame starts to soften and mellow the wax. As this happens the debris is released from the softening candle. Even more importantly this candle now lights the room and allows you to see what you need to see.

Here we have the principle of relaxation. Relax (the wax) release (the debris) and re-learn (what has been hidden by the darkness). This re-learning of who you truly are is what will follow when you allow yourself to relax with me completely on a regular basis, and to release from your being the debris of negative energy and experiences which no longer serve your well being.

You will remember the importance of this advice when you notice the healing effect upon you if you allow yourself to relax fully, if only for a moment or two. You will start to feel the tension flowing out of your system like the ice cube melting in the sun. In true relaxation you regain your sense that life can be good, as the blinkers formed from the build up of negative energy that shut out the good and the beautiful around you fall away.

That first vital step of deep relaxation enables you to go through the healing process of release, and to raise your energies to a level at which you can re-learn the soul wisdom held within you.

When life becomes ever more challenging and the tensions within you become so tangible that they cause you discomfort and unease, it is time to stand back, take a long deep breath, and let it out in a sigh. Then slowly and softly let the muscles in your neck relax, and make a decision that you will free yourself from these tensions at the earliest opportunity.

Be aware that relaxation does not only occur only when you become inert; it can be achieved in movement which is slow and flowing. This type of movement helps the process of allowing the tensions to flow out of your system and back into the universe around you where they can be healed by nature; and you can be healed by your act of relaxation.

It is the conscious act of relaxation and the process of allowing it to fill your heart, mind, body and soul, which allows all these aspects of you to be in harmony with each other. So begins the process of renewal which will enable you and me to move forward on the pathway ahead through this life.

This is not a chore or a challenge I offer you, it is an opportunity to breathe freely, to be revitalised, to be healed, and to regain your sense of purpose and your love of life. I will simply wait for you to understand how important this process of relaxation is, so that we can communicate more easily and the journey can continue.

Concerning The Path of Life - Chapter Seven

Stepping into the Flow

When you have conquered the art of relaxation, your awareness of the importance of flow in all things will have increased. You will know that it is the nature of air, water, and other liquids and gases to flow, and you may also be aware of their presence around and within you. However, you may not be aware that all of the energies of the universe also flow constantly around and within you, for it cannot be any other way. Rivers flow, the movements of dancers flow, the notes of music flow, the drapes of velvet flow, the paint from an artist's brush flows across the canvas, time flows, and on and on and on. In short, life in its deeper and wider sense flows endlessly. The whole of creation is an infinite flow of dancing energy, of which we are all a part.

If you have found yourself in denial of a connection between you and all things universal or soul related, it is good to remember that when you or anyone else gives or receives in any way the action of flow is occurring. This is a flow intentionally activated by an individual or a number of individuals, and as everything is energy which flows constantly, it does not matter whether the giving and receiving involves solid material items or other kinds of energy; flow is still occurring.

This flow can be a gift which passes from one person to

another or a helping hand that offers a flow of positive energy in the form of assistance. It can be information that flows from one person to another and even this can come in many forms, from guidance or teaching given and received, to the pleasure and pain we all experience in this life, which also flows between and around us.

Any thought word or action is a form of flow, and this flow can be powerfully uplifting and therapeutic, or it can be powerfully painful and damaging. Choose carefully your thoughts words and deeds therefore, and be aware of the flow you are creating as you think then speak then act. This guidance applies whether the flow you create is material or experiential. For it is all a part of that magnificent universal dance, and when one dancer is out of step the other dancers are affected. It is thus beneficial to both of us – you the human being and I the soul being - to dance with the flow of life in step with each other, creating a harmonious flow within between and around us.

It is necessary to allow the flow of energies between the universe and the whole of your being to happen naturally, without trying to control it or keep it as you believe it ought to be. If you sense that the energies around and within you are not flowing freely, look at what may have become outdated in your life and allow yourself to let it go. When you can do this you will be like the dancer who finds his or her rhythm, and is once more in step with their dance and the dance of those around them. You will realign with the universal flow, and access the powerful benefits of universal energy.

When energy of any kind flows away from you naturally, it is simply moving to another dimension of the Universe, there to be cleansed and then to fulfil a new purpose elsewhere. This is not a loss, for it is replaced by fresh energy which is so much more relevant to your current situation. If you can remember this you will understand why *at those times when you feel the need to control every aspect of your life, it is important to be able to follow the flow rather than to fight against it.*

When you can summon up the courage to go with the flow, you will be amazed at the increased level of support the universe and its creative forces bring your way. This guidance and support will continue to move into your everyday awareness as it flows from the universe and my vast store of universal knowledge and experience deep within you. As a result you will find the right path when dealing with the issues you encounter in life, and once again you will share the flow of life with me so that we can complete this soul path in harmony.

If you feel a need to remind yourself of the universal flow and your place within it, look around you at the beauties of nature. You only need to stand by a mountain stream to see evidence of this, for the mountains flow down toward the valley and the streams follow them at an ever increasing rate of flow as they journey toward the rivers and then the seas. As they flow into the seas the tides then flow out toward the oceans and in again toward the shore in the natural rhythm of life.

Imagine yourself now standing by such a mountain stream, knowing that if you wish to achieve the progress you are seeking you will need to reach the bottom of the valley. Perhaps you now realise you are uncertain how to get down there. Pause for a moment and take note of the natural shapes of the mountain and the stream flowing down its side, and this will be a reminder of how you can learn from nature about "going with the flow".

Look again at the stream flowing down the hill. You may realise that if you step into the water and relax into the flow of that stream, it will take you exactly where you need to go. Now think of whatever choices you are finding difficult to make in life and picture yourself stepping into the stream of the universal flow and allowing those natural forces to carry you to your destination. This is the flow of life and it will take you to the next stage of your path, sometimes directly and at great speed, sometimes slowly and gently meandering like a mountain stream. When you are able to trust in its deep natural wisdom and sense of direction it will always take you where you need to go.

This is when you will find that life is your friend not your enemy. While it may not always lead you along an easy or lazy path, it will always help you to complete our soul path. Fear and indecision are often your biggest enemies; for they can cause you to lose your sense of of life's rhythm and prevent you from stepping into the flow and taking part in the dance of life.

Life's natural flow will always reach its true destination, unless some artificial force creates a barrier and causes it to divert. If you are able to avoid creating an artificial barrier you will in time reach yours. You will exhaust yourself if you try to swim against the flow, just as you would if you were to try swimming upstream in a fast flowing river.

When you are in a state of denial you are unconsciously creating an artificial barrier and distorting the natural flow of life. In time this will bring to both of us the weariness I have previously mentioned. If you cease even for a moment or two from trying to hold back this tidal wave of life's flow, you will become aware of how much weariness your state of denial has created within your being; and you will know that it is time to allow the universe to help you trust the flow of life.

Remember too that you should trust my wisdom here within you always, and when in doubt which way to go, then "go with the flow"

– Shall we dance?

Concerning The Path of Life - Chapter Eight

All Change Has Its Purpose

Any form of flow is also a form of change; and you will see around you in life the constant flow that creates change. Birth is change; life is change; death is change. Every moment change is taking place throughout the universe as energy continues to flow. On Earth this process is happening at a planetary level, but it is also happening at the levels of nations, cities, neighbourhoods, families and individual humans and souls.

Change will present itself to you at various times during this life whether or not you have invited it. There will be occasions when you have a choice to embrace change or to stay where you are, and there will be times when it is necessary to move on and work with the changes that present themselves to you; even if you feel reluctant to do so.

New beginnings are happening all the way through life, yet many human beings perceive birth as the only real beginning and death as one final ending. Each new beginning is just the end of a previous state, and what you call death is simply the end of one kind of existence and the beginning of another. The conscious part of you is a part of me and we will live on.

Sometimes you will become comfortable with things the

way they are and try to keep them that way. You may fear change because it requires you to deal with the unknown and learn to make it known to you, until once again you are within your comfort zone. It may be that you will seek change only when your present state becomes too uncomfortable to bear. Begin to look more closely at the changes that appear in your life. Remember that all change has its purpose, and nothing will prevent the change that is needed for your growth from taking place in the fullness of time.

You may sometimes yearn for change, and become restless and impatient because the change you seek is not presenting itself to you. You might even fear that it is avoiding you, as though there is an invisible barrier which prevents change from reaching you in the way you hope for. When you are experiencing this kind of frustration you may fail to realise the change that is needed is already happening, it is simply not doing so in the form you have identified as what you "want".

When you feel a sense of wanting in this way you are usually doing so from a limited perspective and from a sense of neediness, as though there is something missing from your life. This frustration occurs when you are focussing on what you miss rather than what you have.

This life you and I are completing together is unfolding before us in the way we have come here to experience it. If you were able (instantly and at will) to remove those blinkers which prevent you from awareness of your greater potential, you would see this immediately and would no longer be anxious and impatient. However, if you never felt the impatience and frustration, the experiences you have whilst working your way through what you see as lack of change would not be gained.

Remember, if you and I had a total conscious connection from birth and all the way through this life, then there would be no point in any of it. I have come here to experience the human condition, and in order to do so I have incarnated into this human body which you may believe to be the whole of you. This is a state of being that sees itself as limited, and whilst it does so then it will remain limited. The blessing in all of this is that when you do briefly re-connect with me, the sensation of bliss is such that it has to be experienced to be understood.

In the process of re-connection you will find yourself experiencing sensations of peace, elation, and love. These sensations are the opposite of the fears that haunt many human beings throughout their time on planet earth. These fears may be familiar to you also, and to be released from them is perhaps the most important aspect of the re-connection process, for fear is the force which is in opposition to love.

Even if you are not yet aware of it, the power is within you to choose the change that will take you where we both truly want to go in this life. For most of the time your everyday consciousness will be unaware that what you are seeking is to find my path - the path of your soul, the map of which is held within the deeper levels of your consciousness. When you are able to work with change it will empower you to take that further step toward retrieval of this map. In gaining the ability to accept that change is taking place somewhere out of sight of your human understanding, you are beginning to work with change at its most powerful and beneficial level. This will always be a good thing in relation to our progress as we live this life together.

It may help you to understand the deeper nature of change if you can imagine yourself standing on a beautiful gleaming multi coloured floor. The design of the floor appears to be completely abstract, made up of straight lines, curved lines, and circles. As you look down, you find your eyes following the shapes and colours swirling and twisting around. They weave in and out of each other almost as if they are alive, and as you watch they fade away and then become vibrant again. But, there in the centre directly under your feet brightly coloured and dazzling white star shapes flash and sparkle, reaching outward as though they are escaping from the centre of the design.

How many different colours do you see in this abstract design? What direction do the lines take? Can you see where the colours or the lines start or end? They will seem to swirl one way then another, turning this way and that in a constant process of change, almost like the effect produced when a kaleidoscope is rotated. Even when you manage to answer these questions, you may be unable to see what the result of this process will be, or when it will end. But, clearly flashing out from the centre are those sparks of light that are symbolic of the energy at work when change is taking place.

This image is a reminder of how varied and continuing

the process of change is, and how it comes in many forms often from where you would
least expect.

If you look around the edges of the floor away from the central image, you will also see smaller less noticeable shapes, and these are symbolic of the changes only just starting to move into your life. They are quietly awaiting their time to enter your life experience, dancing with the flow of the universe, just out of reach and out of your everyday awareness. Remember the nature of change is such that you may often be unable to perceive or understand it until it has taken place and you are looking back at what it has produced. Now picture again the swirling shapes in the floor and the brilliant sparks of white and coloured light being released from the centre. Feel those coloured sparks flowing upward from the floor and filling you with vitality. This is the vital force of change in your life bringing new energy and new opportunity.

If the change which comes into your life is is unexpected, unwelcome or confusing, take a moment to see it as that vibrant image you were standing on as you completed the visualisation. Then consider whether it is bringing with it all the elements you will need, to work with that change and to make it work for you.

When you are able to work with and accept this kind of change, it will empower you to take a further step toward connection with my universal wisdom, and toward the time when we will return home together to our source. For it is through you that I experience and learn the soul lessons of this life. It is when we return to oneness that sensations of love, peace and tranquillity will be the rule not the exception, and there will be no fear of change.

Concerning The Path of Life - Chapter Nine

The Deeper Value of Solitude

Solitude can be the act of distancing yourself physically from all other human contact, or even from much of the usual stimuli around you in life bringing sound, vision, and exciting the senses. It can also quite simply be those quiet moments when you are still and able to step away from your involvement in the busy world around you. Even the act of standing back and considering the changes that have taken or are taking place, is a form of solitude.

Each human being will view solitude in his or her own way. So what does this word solitude mean to you? Is it something appealing which provides space and privacy you long for, or something to be avoided; because in solitude you feel lonely or isolated? You may even feel threatened without your usual companions close by to make you feel safe and in a familiar place. If you feel that solitude you long for is eluding you, step back from your search, and ensure that it truly is a search for a destination and not an act of fleeing. Only then will you find within it the insights and answers you may be seeking.

When you realise you are never alone and can never be alone, your perspective on solitude will change. If you fear solitude and associate it with loneliness, remember that in the peace of solitude you can commune with me and discover you are more than you dreamed you could be. You can experience an increased sense of security, and the knowledge that when you believe yourself to be alone you are always guided and supported. Even at those times when you think to be alone is not what will bring you peace and contentment we are never apart. I will simply have slipped into the shadows of your awareness, respecting your wishes and awaiting your call for guidance and support.

It is a natural human response to to put in place barriers against the effects of anything that feels uncomfortable. You may do this at such a subtle and unconscious level you will be unaware you are doing so, and your awareness of these barriers may come only when a source of stress is removed and your system no longer feels the need to retain them. The releasing of these barriers can sometimes prove difficult and at such times solitude may be what you need in order to safely put them aside and move forward freely without the encumbrance they have created around you.

In true solitude you will be able to move away from the clamour and noise of the world you live in, to find awareness of peaceful silence even though the clamour and noise may still be close by. When this happens you may find yourself involuntarily taking a deep breath and letting it out in a sigh, thus letting go of the tension the energies of those around you has caused to build up in your energy system.

If you reflect on a time when you have experienced at

least one difficult period in your life or have known someone else who has done so, you may find it has been due to the loss or illness of someone close or even your own ill health. Perhaps instead it has been one of the many other distressing periods that human beings experience as part of life on planet earth. While you soldiered on and dealt with whatever came your way your fortitude was strong, and often those around you expressed their admiration for how you were "coping". Then when the pressure was removed and the trauma or crisis had ended or been dealt with, you began to sense that it was a safe or appropriate time to deal with the effects of the pressure.

You may have realised that during your period of coping you had unconsciously turned away from the distress and pressure. Then suddenly it descended upon you, as if whatever higher powers there are had decided to envelop you in a dark cloud, and one that was far too heavy for you to resist or even hold at bay. Just when you felt you should be sighing with relief, or even perhaps jumping with joy, you felt utterly deflated or defeated, even at the point of collapse. The whole sensation was then added to by your inability to understand what was troubling you. Here you were dealing with whatever 'life' had to throw at you, and when it had offered you a break you felt unable to cope.

The longer you continue your busy and often stressful life without allowing time for solitude, the greater will be this build of such pressure from the various situations you encounter in life. In solitude you can listen to my voice, benefit from its wisdom and its reassurance, and relax enough to release the energetic debris from your system. You may recall that I mentioned this to you when I spoke of the importance of relaxation. In solitude you will find the peace that allows you to relax and to hear my offerings of guidance and support.

When you mention to others of hearing an unfamiliar voice speaking to you in the silence and the solitude, there are those who will suspect you are descending into a state of insanity. But the voice I speak of is not the kind of voice heard by a mind that has lost its sanity. It can be felt as a sense of clarity, or experienced as some incident that you might describe as coincidence. An opportunity may arise that you had not foreseen, or life may suddenly or perhaps gradually begin to take you in a new direction.

There are numerous ways in which I may speak to you, but if you do not make space in your life for periods of solitude, you will be less able to hear my voice above the noise of the world around you; which you may by now have realised seems to have become louder with each passing year of life on planet earth. You will no doubt have heard of the "still small voice" and this is a very apt description of those occasions when I speak to you. There are times when a human being hears the voice of their soul and attributes it to God - Buddha – Jesus, Angels, or whatever else they may see as representing the infinite power behind creation.

My voice does not shout for I am in no hurry. I understand that all is well, and I will wait quietly until you are able to step into your solitude and hear me.

So, how do you perceive solitude? If you are unclear about your feelings on this subject imagine yourself walking peacefully along a beach with the silvery glow of the moon lighting your path ahead. If you see this image as dark and forbidding and feel you are a lonely figure walking in the darkness of night, then you will most likely avoid solitude wherever possible, because you will associate it with isolation, loneliness, and even fear.

However, this is a peaceful scene, the sky has a gentle glow and the moon is shining down on you as you gaze out across a calm sea. You are able to focus your mind clearly for there is no one to interrupt or to make demands upon your time, and no one to disturb your train of thought. Nor do you feel a need to look around for someone to join you, because you are quite happy to be in solitude.

This is when you have found the deeper value of solitude in connecting with me and being able to listen to my voice. Take note of the peace and serenity of this scene, and know that such solitude is where you and I can meet, and where I can share with you the wisdom I have accumulated over many life times.

In the midst of the chaos and confusion that often surrounds you in life you may at times yearn for complete and endless solitude. Remember that whilst it is an important aspect of your life, a state of solitude is not your life. To live this life fully you will need to return to the world of chaos and confusion and use the clarity and understanding I have been able to offer to you in your peaceful and undisturbed time. This is the real value of solitude and it is what helps you to follow your path of the soul through the turbulence of this life.

Concerning The Path of Life - Chapter Ten

When Knowledge Should Remain a Mystery

In those quiet and undisturbed moments I have spoken of, you may find yourself attempting to unravel the mysteries of life, the universe, and your deeper nature. So what do you mean when describing something as a mystery?

There have been mysteries from the beginning of time, but a mystery only remains so until you discover it's secret or reveal its true meaning. Some mysteries remain, but over time many have been explained and no longer have any sense of mystery about them. Somewhere in space and time there is an answer to those mysteries that have not yet been explained. When you encounter a mystery for which the answer does not become available, know that this does not mean there is no answer. It is simply that the time is not right for its discovery.

It is in the nature of human beings to be curious, and a healthy curiosity helps you learn how to live your life fully. But, as part of the seeming duality of human life there is also a negative aspect to such curiosity and this can take two forms. The first of these is to allow your curiosity to get out of control, and insist on knowing things before the time is right for them to be known. The second is to gain knowledge in a less than honest or honourable way. When knowledge is gained in this way it is often so that the knowledge may be held in secret, until such time as it may be revealed to achieve personal gain or great power. It may also be used to control others who do not have the knowledge in question.

There is also another way used by some to gain power, and that is to access knowledge and release it in the certain understanding that such release will harm someone, thereby removing their power and rendering them vulnerable and able to be controlled. Of course it is not always negative to gain knowledge and then release it to others; indeed without this happening some of the most wonderful discoveries humankind has made would never have taken place. As a result, life for many human beings on planet Earth at this time would be considerably less comfortable, less enjoyable, less healthy, and probably shorter.

There are occasions when knowledge should remain a mystery, at least for the time being, and when it seems that this is so, be patient in awaiting its release or in releasing it to others. This can sometimes prove difficult, but if you understand what I have just said you will see that a mystery should be handled with respect with honour and with patience.

While it is true that knowledge is power; the important thing is how you will use your knowledge once you have gained it. You may believe that a little knowledge is a dangerous thing and this can be true. You would not place a small child at the wheel of a fast car, because it is not capable of driving the car; nor will the child be ready for the knowledge of how to drive the car. The potential consequences of this and the potential danger to the child are not difficult to imagine.

If you hold the answer to a mystery, it would be wise to consider with care the timing and circumstance of its revealing, and to be sure that those who seek the answer are ready for the understanding or knowledge you reveal to them. Be certain also that this knowledge you intend to release (which will of course cease to be a mystery upon its release) will not be used for a negative or harmful purpose by those you have passed it on to. Consider this also in relation to the mysteries for which you seek answers, and remember the story from Greek Mythology of Pandora's Box. If you are unfamiliar with this story I can tell you that the box in question held not one but many mysteries.

The story goes that Zeus the king of the gods offered Pandora, the first woman on earth, to the brother of the god Prometheus as an act of vengeance against him. Pandora was then instructed by Zeus that the box should not be opened. However, Pandora was human and she had within her the human qualities of curiosity and impatience. Zeus knew this was so and had filled the box with all the ills of the world, amongst them war, famine, pestilence, illness, wickedness and malice. When Pandora could no longer control her curiosity she opened the box and these 'ills' were immediately released into the world. Like many mysteries released prematurely the 'ills' could not be returned from whence they came. The only thing that was not scattered was hope, of which I will speak more in due course.

It may help you to see this principle of mystery more

clearly if you are able to visualise a large and beautifully decorated jar. For in the original version of this Greek myth 'Pandora's box' was actually just such a jar. From the top of this jar a beautiful golden bird is emerging with the answer to a mystery. Imagine that the mystery this bird is about to reveal on leaving the jar is one upon which you are impatiently awaiting clarity. Now, as you visualise this scene you see that in place of a lid on the jar there is a radiant guardian hovering above it with wings out-stretched as though to shield the the jar and prevent the mystery from being revealed.

Look again at the bird in the opening of the jar, and see how brightly coloured its wings are and how dazzling the light is within the enclosed space around it. Now take your focus to the guardian at the top of the jar past whom the bird must fly for the mystery to be released. This guardian is strong and wise and she is a reminder that it is your inner strength and wisdom you will need to call upon when the answer to a mystery refuses to reveal itself to you. As you picture the bird and the guardian with your mind's eye you may realise they are all exactly where they should be, just as you are.

The guardian is not suppressing the mystery as a lid to the jar would do; she is protecting it until the time is right for its release. When you consider this you may also find growing within you a sense of peace replacing your impatience to find the answer to your mystery, and a realisation that when the time is right the knowledge will have far greater value to you than if it is released too soon. The realisation expands and you become aware of whether or not the time is right to release any mystery for which you hold the answer. The realisation I refer to is always held within you, in the depth of 'our' being where uncertainty has no place.

Let this story of Pandora and the visualisation I have suggested, help you to remember there are times when a mystery should perhaps remain so for a little longer. How you see it depends upon where you are looking from and when you are looking. A mystery today may have a clear, beneficial and simple explanation tomorrow – when the time is right.

Concerning The Path of Life - Chapter Eleven

To Achieve True Mindfulness

At first glance you may find yourself defining this word mindfulness as meaning the use of a little extra focus or consideration, but it can be so much more. In practicing mindfulness you will discover the value of directing your mind to positive use instead of your mind controlling you. It can be a powerful tool when you learn to use it fully and can summon it at will.

To give the fullness of your human mind to only one thing is not always easy; to succeed in mindfulness practice is required. It is important to take time and not to lose heart, for you live in a world of constant distractions. There may be times when it seems as if the universe is trying to take you away from the real issue, by drawing your mind one way and then another. But with practice mindfulness will overcome these distractions.

When you are listening to someone speaking to you it can become most disconcerting if someone else nearby begins to address you at the same time. The human mind cannot efficiently focus on more than one thing at a time, and this is so whether that thing is a voice they are listening to or an issue that requires attention. You may at times have tried to do so, but will have discovered that each separate thing you try to focus on simultaneously is in fact only receiving a part of your attention.

When you are in a negative state of mind such as fear, anger, frustration, resentment or other thoughts of a similar nature, you may feel you are being very mindful. This is because your mind is completely enveloped within those feelings and thoughts. But to be in any of these states is the opposite of mindfulness, for your mind is running amok in a frenzied and uncontrolled way. If you are able to stop for a moment and consider how you feel at such times, you will realise this is not you focussing your mind it is your emotions taking control of your mind, and doing it so strongly that it feels unable to focus on any emotion or thought other than the one that is controlling you. If the mind is angry or fearful or it is filled with bitterness and regret, and it is empty of positivity. This is because your emotions have become the master of your mind. They are ruling every physical and mental sensation with negative force, and this force is like a poison filling your mind and your body.

Next time your mind is in this state, take a deep breath and let it out slowly taking your awareness to the unpleasant physical sensations such a state of mind is bringing you to. What you will find is that this unpleasant emotion has almost taken over the whole of your being. From the point that the unpleasantness was triggered it has affected you physically, mentally, and emotionally. In addition, it is separating those parts of you from your spiritual aspect, the calm centred and wise aspect of your consciousness.

You will see I have not said this emotional tidal wave has swept through your soul, for while I will experience these feelings with you I will not be overwhelmed. I am your stabilising force, the part of you that awaits your call for help. This is help you may require when becoming mindful of the need to regain your equilibrium and re-connect with your spirituality. For in doing this you may once again be master of your emotions, your body, and your mind.

If you wish to master the skill of mindfulness start your practise in a quiet space where you will not be disturbed, for here you can learn to perfect the art of focussed thinking. You may not find this as easy as the quiet space would suggest; and you will perhaps discover that external disturbance may not be all that distracts you from your mindfulness. The human mind is forever active, buzzing this way then that and just like a bumble bee never flying in a straight line. It may settle for a moment then it will meander off again in another direction, as the perfume of a new flower attracts it. To achieve true mindfulness you need to focus on the one bud in your thoughts that you wish to bring to flowering, and so without doubt practice is required.

When you are able to achieve such focus easily under peaceful and undisturbed conditions, you may enjoy the challenge of holding on to your focus in the midst of the various distractions in life. There are many different levels of distraction that can divert you from your practise of mindfulness. Still, if you work your way up to the higher levels gradually, you will eventually find you are able to achieve mindfulness on whatever subject you wish. What is more you will be able to do so under any condition or circumstance. If you are able to reach this stage you will know which things are worthy of your mindfulness, and which are simply distractions from a playful universe.

When you have reached a point in your life where you start to consider your own personal growth and development, and you wish to seriously consider the deeper issues of any aspect of yourself, mindfulness is a very useful self help tool with which to work. If mindfulness escapes you, remember what I have said about beginning your practise of mindfulness slowly and increasing the challenges gradually. Then you will in time be able to find mindfulness whenever there is a real and important need for it in your life.

To reflect on the nature of mindfulness, visualise your own face calm and serene in appearance. You may find this difficult to do, so it may help to recall a moment in your life when you felt a sense of peace and tranquillity. Feel the furrows smooth from your brow and allow your jaw to relax. Now focus your mind's eye on a point in front of you. Picture a smooth white pathway directly ahead of you, stretching out into the distance until it almost disappears. Imagine you are quietly and peacefully walking this pathway searching for a small pebble on the ground. As you walk your focus is completely directed toward your search for the pebble, and your mind is steadily working on finding it. Now you see that the pebble is directly in front of you and you pick it up. You hold it in the palm of your hand and look at it calmly in an unhurried way. Consider how heavy or light it feels in your hand, search it for speckles, markings or indentations, and note whether it is perfectly round or slightly misshapen. Remember, you are totally mindful of this pebble and wish to know everything about it.

When you have learned everything you wish to know about this beautiful pebble place it gently back on the path then return your mind to where it was before you took your focus mindfully on to that one small pebble.

This exercise in mindfulness can be focussed on any issue of significance in your life or on some small and simple thing. It is important that you are able to focus your mind totally on the issue before you, to the exclusion of all else. Quietly and calmly explore and examine it, and take the information you have gathered to be used in a wise and positive way.

When you can achieve this level of mindfulness you have found fullness of the mind, so that it is working to its highest potential and fully directed toward the object of your focus. Now you are restoring your mind to its rightful role as a servant you can direct at will, rather than as a master which will go wherever it wishes without your consent.

Concerning The Path of Life - Chapter Twelve

True Vision Sees Past All illusion

Vision is to your eyes as hearing is to your ears, but this is simply a comparison between your vision and hearing as physical functions. When I offered you an exercise in mindfulness I was guiding you toward working with your inner vision.

Visions have been experienced throughout the history of humankind, but these are visions of things not normally seen by the physical eye. This word vision is also often used to describe a mental or spiritual experience of seeing. This could be described as inner vision, for you are not looking outside of yourself but looking inward in a non-physical way when you have this kind of experience.

In addition, vision can be the ability to perceive the best possible potential in people events or situations and to make them come alive. This is a vision that is a sensing, rather than a seeing in the way you might understand vision to work. It is a vision that comes from looking through my eyes, and it is good to remember my eyes are always available to you. When you avail yourself of this way of seeing, you will find you have a vision filled with a greater degree of creative and loving strength.

The opposite of this is when your eyes see through a filter

of fear rather than love. This is when you are seeking validation that your view is "the right view". This type of vision sees with judgement and seeks to find fault and weakness rather than purity and strength. When you look from this perspective of fear, you will always see what you expect to see, and it will usually be something of a fearful nature.

As we walk this path of life together, Some of your experiences will be those I have come here to seek for my soul expansion, and which I have made a pre-life agreement to share with you. When you encounter these experiences they may affect your view of all that is around you. The filter through which you view life may become distorted from the effects of the experiences, and lose its original focus. This is not true vision it is looking out into the world around you through a filter that has become clouded and discoloured by fear and other negative emotions. This filter will prevent you from seeing the light of goodness and potentiality shining out from what may be directly in front of you. When you find this happening and it is becoming more and more difficult to see the good around you, it is time to "clean the filter", to refocus, and to allow the light of love back into your vision.

When you do this, and you look again through the clarity you have gained, you will find your reclaimed vision may give birth to a wonderful creation or a glimpse of what may come to pass. True vision sees past all illusion into the source of creation. This is a vision with the power to change lives, and it is the right of each human being on planet earth. Remember you can find this vision when you look through my eyes, instead of simply using your physical ability to see. I offer you my vision freely and with love, for the eyes of the soul see the soul, just as human eyes see the human being, and the eyes of the soul never lose focus, nor are they ever clouded by a distorted filter.

In seeing through my eyes you will discover many wonders around you, and the potential for goodness and sometimes for 'greatness', in those you encounter. You will see opportunity where once you saw closed doors, and you will understand that sometimes patience is required in order to allow those around you to fulfil their promises, intentions, and even their potential. With this vision you will see past the apparently hopeless to the wonderfully possible.

Remember, when you allow yourself to think calmly and unhurriedly, or when you refuse to bow under pressure from the views of others which you know to be misguided, I am speaking to you. This is when you will begin to see with soul vision, and you will see past masks often worn by others to protect themselves, but those masks hide the beauty in their souls. You will also see the truth of their intention and whether it is genuine, or whether at a human level it has an intention to harm or cause injury to you or to others.

To sense more clearly this soul vision sit quietly for a moment or two and imagine you are sitting before a ball of sparkling clear pure quartz crystal. As you gaze at the crystal you see images begin to form within its perfect clarity. It is as if you are watching a film through the clarity of the crystal. There may be people you know and who you are fond of. When you see these people smiling you find yourself smiling too, and feeling aware of your affection for them. Alternatively if they are filled with sadness you feel a heartfelt compassion for them.

But then the image changes and you see someone you do not know. This is a young boy who has slipped away unnoticed. He is in a market place stealing from the stalls when the stall holders look away, and you feel a sense of impatience and anger at his laziness and dishonesty. You notice he is not poorly dressed or apparently in need, but he is untidy and appears to have no self respect.

Now, look with your soul vision to see if there is anything you are missing, and remember you are looking through my eyes. Use this vision now that you were granted at birth, but may rarely or never have used when viewing the world around you. As you do so, you begin to see sadness in the boy's heart and pain from a sense of loneliness and despair. You also see he has a fine mind and great potential. However, it appears his potential has been ignored by those around him and he has been given no support or encouragement from the significant adults in his life, other than to follow a negative path.

You begin to understand that his actions may not be what they first appeared to be. Perhaps they are a misguided cry for help and for some recognition of his finer qualities. Perhaps they are fuelled by a desire to escape from the environment that he lives in. This boy is of course symbolic of many human beings who are young or old, rich or poor, weak or powerful; but who are in need of someone with the desire and the vision to see past the surface illusion they present to the world. This surface illusion indicates only weakness or laziness, but soul vision looks into what really is or has the potential to be, and where it can be revealed and encouraged to flower.

This is a kind of vision that works miracles. It connects you deeply with me and my guidance; so remember this when you find yourself seeing only what is on the surface, and pause to look again with "vision". This does not mean everything which is apparently negative will suddenly become positive, it simply means that you will be more able to see the truth of what is in front of you, rather than what your fears or prior conditioning expect to see.

Learn to see what is beyond logic and rationale, and what would often seem to be an impossible outcome; and begin to see the deepest yearnings and the fondest hopes of yourself and others as a real possibility. This is when you will have learned to look through my eyes and found the "vision" that will change your experience of life for the better. In doing this you will help us both on this journey of our soul path.

Be aware that in using your own soul vision, you will be helping others to use the eyes of their soul in order to have their own clear soul vision too.

Concerning The Path of Life - Chapter Thirteen

When True Revelation Occurs

Revelation is generally understood to be a simple revealing of knowledge or information not previously held. This brings me to suggest once once again that you look up a word in a dictionary, for although you will see that it is usually described as a shock, surprise or disclosure, it could also be described as another kind of vision. Here we have another word which can mean so much more than the dictionary would have you believe.

You may not always realise that from the point in your life at which true revelation occurs, there is a change of perspective taking place deep within you. The experience of revelation will sometimes cause your world to be turned upside down in an instant, but at other times your awareness of the change of perspective that is taking place will begin to surface in your upper consciousness gradually, and arrive in your everyday awareness at a later time. Whilst this can seem sudden there are times when it has been making its way to the level of your everyday awareness for a while.

It may be that at some point you have noticed some new information being revealed to you, and then you have dismissed it because at the time your mind was busy focussing on some other matter. However, there will have been a shock wave forming deep in your being at that initial moment of revelation. This shock wave will resonate outward until it reaches the upper levels of your awareness, and that is when you will have what is often described as a "light-bulb moment" or "brainwave".

Deep down at an instinctive or intuitive level, your thoughts and decisions will immediately be affected by the change that has taken place when true revelation occurs. From that moment onward you will perceive the world around you in a different way. This difference may start in a small way, but if a real revelation has occurred at some level of your consciousness it will become increasingly significant until it reaches a level you are acutely aware of. It can be as if one door opening in your mind has caused many other doors to open in a short space of time, or even simultaneously.

When you experience revelation, it often happens following a decision you made previously at some subconscious level. This is likely to occur if the earlier decision was to allow the knowledge now reaching your awareness to remain dormant temporarily, so that it could be processed at some time in the future.

When you become aware of some new knowledge, or experience a sudden change in perspective, you may feel you already had this knowledge, and you are only now seeing it for the first time in a clear way. However, the conscious revelation will have occurred because the time is right and because you have seen with soul vision and listened to my voice.

If you find yourself saying "this is a revelation to me" the experience can take on biblical proportions in your life. True revelation is a deep life changing gift, which you will receive when you and I are in harmony of thought and understanding. The significant changes you can benefit from as a result of true revelation will take place only if you are able to recognise why the revelation has occurred to you at a particular point on the path of your life. Therefore remember what I have said to you about mystery and its revealing when the time is right.

If you allow this revelation to reach those upper levels of your mind, it will present a time of opportunity for the two of us to walk this soul path in harmony, if only for part of the way until the next "lesson" is due to take place. As a result you will find you are able to open your mind to the possibilities this deep understanding is presenting you with, and more importantly to fulfil the potential of those possibilities.

The practice of mindfulness will at times create the experience of revelation in your life, and it will be experienced as a moment of total clarity, of instant understanding and a complete absence of doubt or confusion. The revelation which brings such sudden and complete clarity is not granted to you accidentally or incidentally; it is a part of your life learning process, and a part of the path of the soul that meets with the path of the human condition. This experience of revelation you are undergoing will have a purpose for both of us.

To align your mind with this concept of powerful revelation, sit quietly for a moment and close your eyes.

Imagine you are gazing out into a deep blue starry sky. As you look into the heavens you see a haze of light growing in the sky directly above you. This light is soft and muted reflecting gently the blue of the sky within which it is centred. It swirls and spins like an early morning mist or a milky-way galaxy of stars. It is vague and indistinct, so you are unable to focus strongly on what you sense is there to be seen, and you find you cannot quite reach it with your inner or outer vision.

Then, out of the centre of this gentle mist a dazzling ball of light appears and starts to expand growing larger and larger before your eyes. As it expands you see that it is filled with a multitude of colours and forms, just as you would see if you were to zoom in closer when looking at a galaxy. Here you are gazing into this deep blue sky filled with clusters of brightly twinkling stars, and endeavouring to see more clearly what you seek. In the next moment, a hazy mist begins to form, and then with a sense of shock and awe you see this ball of light and colour instantly expand and move toward you, a thing of beauty and wonder.

The soft mist you first saw is symbolic of the sense you might have just before a revelation occurs, and although you are not yet aware of the result it will present you with, it represents change and progress occurring in your life. Then the revelation occurs, and suddenly there is the appearance of this dazzling ball of colour and light, and this is the sensation of true revelation. It is a feeling that may cause you to ask yourself where this sudden information and awareness came from.

This is how revelation will arrive in your life, as if appearing out of nowhere. Then suddenly all is profoundly clear, and you have a significant understanding of some issue or aspect that is important to you and the world you live in. When such revelation touches you a revolution is occurring.

For it is the experience of human and soul living as one, hand in hand, heart in heart, mind in mind; and it is known as revelation. Be prepared for its occurrence in your life and use the ability to be mindful, and to use the knowledge and the vision it will bring to you wisely and well. Know that it has come to you for a reason and with a purpose as we walk this path of the soul together.

Concerning The Path of Life - Chapter Fourteen

Truth is Everywhere and in Everything

If you recognise the experience of revelation I have described, you will realise it is powerfully linked to a sense of awareness about what you might call "truth". Once again let us consider the real meaning of a word, and search the dictionary for that meaning. So what does this word truth really mean? In a dictionary you will see it is offered as meaning the same as words like fact, or reality. So what is the real, factual or "true" meaning?

Listen to politicians or philosophers debating, and you will discover each of them believes strongly that their own "facts" or "reality" are the "truth". However, these may not be the facts or reality of their opponent in the debate who also believes their version of the truth is the only one. It is not only politicians and philosophers who see different truths from the same facts, for many human beings claim to live truthfully and to be seekers after truth, and yet they still see many different truths.

Truth cannot be chased after, and it cannot be manipulated or imprisoned. Whether you have a religious belief or no religious belief at all, consider the words "the truth shall set you free" so famously attributed to Jesus Christ and which are so timeless and meaningful.

Although truth cannot be imprisoned, it is always held deep in your soul consciousness. Here it is safe and free to leave and be revealed whenever you genuinely wish to discover it or pass it on with good intention. The truth you find may depend upon where you and I are on this path we walk together. As we do so our knowledge and experiences will grow. What you perceive to be the truth therefore will appear in various forms in an ever-shifting image as you go through life. You will learn a little more of the truth with each step you take along this path with me. With each new piece of the puzzle, and each new part of your life that unfolds, you become wiser. The paradox of human life is that as you gain this increasing wisdom, you will also have a sense that you seem to know less and less.

The absolute truth is so vast that it encompasses all that is, all that ever has been and all that ever will be. As human beings walk their paths through life, they grasp - piece by piece - morsels of the absolute truth they are able to understand at each point in time. Each of those morsels will be a part of the whole truth, and yet each of them may be different, but they will be what is needed or meaningful for the human beings who have grasped them.

There may be times in this life when you feel that the morsel of truth you hold is the real and complete truth and that you need to reveal this truth to another, to" 'put things straight" to "sort things out" to gain or offer some form of justice. However, when you think your truth is the only truth, you should remember how many others believe this to be so. All human beings see through their own eyes and from their own perspective. It is therefore inevitable that each human being will see a slightly different truth. This is the nature of the human condition.

The vastness of absolute truth is simply the natural universal law, which in its totality is far beyond human understanding, unless it is seen through the eyes of the soul. When this happens the human being who has seen his or her soul truth may be unable to find the words to describe it.

Just as "truth" is experienced by each human being in a personal way, it is also the way of life on planet earth that time moves on and the world changes; and because of this from a human perspective the truth changes also. Just like the universe we are a part of, our understanding of truth is constantly unfolding before us.

If you believe that someone is deliberately distorting a particular aspect of the truth for their own gain, and this distortion does not serve the higher good of all, you will know the distortion should not be passed on to others as truth. For it is merely an illusion or pretence of being the truth. Woven within its roots are fear and anger and they will in time suffocate it. If this happens, this so called truth will eventually lose all of its apparent substance and will fall apart. The strongest weapon against such a distortion is pure love, for anger and fear will fuel the energy that has produced such a false "truth".

Remember I have said that at any time you truly wish to see through my eyes they will be open to you and they will show you the "truth". When you are able to view things in this way it can help you understand the truths of others. Whilst it may seem to be a contradiction in terms to say there are different truths, it has ever been so. Whilst souls walk their paths each within the vehicle of the individual human being it will always be so. If your search for truth at this time is an honest one, be aware of the nature of truth and take comfort in this knowledge. Remember I have said each person's truth is seen from their own unique perspective. Each human being is focussing on a different aspect of the bigger picture, and as in truth, we are all one; the whole truth is collectively being seen and understood by all of us.

You could liken this seeing of the truth to a choir of people singing together and producing one beautiful song. As the choir raise their voices in unison the sound is moving and beautiful and will touch the heart, but if each individual voice sang alone a song that was written for a choir, it would seem to have no essence, no substance, no strength, and it would seem incomplete. The same is true if only one verse of the song was sung in isolation. Whilst the verse would be complete the whole "truth" of the song would not be heard.

Reflect for a moment on the path of your life and this journey of the soul. Then reflect on the paths of all the other millions of partnerships between souls and their human counterparts on planet Earth at any given time. You will see that souls come and go as the body that holds them is first born then ages, withers and dies. This is when the truth of that human life is no longer alive to human perception. However the soul lives on unseen and without the human race being aware of its continued existence. So here we have two truths, both valid. The human being is perceived to have died, and yet its soul and driving force lives on in another dimension.

If you look at it another way, one verse of the song one chapter of the story is complete, but that is only part of the song, part of the story. Nevertheless for those who see that a life is ended this is the truth. For those who perceive that the soul lives on this is the truth. So here we appear to have two truths each as valid as the other.

Each human life, each soul that exists, each event that takes place, and each year that passes; all of these have their truth, and yet that truth is in a constant process of evolution. You will never find pure truth in hard scientific fact; for it has more depth and but also more simplicity than science or technology can ever demonstrate.

Truth is everywhere and in everything, yet it can seem to change at any moment, and it will be seen and heard differently as each human being hears their verse of the song, their chapter of the story, and only the universe sees and hears the whole of the song.

Concerning The Path of Life - Chapter Fifteen

The Responsibilities that Liberation Brings

You may at times become subject to captivity or loss of freedom of one kind or another. Whatever form your captivity takes it is likely you will long for liberation. If you believe freedom is a human right then physical captivity, even restriction, repression, or limitation of free expression will cause you to feel trapped, and to believe it is not a natural or happy state to be in.

When you seek liberation for yourself or others, know that whilst liberation may bring a much yearned for freedom, it will place upon those who are liberated responsibility for choices to be made, actions to be taken, and directions to be followed. In order to be free, there is a need to be strong. Make certain, therefore, that you or those you liberate are prepared for and accepting of the responsibilities that liberation bring.

Whilst liberation can be a truly positive aim, it is good to remember that if these considerations are overlooked, there may be those who will accept their freedom without taking on the responsibilities that come with it. There will also be those who may protest that they are imprisoned and insist they have a yearning for liberation; when at some level of their consciousness they do not really wish to be free at all. The reason for their reluctance will be that they are unable or unprepared for the responsibilities which come with freedom. This reluctance to become liberated is usually unconscious and fear based, and they will believe they truly are a victim of their captor. This will be so regardless of whether that captor is a person or persons, or even a set of circumstances. As a result their actions will reflect this belief and they will do little to seek liberation in any meaningful way. You may even find them making excuses when a helping hand is offered.

This life will present you with any number of situations in which it is natural to feel the need for liberation. These may come in the form of significant curbs to your freedom, where you are physically restrained from moving at will, or they may simply be places you find yourself in and you wish to be physically elsewhere. Then again there are situations which you will be unhappy with and wish for them to be different than you find them. The various forms of captivity are manifold, and there are no limits to how they may challenge you as you go through life.

Some of the prisons human beings find themselves in are self created and the reasons for this are also many and varied. Perhaps they have taken some action which they were aware would result in physical imprisonment. Alternatively, they are in a situation which they find uncomfortable, but they seem unable to summon the will or courage to detach from it. If you find yourself in this kind of situation you cannot look to others to free you from your imprisonment. You will need to be the creator of your own liberation, and it will be within your ability to do so.

If you find yourself in a self imposed state of imprisonment, you may begin to realise that you are frequently complaining about your "prison", and repeatedly stating that you have no opportunity to liberate yourself. But deep inside there is a growing awareness that liberation is within your reach, if only you can find the courage to take the first important steps toward it and toward a new way of being.

It is true there are many forms of captivity, and amongst them are those where all autonomy is removed. There are also many more where the human being concerned simply finds they are prevented from making the necessary choices which will bring them the desired freedom.

When I say this, I am deeply and poignantly aware there are forms of imprisonment which were decided before this life began, and that are a part of an individual human being's path of the soul. If this is so, these experiences of imprisonment whether physical or psychological, have been chosen to provide expansion and development for the soul which has chosen to experience it before incarnation into the human condition.. If this is the nature of the experience then I can only offer you whatever strength you will accept to help you through it.

This kind of imprisonment will often involve having all control over the direction of a life being taken by force. If the individual concerned has done nothing to warrant their imprisonment, they will without doubt achieve significant soul progression as a result of their suffering, whether it is mental emotional or physical. However, this does not mean those with compassion should stand idly by when they have the power to bring an end to such captivity or ill treatment.

I am also aware that it is sometimes not possible to completely understand such experiences from your human perspective, but if it was there would be no lesson, no development, no expansion. The "experiences" would have had all challenge to the soul removed from them at the outset

Whatever the circumstances of their captivity, those who are liberated will need to be prepared to live freely and take control of their lives once again. For captivity also conditions the captive to think like a captive and such thinking is no longer useful once liberation is gained. Guidance may be needed for the one who is liberated, to help find a new way of being and to think and act from a liberated perspective.

To help you examine the concept of liberation and its responsibilities, I ask you to consider the image of a beautiful richly coloured butterfly soaring joyfully up toward the sunlight and liberation from the captivity of its chrysalis. If you had watched the butterfly emerge from its chrysalis you would have seen that at first it could not fly, because its wings were still wet from imprisonment inside the chrysalis. The prison of its chrysalis did not require the Butterfly to learn how to fly or to survive in a world containing many threats to its survival. Now it is free, but it is also self-sufficient and responsible for its daily life and its continuing survival. The butterfly's responsibilities range from pollinating flowers to providing food for other insects and birds; even as a caterpillar they have their place in the world. So you see even the tiny but beautiful butterfly fulfils its responsibilities once it is liberated from the chrysalis. This tiny creature cannot see what lies ahead as it becomes liberated, but once it moves out into the world it simply allows its responsibilities to present themselves and then fulfils them naturally until it is no longer able to do so.

This analogy of the butterfly reinforces the importance of patience and acceptance of the responsibilities that liberation brings, sometimes without prior knowledge or understanding. The chrysalis no longer imprisons the butterfly when it becomes ready to emerge into the world, and the butterfly has the patience and innate wisdom to wait for its wings to dry so that it can fly out and fulfil its other responsibilities.

Remember too that liberation for human beings usually brings increased power and with power also comes the responsibility to use it wisely and well. For when power becomes corrupted it simply starts to create a new form of captivity for someone else.

It is true that to liberate another from an unjust situation not created by them is admirable. It is also true that even when the captivity is of their own creation, the support of a fellow human being may be needed in order to gain freedom. Nevertheless, there are times when liberation from a self made prison can be achieved, when you follow the guidance of your soul and accept the responsibilities that freedom brings. Remember always that liberation without consideration may cause a new form of captivity for someone else or even for you if you allow this to happen.

Concerning The Path of Life - Chapter Sixteen

To Understand What Wisdom Is

Wisdom is often associated with those who have lived for many years. It is easy to see the logic of this, because these elders of any society have had a longer period of time in which to acquire their wisdom. The younger members of a community will be taught that before they can become wise there is a need to acquire knowledge; and before they can possess knowledge there is a need to complete a process of learning. These processes of acquiring the knowledge and then turning it into wisdom can take considerable time, and as a human being you may reach old age before you complete them. These are the reasons for the association between wisdom and the old.

With sufficient effort it is possible to absorb large amounts of knowledge into your mind over a short space of time. However, the true purpose of the knowledge accumulated can only be realised when you have had the opportunity to use it. This use of knowledge is called experience, and this cannot be condensed to create "instant wisdom", it usually has to be achieved in what you might call "real time".

Wisdom does not come from a theoretical knowing of information or facts, but from experience gained over time. It is for this reason that the process of acquiring wisdom will inevitably take more time than the acquiring of knowledge. The journey to becoming truly wise is not a journey which can be approached with haste. It will follow a proper sequence of acquiring knowledge of one sort or another, then absorbing and digesting it, and finally learning the real value of that knowledge in the context of your life and the lives of others.

The path of experience is personal and unique to each human being, and so you can see that for some it may take almost a lifetime to have the necessary experiences to be able to turn them into wisdom. For some, the acquiring of such wisdom is not complete even within a lifetime.

Those who lack the patience and ability to give themselves that all-essential time for contemplation and communication with their soul wisdom will discover they have knowledge that turns out to be simply words on a page or in their head. You could perhaps describe it as a purse filled with knowledge but empty of the wealth of wisdom. This is the result when human beings become impatient and do not stop to listen to the wisdom of their soul.

It is regrettable that nowadays in many parts of the world, the old are being relegated to the "back benches" of life's debate, and their wealth of knowledge which has had the time to mature into wisdom, is being ignored or dismissed. It is sad to see such valuable wisdom lying fallow, when it could be of great benefit to humankind if only it was recognised and acknowledged. What is even more regrettable for the human race is that such wisdom will die with those wise human beings and will return home with their soul. It will not of course be lost completely, but many people on earth who could have benefitted from it will not do so. You will see I have said such wisdom is not lost for it is only temporarily removed from the earth plane. When that soul returns to planet earth for the next stage of its human path the wisdom it has gained will return also.

There will be times in life when you encounter a natural and instinctive wisdom, in those who are far too young to have attained it in the usual way. This means they have not gained their wisdom from the process of learning and acquiring knowledge over time. Those who encounter such young people are often at a loss to understand how they have acquired wisdom that is considered to be "beyond their years". This kind of wisdom comes directly from their soul, and it may have been waiting many lifetimes for the right time the right place and the right circumstances, for the human being in whom the soul resides to call it up. For when this time and place occurs the wealth of wisdom may be returned to the human race, and its value will eventually be recognised and used.

In certain parts of this planet you call "Earth", the bird known as the Owl is a symbol of wisdom and learning, and those human beings who are perceived to have wisdom are often described as a "wise old owl". The owl is a bird which hunts its prey at night, and has wonderful night vision and incredibly powerful hearing to enable it to survive. The ability to see and hear things that most human beings cannot normally see or hear, may explain how this wild and simple creature became such a widely known symbol of wisdom.

When you think of wisdom, picture in your mind's eye the owl that is so often a symbol of it, and there by its side, young and innocent in appearance, its offspring; a small, defenceless and inexperienced baby owl. Let this image be a reminder that it is sometimes a narrow and limited way of thinking to see wisdom only in the place you expect to see it. Whilst the mature owl has gained experience in hunting for food and surviving, it may well have encountered danger whilst gaining the experience. As a result the owl will be wary and perhaps fearful. When living within the human condition this is not a wise way of being; for fear can make you hesitant and disconnected from your soul and its wisdom.

Children in their innocence and simplicity unaffected by the complexities and influences of this world often have a close connection with their soul and therefore may give forth great wisdom. When you meet with such wisdom, be aware that these human beings may be young, but their soul will be old and will have been travelling their path through many human lifetimes. Such a soul will be powerful, and its human counterpart will find its voice easy to hear and its eyes easy to look through. What you are seeing is soul wisdom.

It is wisdom in and of itself to be able to acknowledge the wisdom of the elderly, gained from extended life experience. However, it is even wiser to be alert to the wisdom found in those who are not old enough to have had such a wealth of experience in their current lifetime, nor the time to turn it into wisdom. I am reminding you here to acknowledge the wisdom gained over many years and to respect such hard earned wisdom, but also to be aware of the soul wisdom that has been gained through many lifetimes, and which sometimes comes forth from very young human beings.

If you wish to understand what wisdom is, do not look always to those who shout their so called wisdom from the rooftops, but to those who are quietly continuing to use for the best outcome, the knowledge they have gained and transformed into wisdom. This may be so whether they are old and their wisdom has been gained in this lifetime, or they are young and their wisdom was achieved in the ancient past of their soul.

For the truly wise do not announce themselves with banging of drums or clashing of cymbals, they simply live their wisdom and offer it freely to those whose eyes and ears are open enough to recognise and gratefully benefit from it.

Concerning The Path of Life - Chapter Seventeen

Hope is Essential to Your Being

When you come into this life as a human being you may have been fortunate enough to have arrived with a soul who has an enviable store of wisdom, or you will spend years of your life acquiring it, in order to increase the wisdom your soul already has.

If it is the former and considerable wisdom is present within you from a young age, you will know early in life that hope is essential to your being. You can lose all else but if you still have hope, you can overcome your difficulties. Until the last thread of hope is lost you will not give up the fight, and the vital spark of meaning will remain in your life. This is the nature of hope while travelling within the human condition

Never forget that hope has power beyond understanding, and whilst you still have it you can work your very own miracles. Hope is not bound by logic or rationale; it is literally a lifeline when you are drowning under the weight of challenges which defy all your efforts to rise above them. This supporting and sustaining nature of hope is a part of the natural essence of how I connect with you, to help you overcome the challenges of the human life path.

With sufficient hope what is seemingly impossible can

sometimes become possible. Even in the face of utter defeat you can have hope in your ability to re-build, and rise like a Phoenix from the ashes of your defeat. Hope will keep you aware of the potential for success in your efforts to overcome many of life's challenges. So, when you feel you are losing hope in any situation which is close to your heart, know that hope can never be taken from you; it can only be only given away. Sadly when human beings are vulnerable and buried beneath the weight of their grief or fear, they may be unable to hear the gentle voice of their own soul guiding and supporting them. When this happens they feel at their weakest, and they loosen their grip on hope, thus allowing it to slip away and believing it has been taken from them rather than released by them.

You do not need the permission of another to hold on to your hope, and you do not need to offer explanations as to why you are holding on to your hope, you simply need to continue to hope, even to hope against all the odds that may whisper in your ear and say hope is lost. When I say these words I do not say that all reason and sanity should be dispensed with, for it is possible to hope, even in the knowledge that your hope does not fall within the bounds of reason and sanity. Still, you can retain those qualities and a sense of hope within your being.

So if you believe there is no reason to continue hoping, search your heart for my guidance. You may be surprised to find the kind of hope that helps you to let go of a situation or set of circumstances and move forward in your life. This is when your own healing can take place. Remember that while doing this, you can still keep just one small seed of hope quietly thriving and completely un-observed by others deep within your being. That seed of hope can lie there ready to be called upon in times of need or desperation. It will revive you and carry you onward to reason and logic to sanity and optimism for your current situation.

This does not mean you should wallow in a stagnant situation, it means you can draw on a strength that lies within me, waiting for you to call upon it. This hope is not narrow and it does not dictate specific outcomes, it simply trusts that all will be well. It trusts that for the expansion of your soul, and the completion of your soul path through this life, you are where you are meant to be, in the company of whom you are meant to be with, doing what you are meant to be doing.

Hope allows you to open your mind to the good and the kind, the positive and the optimistic, and to survive and thrive. It will help you to defy those who would beat you down and destroy your hope for the future. For hope, like its sister, trust, can be held on to whilst remaining grounded and centred in what is sometimes described as the real world. In retaining your spark of hope you may find a realisation dawning upon you that there is so much more than this "real world", and there is so much more reason to hope than this "real world" would have you believe.

If you are tempted to discourage another person from hoping, consider deeply how vulnerable they may be at this time, and how much you may be encouraging them to give away by persuading them to give up their hope.

This is when it is time to think carefully before you take the risk of encouraging anyone to allow the last spark of hope in their heart to be extinguished.

If it is you who are in this place of grief and fear remember that the choice is yours, and be strong in holding on to your hope for as long as there is breath in your body. When you feel you have reached your lowest ebb and your grip on hope is slipping away, hold on to the hope that it will return, for it can do so if you create a place in your consciousness and in your heart for it to grow again. Hope is like a tree which may appear to have withered and died, only to grow afresh when Spring arrives.

As you complete your journey through life you will have periods (however brief) of peace and tranquillity, and these are times when you feel a warm glow of contentment with your experience of life. However, it is in the nature of the human experience that such peace and contentment can be swept away in an instant by events that can overtake you unexpectedly. My journey through this life of yours can at times be like a gently winding stream, sparkling in the sunlight and filled with gentle images and thoughts of wonderful things, but it can suddenly and without warning become violent rapids of water filled with fear and despair. This path of the soul we walk together through each day that passes will often bring the unexpected, and although what it brings may be wonderful uplifting or exciting, it can also bring pain and anguish.

It will be of help to hold on to the power of your hope at

such times, and if you are able to visualise your difficulties as a hill to be climbed and your hope to be the top of that hill which you continue to reach for, there will still be hope for you. Always focus on the top of the hill and reach out to it, remembering that you may need to make the journey toward fulfilment of your hope step by step, stage by stage, and you may need to allow yourself a period of rest every now and then before you reach the top. Do this in the knowledge that your re-discovery of hope will in time become a resting place where you can look back on your time of trials and be refreshed and reassured.

This is when you will know that you are once again equipped for the next stage of your journey. Use this mental image of the hill to remind you how powerful an influence hope is in your life and the lives of others, and of the vital role it plays with regard to your survival. For it will remind you that hope is not completely lost it is always waiting for you to rediscover it at the top of that hill.

If you take the time to look more closely when your world seems to be falling apart, you may realise that the falling apart has already occurred without you being aware was happening, and now it is in fact slowly coming back together. If you listen carefully for my voice you will always find your own spark of hope, and it will take you onward when you would otherwise lose faith in yourself and the world around you.

You should consider deeply what the implications of persuading anyone to give up their last spark of hope might be. If you encounter someone who appears to have succumbed to such a loss, then remember the tree that fills again with fresh green leaves each spring, and quietly support them in the process of seeing the new shoots of hope open in their heart again. If you can do this you will be reminded that your own fresh shoots of hope can grow again within your heart.

Concerning The Path of Life - Chapter Eighteen

In Unity

When someone uses expressions such as, "united we stand - divided we fall" or, "there is strength in numbers" they are often seeking continued hope of success or achievement, but they are also referring to the concept of unity.

It is true that if you fortify a thing by adding to its substance or volume it generally becomes stronger. Nevertheless there are times when all the substance or volume is as nothing if there is no unifying bond. It will simply drift into its separate parts, and will become weaker as a result of that separation. Then there is a state of staying together and refusing to become separated simply from fear of the consequences of doing so, or a fear of being alone and isolated. When this happens, human beings seek to justify their fear by using another well worn expression, which is "better the devil you know than the devil you don't know"

There are also times when individuals remain as part of a group or within a relationship or friendship without any real purpose for doing so. This may simply be because they remain out of habit, or they cannot summon up the physical, emotional or mental energy to detach from something that no longer has real meaning for them. They may fear repercussions, or demands that they explain their decision to leave. If they feel unable to deal with either of these consequences they become a disgruntled and disruptive part of the so called unity, whatever its nature may be. In doing so they create ruptures in the fabric of the union and rather than adding strength they are weakening it; for none of these is in the spirit of true unity. If a union is built on fearfulness, stubbornness or laziness it will eventually collapse.

Fear will weigh down the strength of a union, because the energy of fear is heavy. Stubbornness will create obstacles within the union, because stubbornness is rigid and refuses to move, so that the light of truth or progress is unable to shine through. Laziness will hold back any progress or enlightenment of a union, because laziness makes no effort to move forward; it simply relies on the efforts of another or others to get where it wishes to go. Any of these variations of false unity will collapse under the slightest pressure, just as a wall would if you place bricks loosely together, but do not use mortar between them. You will be able to see that a wall built in such a way would fall at the first push.

However, whilst you will know this to be true, you should also consider that appearances can be deceiving. Because the shape of a brick is uniform and has no uniqueness or individuality it will easily be loosened and any wall constructed without the necessary bonding will fall apart. But, a stone wall made of individual stones which are just the right shape and fit for each other, will stay as solid as any wall which has been cemented; if it has been built with skill and a passion for building unity into its design.

There exists also an appearance of unity which seems smooth and perfectly dovetailed on the surface but is falling apart behind the facade. There are also relationships of different kinds which appear to be turbulent and erratic, and yet the relationship (or unity) sustains beyond what may be expected or anticipated. These relationships are like the stone wall perfectly put together with skill and loving care, so that even though all the angles of the stones it is built from are different and appear to be uneven, it still holds steady and strong.

If you look more carefully at what appears to be unity you will see that true unity is held together by a meeting of minds. Even stronger unity is created where there is heartfelt love, or a shared passion, which binds it together, and helps to overcome bumps in the road and difficulties that may lie ahead.

The creation of the universe, including human beings and all other living things, has a unity which has been lovingly put together to create a complex and yet perfectly united whole. For each aspect and being plays their own role within the whole of the universe, and each time a part of this complex universe is unnecessarily extinguished, it affects all of the others directly or indirectly. The individual consciousness of each human being is still journeying towards an understanding of this, and it is now beginning to be understood by some human beings on the planet at this time. The wonder of this oneness is that as aspects of it cease to exist the unity that is creation adjusts, adapts, rebuilds, and evolves.

True unity within the human condition is a meeting of hearts and minds, and it is filled with a love that is deep enough to withstand doubt and fear. It is a total bonding, and when you re-discover your awareness of this universal unity, you will see more clearly the connections between yourself and others; rather than seeing the differences. This is when your understanding of true unity will become your greatest strength. This is a unity that cannot be weakened or broken. It may simply be that in travelling the path of physical experience you have temporarily lost sight of it. In returning to your roots, to your centre, to me for guidance, you will strengthen the unity that is creation, and you will become strengthened also.

When you wish to consider more deeply the nature of unity, simply close your eyes for a moment or two and imagine a group of people all connected to each other and forming an unbroken circle. Whilst this may seem to be an obvious symbol of unity, it is not the circle which is the real symbol here; it is in the detail of the image which you may not notice at first glance. For these people are not just linked they are entwined and their heads move forward to make connection with each other. Here we have a meeting not just of bodies, but of hearts and minds; we have a group of human beings forming a union that thinks and acts as one. Look more closely now at the image in your mind, and see that there is coloured light shining around and between these people. If you were to open your eyes and view such a group through your physical vision, you might not see this light, for it is the energy of each individual person joining together with the others and forming the energy of unity. This is a sharing, loving, giving of strength, bringing to the group a sense of the powerful energy or movement that is bringing the figures closer together. This is real unity, the kind that has strength to hold and sustain itself whatever challenges it may face in the future.

When you encounter anything that is considered to be unity whether it is in others or between you and others, stop for a moment to consider whether it is simply a facade or a solid and powerful unity, such as the one you see in this mental image. This pause for reflection will help you to sense whether the perceived unity truly does have a sound basis and a positive purpose. If you connect with your heart and with your soul you will begin to *feel* whether it is good sound unity or just a facade.

This unity I have described is a perfect example of unity that exists between the two of us. You may recall what I have said already, about "you" the human being and "I" the soul being, each existing in our own right; and yet although it does not seem possible when considered with logic and rationale, we are also indivisible from each other, for I am built into every atom and every cell of your being and thus it will always be throughout this life.

We will not fight or disagree; we will not lose our love for each other, even when your awareness of me is sleeping. For I am you and you are me; we are one, we are whole, we are in unity.

Concerning The Path of Life - Chapter Nineteen

Power Such as This is Within You

The words "control" and "power" are often used in an interchangeable way. For instance, you may perceive that to control is to have power over, or to have power over is to control. But these definitions when considered together almost always refer to ways of restricting individuals, groups, or even whole nations. To be truly powerful the control must first be applied to the "self" and it does not matter whether this "self" is an individual human being, or a larger body of people or circumstances.

You are living in a universe so vast and yet so powerful in the beauty of its self-control that you only need to look around you in nature to see how everything works together and has a purpose and design. While nature can at times appear to be destructive, when studied in depth it becomes clear that the greatest power of all is not restrictive and controlling but structured and creative.

In nature there is of course a natural order and sequence, and these are all interwoven in some way to co-exist with each other. Even those areas of creation which have the appearance of being destructive are never so without reason or purpose; they are a part of a process of breaking down the old so that it may be re-created in the new, and balance can be maintained. Even when you turn your gaze away from planet earth and into deep space, you will discover that stars and planets are being born and dying away in a constant and continuing process. Although these events can seem destructive in their power, as human scientists search ever more deeply into these cosmic events, they begin to discover that what appears to be a death or destruction is usually an event that produces the birth of new stars or planets, and it seems that this is the way it has always been.

Humankind is the only species on this planet that destroys simply for pleasure. This is power misused and abused, and it has no positive or creative outcome. Such a use of power does not serve the future of humankind or the planet that human beings live on. As the human race moves ever further out from the boundaries of planet earth, they are in danger of taking this destructive perspective with them in to all that lies ahead of them.

You will be walking your soul path more faithfully and truly when you are able to recognise and own the power that lies within you. When you see this pure, unadulterated power in others, be aware that whilst you too have that same power, it can never be controlled by another unless that is what you have chosen to allow. Resist wherever you are able to, the temptation to use your power for the control of people or situations purely for your own benefit. This is not *use* of your power it is *abuse* of your power.

When you recognise the need to control your own thoughts, words, and actions and can use that control wisely, you are on your way to becoming truly powerful. If you have concerns about power, whether it is your own power or that of another, first recognise the difference between restrictive control and true constructive and creative power. Remember I hold that greatest power deep inside of you. I am your strength, your power, your vision, your clarity, your structure and your discipline; but above all these I am love, the power that creates and heals.

Look around you in this world and even back through history and into the ancient past. You will see those who have used power to create something outstanding. However, if you look more closely you will also see they often did so from a need to increase their own power. If you continue to explore these events, you will also see that abuse of power usually produces an event, occurrence, structure, or civilisation, which will in time go into decline. The reins of such power have always eventually been grasped by another or others. All civilisations have their day, and those that become a major "power" eventually give that power over to another more "powerful" civilisation. For these civilisations are initially and ultimately about having power over others, and they will eventually have need to do battle for the power they wield. For often, (despite appearances to the contrary) this is a destructive and restraining power.

Human beings as individuals and groups often allow instincts of fear to guide their actions, and when they do so, good does not usually come from those actions. If you do this you may temporarily gain the power that makes you feel safe for a while. However, when you allow fear to take the reins of your power, it will be destructive and limiting rather than creative and evolutionary. Only when you offer the reins to love will the truly positive and life affirming creations begin to arise in your life and the lives that you touch. When you are able to work from a base of love instead of a base of fear, this is when you will find the desire for your power to do good for others increases. As a natural consequence you will find also that your inner power is increasing in proportion to your release of the need to have outer power.

If you look at what remains from the greatest civilisations, you will discover an important lesson. When you explore these great civilisations carefully enough, you may be surprised at what the evidence reveals. For you will see that each soul who has lived on this planet has or will have had some spark of goodness somewhere within their being, no matter how insignificant it appears to have been.

If you wish to have a clearer picture of the real nature of power both negative and positive, I would ask you to close your eyes and imagine you are looking at a star of intense coloured light spinning around. At the outer edges of the star there appears to be an invisible barrier or restrictive force that is preventing the sharp points of spinning light from shooting straight outward, and is causing them to form a curved spiral shape.

Now look again at those points and you see they are fiery red, a colour which often indicates an aggressive energy, strength, or power. Move your focus inward to the centre of the image and you will see the colours soften and become lighter, and then more muted, and in the very centre is pure white. This is symbolic of the appearance of power you may often see in the people and situations you encounter in life. For you may come to realise that beneath the fiery aggressive exterior there is a much softer calmer and more pure interior and the aggressive or assertive image is just a facade, used by those in fear to protect themselves from some perceived threat to their power. It is for this reason that the edges at the outer limit of the image I have described are curving in to protect themselves, rather than because they are pushed in by some external force,

If you look even more closely at this mental image it will become clear that the softer more muted energy is in fact deceptively strong, and the pure white light deep in the centre has power beyond description. It is the ultimate power which is at the centre of every human being.

Know that power such as this is within you if you choose to acknowledge it. But remember also to respect this power within yourself and others, and use your own power in constructive and creative ways. If you search within and listen to my voice, you will know this to be true.

Concerning The Path of Life - Chapter Twenty

Universe Within a universe

"I am the master of the Universe". In having just spoken of power, I would ask you what more powerful and sweeping statement than this could there be? For what more is there to be master of? When you say "universal" you will often be referring to something that is all encompassing, or in more practical terms, something that will fit all, suit all, adapt to all, or that all can be adapted to.

When you speak of the universe, do you know which universe you speak of? Is it something so vast that you are smaller than a grain of sand in the desert by comparison? If you saw yourself from the viewpoint of an atom, then you would see that by comparison you are as vast as what you understand to be the universe. Know that each thing you consider is relative to something else, and what you perceive as vast may be as nothing in relation to vastness you cannot presently comprehend. This relativity of sizes is contained within an even more vast range of sizes than the human consciousness can yet begin to understand.

The universe most apparent to you will be that of your physical structure, and even this is made up of so many aspects and differently functioning organs, glands, hormones, blood cells, muscles and bones. I could go on and describe physical aspects and attributes the scientists have not yet discovered, but I am sure that what I have said is sufficient to make you realise that your "body" is a universe.

Within the physical aspect of your being is the brain, and this is generally believed to be what instigates everything you do consciously or unconsciously, and what keeps you alive. For without the messages the brain sends to all other parts of you, it would not be possible for you to continue living as a human being. This is why the brain is one of several vital organs in your physical system, without which you cannot continue to live physically unless they are functioning at a certain level.

You may be aware that the brain is not seen as a living organism because it does not meet the criteria of a living organism. For instance some of the qualifications needed to be considered alive, include feeding and reproducing, and the brain fulfils neither of these functions. When you begin to understand only a small part of how the human brain works, you soon realise what a miraculous and complex physical machine it is. If you undertake a more detailed investigation of how the brain works, you begin to see that the scale of its operations and efficiency levels begin to take on an almost mystical quality.

While the human brain is not an organism it is an organ. It is a part of you that can be seen and touched and it exists in a physical sense. The brain works to connect information between various parts of itself and of you, and it uses electrical impulses to do so. It could well be described as one of the universes within the universe that is the whole of you, but still it is a physical organ.

Then there are the universes of your mind and all of the various and complex levels of your consciousness. When you look at what makes you function as a whole you cannot ignore the presence of your mind, which is a concept rather than a physical entity, and yet it is still quite real. Here you have the part of you that connects the physical to the non physical. The brain sends the electrical impulses and the mind uses some of these impulses in a non physical way to think, consider, muse, anticipate, remember, and so on. But then you may ask - is it not the mind that sends the knowledge to the brain so that it knows what electrical impulses to send and where to send them?

The workings of the mind truly are of a universal nature, for they are intangible, unlimited, and infinite. While the physical actions you can perform as a human being are contained within the scope of physical ability, the mind can think of anything it so wishes. The mind has the ability to imagine beyond what you may see as normal limits and understanding, for it is a direct line to the forces that have created all that is, all that ever has been, and all that ever will be.

You will be aware of the universes of your emotions, each level being intricate and varied, and contains abilities and complexities that human comprehension has not yet completely conquered. Beyond these are the different layers and aspects of your energy fields; from the physical through to the higher or divine awareness, and each is a universe of its own kind. To reinforce what

I am saying, each of these is a universe in their own way, and yet they are also a part of your universe, and the greater Universe which is the oneness of all that is.

Deep within you is my universe; the universe of your soul. But whilst it is true to say that I am deep within, I also permeate every aspect and field (physical and non physical), every atom and cell, every organ and gland, everything that is of you I am within and a part of. In considering this you may begin to understand the miracle of the universe and the eternal and beautifully intricate nature of creation, and to realise how grand the "grand design" really is.

As an individual human being, you are vast compared to an atom, and yet you are not even as an atom compared to the entire universe. You may struggle with the concept of infinity and of parallel universes, but how can you dismiss these with so little understanding of the universes I have mentioned, which you experience on a day to day basis.

The journeys into space which are now being made by human beings from planet earth begin to reveal how vast the universe is, and how much more there may be that has not yet reached human awareness. These new discoveries are all of a physical and material nature, made of gas, rock, iron, fire and ice to name just a few of the substances that form what is slowly being discovered by human scientists. Think what is yet to be revealed .In your three dimensional existence, you can see only so much of the absolute universal creation. How many more wonders might there be that are not of a physical or material nature; wonders that the human eye and the other physical human senses cannot perceive?

The explorers of the human race are still focussing their explorations outside of themselves. The real progress will be made when the explorations begin to go within. When the journeying to the universes that are ethereal, spiritual and beyond the human condition start to be contemplated and taken seriously, the path we travel will be moving onward and upward. That is when we will be working so much more closely with each other.

When this inner journey of discovery begins to take place on a wider human scale, your perspective on all matters will be widened and deepened, and you will become increasingly aware of the wonders of the whole of creation. When you consider the universe therefore, keep your brain active but also keep your mind open, and remember there are worlds within worlds, and you, too, are a universe within a universe, within a universe.

Book Two
Concerning Love

The thoughts expressed here concern issues around love and loving relationships experienced as you travel your soul path through this life.

The word "love" is often misused and associated simply with romantic love. However, when you consider the real nature of love, it becomes clear how many different areas of life there are where love (in its broader sense) is involved, and how many different forms love can take.

Concerning Love - Chapter One

The Most Significant Birth Experience

The most significant birth experience you will have in this lifetime is the moment you emerged as a newly born human being to take part in life on Planet Earth.

You will recall that when this life began I could not speak to you, because we were both still under the influence of the "sleep" that veiled my soul memory from you. A sense of "self", or of the human being you are (different in personality and physical features from other human beings) would not develop until sometime after your birth into this life.

There will have been other times when you have found yourself at points of new beginning, and this will continue to occur at different stages throughout your life. Each time this happens you may feel as though you are at the start of a new and different path. These events can make you feel as if you are turning a fresh page in the story of your life, and they can be exciting but also challenging.

As we walk this path together and you continue to experience your various new beginnings, you will be aware they are not physical births, but may feel they could be described as birth experiences. These are simply milestones that indicate a new and different stage of the journey taking us forward on our shared soul path.

When such times occur, they may be changes in location, physical, mental or emotional development, perhaps even spiritual revelation. There are many "births" as you go through life and it is from these experiences that the human expressions, "I feel like a new person" and, 'I feel like a different person' have come to be used.

You will no doubt by now have undergone a number of experiences, and relationships with other human beings that were relevant to you at the time they began. However, everything and everyone has their right time to exist in a place or situation, within a relationship or with a connection. Some relationships are relevant and healthy for a whole lifetime, whilst others run their course and then need to be released, so that each of those involved can move forward on the path of their own soul. This means there may be times when your new beginning feels more like an ending or a death rather than a birth. But remember that for a new beginning to take place there will need to be a space in which it can be born.

When you have read all of these, my thoughts, and can bring to mind what I have said about change, you will see why I do not devote a part of these discussions to the experience of death. What you call life is simply this stage of my path we share and in which we are existing within the human condition. You may recall that when your physical body (the part of you that enables the human condition to be experienced by me) can no longer sustain life, I will return home. The essential part of you which is your human consciousness will live on in me, and in time we will begin the next stage of the journey.

This means the whole of what you might describe as "you" does not expire completely. For after your physical death, your consciousness and all that you have experienced through this lifetime, will become a part of me and my continuing path through existence. What you call "death" is simply the catalyst for me to prepare for the next stage of my soul path journey.

It is a normal part of being human to become emotionally attached when in a relationship with another. There are many reasons why relationships end, but it will usually be because it has fulfilled a lesson within the soul path of those involved. If this happens to you before you become aware of this fact you may experience emotional pain. Remember, therefore, that if you are the one who first has such a realisation, there is a need to be gentle and compassionate with the other person when the time comes to let go. If you do so you will both be able to move forward with less pain.

Whoever first realises the time has come to make space for a new beginning, the realisation will eventually come to all concerned. It may simply take a longer time and further experiences for some than it does for others.

Endings are always followed by fresh beginnings of one sort or another. If your fresh beginning is a new relationship you may feel innocent and trusting, seeing only good in those with whom you are entering into that new relationship. You will quite possibly believe this will last for the rest of your life and be eager to move forward.

You might feel as if you are undergoing a re-birth, and your emotions at such a time may be positive and constructive, fulfilling the purpose of strengthening the new relationship. Sometimes however, there may be a feeling of unease or mistrust around a "birth" or new stage of the journey, for when you enter into a new relationship, there is a need to be able to deal with the changes it brings. It is at times like these you will be required to step into the unknown and re-discover the sense of familiarity you had acquired in your old situation or relationship.

On the other hand, there may be times when you find it easy to rediscover that sense of trust you had as a new-born child, clear of doubt and suspicion or fear and withdrawal. If this is the case, there will still be a need to retain the wisdom you have gained from your previous relationships in life, and even (at a subconscious level) from the memories of my previous life relationships.

These are times where you need to use the sense of "vision" I have already spoken of. You can do this by seeing people through my eyes, as they really are, not just as you would wish them to be or as others may tell you they are. This does not mean you cannot love them if you find they are less than perfect, for then you would give your love to no one. There is a need for healthy balance to be established, and it can be found with a loving heart and a little soul wisdom

Imagine now that you are gazing into a deep blue night sky filled with stars and lit by a large, bright full moon. you see a rainbow arc forming and reaching from the depth of that night sky toward planet earth where you are standing. As you look even more closely, you see a spark of brilliant light travelling along the rainbow arc and you realise it is the soul of a tiny new infant completing its journey to earth as it prepares to begin life as a human being.

While you may not remember the time when you and I joined the human race together, as you look at this soul approaching the planet to join the rest of humankind, you may be reminded that it is a time of new beginnings and of innocence. It is the starting point of this journey called life. This soul has moved on from any previous existence and is about to "start again". It is preparing to merge with an infant soon to be born. If reincarnation makes sense to you, then this concept will be easy to relate to.

Whatever your beliefs may be, this is simply a visual reminder that at any time during this life, you can, if you wish, view things from the perspective of the new born child. This is a perspective without prejudice or pre-condition, yet it still retains the eternal inner wisdom of the soul with which you become unified at the time of your birth.

Remember what I have said about wisdom and power, and you will understand more clearly what is truly important. If you are able to take a quiet moment to sense my loving guidance when entering a new relationship, you will be taking a step closer to our ultimate union, just as this soul is preparing to be united with the human infant. You simply need a brief period when your mind and heart is free from the many distractions that life and its various relationships can present you with. Remember also at such times how valuable the the practice of mindfulness can be.

It is important to be aware that a loving heart does not subdue its own identity and give away its energy space. This infant and its soul are not coming into life on planet earth to offer their personal space to another; they are coming to take their rightful place and help to fulfil the path of the infant's soul.

When a "birth" situation occurs in your life, know that it is always right to share with and have an awareness of the "other". This is the way whether the "other" is a person or a situation; for it is love in action. We are all a smaller part of the greater whole of creation. Each time you fail to offer love or compassion and instead offer pain, you are doing so to yourself as well as to another.

Never forget that the human race has lived through many dark ages, and these have left their legacy of limited understanding about the meaning of the word "love". Some human beings think only of romantic love when they use this word, and others think only of friends and family. But, love is at the root of all survival, all renewal, all new beginnings (or births). It is the creative force of the universe and all that is, and when it seems lost, this is fear which also has many names and many forms.

Do not forget to offer love at each new beginning or "birth" in the course of this life. It does not matter whether it is to a person or to any other living being. Remember how many different ways love can be offered.

Remember too that there is also a need to love yourself, and this planet that is your home and that sustains and supports you.

Concerning Love - Chapter Two

Releasing Miracles of Wonderment

The concept of wonderment may bring to mind for you the sensation you experience when entering into new relationships, or perhaps the innocence of your childhood when you were able to see wonder in so many things. During those early years of your life, your sense of wonderment will have come from such simple experiences as seeing a reflection in a mirror, the colours of a rainbow, or bubbles floating in the air. As a child you could enjoy this sense of wonderment completely without any feelings of foolishness, for when you were very young you had not yet developed a consciousness of how others perceived you. There would be no sense of apprehension or awareness of the challenges which may lie ahead of you in life.

But then you would begin to acquire a sense of self-consciousness, and an awareness of how you appeared to others. So you no longer wished to appear innocent and filled with wonder for fear of being seen as naive and foolish. You will then have begun to experience some of the challenges that are a part of this life and perhaps replaced your sense of wonderment with one of doubt and suspicion. This will have prevented you from enjoying those simple experiences you had as a small child, in that same uncomplicated way of accepting them purely for their beauty and the pleasure they gave to you.

However, it is not wise to become conditioned in such a way that you let go of your capacity for this experience of wonderment. Remember you are constantly surrounded by beauty and miracles large and small created by nature and your fellow human beings. Do not allow the challenges of life and the teachings of others to cloud your ability to see these wonders.

As you learn and grow, you may begin to find stirring within you awareness of my presence deep inside your being, even though you are still uncertain exactly what it is you are becoming aware of. This awareness brings you opportunities for wonderment of an inner nature. When you begin to connect with me and allow opportunities for communication between us to grow, the sense of wonderment becomes even greater, and it can grow and evolve throughout the whole of this life.

Remember, too, that in the most negative situations you may encounter there can be reason to find a sense of wonderment. Even in the darkness there is always the divine spark of creation. You will find after tears there will be laughter, after anger there will be calm, and after war there will be peace. If you remember this and your search is sincere, it may help you to hold on to your sense of wonderment, even if it is only from some small act of kindness you would have failed to notice and appreciate had you lost your capacity for this profound experience.

As you grow and change and your awareness of my presence within you also grows, your experiences of wonderment will change too, becoming deeper and all encompassing. So it is that from the simple innocence of a child who finds wonderment in a bubble floating through the air, you will begin to experience a sense of wonderment in the nature of creation, in exploring the different layers of your being, and in remembering who you truly are.

To experience wonderment is to be touched by your soul and to recognise that touch, and in that recognition you will radiate your experience out to all you meet. Whilst you are savouring your sense of wonderment, you are in turn empowering others to connect with their souls and to perpetuate this wonderful energy onward without end. If you wish to consider this concept further, look at the face of a small child experiencing a sense of wonderment. It is likely to be at some simple event or occurrence. For these small human beings have the capacity for wide eyed wonder at almost everything they see around them.

While I urge you not to lose your sense of wonderment, having lived through many previous lives, I know that as you face the challenges of your soul path, it is possible to lose the ability to experience this sensation. For these challenges will often appear to you as setbacks and misfortunes which life has placed across your path and cause you to focus on what you perceive to be negative experiences of your path through life.

This loss of wonderment can happen gradually from an early age, and you may be unaware that it is fading away. Then one day you realise you have become cynical about your interactions and relationships with others. You are unable to feel a sense of awe and wonder about anything you encounter, and you view things from a suspicious and sceptical perspective. If there is still a trace of this sensation left within you, make sure you hold on to it, and if you discover it has disappeared completely, seek it out without delay. For throughout your life in times good or bad, you will experience events large or small that can produce a sense of wonderment, so long as you have not allowed it to fade away from your senses completely

Those events perceived from the innocence of childhood with a sense of wonderment, may have passed into your history, and with time and greater understanding of them, they will have moved into the realm of the mundane. However, there is no limit to the wonders that surround you and lie within you. As a child you will have looked outward for the wonders to appear, but as you travel your path through life with me, you will begin to see the wonders I see, and even to feel them deep within you in the silence. Remember to keep open the channels of communication between us. Look into the innocent eyes of a young child who stands in wonder, and know that you can still experience wonderment at an ever increasing level. You simply need to allow yourself to feel your sense of wonderment, without any concern about how others may judge you.

When you experience this sense of wonderment at even the simplest of things, you give permission to those around you to do likewise, and help to release them from conditioning that has isolated them from their own sense of wonderment. You in turn will be releasing miracles of wonderment into the world; miracles that became suspended as they were buried beneath conditioning based in fear. Such fear leads you to believe that to be cynical and sceptical protects you from disappointment and reduces your vulnerability. But to live in such a state of fear is to live in a state of vulnerability, quietly and desperately waiting for disappointment to occur.

Life often presents challenges and unexpected outcomes; but when you are able to accept this and know that these are all a part of my plan for us, you will understand that each challenge contains a lesson and an opportunity for growth. This is when you will be more able to work with the lessons presented to you. Then you will move forward on the path of your soul, ready for the wonders and beauties that are also a part of life. When you can do this you will truly be in communication with me - your soul.

Your eyes, which are the windows of the soul, will see the beauty around you more clearly, and what is just as important they will see the beauty and wonder that is within you and within each soul you encounter, even if the human counterpart of that other soul is still searching for their own soul connection.

Concerning Love - Chapter Three

Listen Carefully When Displacement Comes

Have you ever felt like you are being tossed this way and then another, until your head feels as if it does not know which way round it is and you no longer know your proper situation or position. This will be very different from the feelings of wonderment I have just discussed with you. The feeling I am now describing is one of something known as displacement.

Imagine yourself being spun round and round until you get just such a feeling. When you have stopped spinning, you feel that you no longer know where you are or in what direction you are facing. You may even reach out a hand to find support until your dizziness subsides. However, if you allow yourself to remain calm and still for just a little while, you find you are able to take your bearings and know exactly where you are.

If you feel that something no longer has a place in your life, you are likely to consciously remove it and displace it from your experience, and this may feel positive. However, there are many different experiences of displacement in this life and not all of these will arise from circumstances of your choosing. When this is the case the experience can leave you with a feeling that your sense of purpose or identity, your status, or the place you see as home has somehow been removed. Most human beings find this experience leaves them feeling uncomfortable, as if they are no longer in their rightful place or position, and you may react in just such a way.

If you listen carefully when displacement comes, you will find it is simply telling you it is time for the next part of your journey, where your new rightful place awaits you. Listen in the silence for my guidance and you will realise that in the greater plan your position can never be displaced; it can simply progress. What you may see as a loss is really a gift on this path we walk together. If you find yourself in this kind of displacement experience, and feel troubled or that your position in life is under threat, go deep into the silence and listen to that still quiet part of you where your soul wisdom is and unease subsides. For this is a part of you which helps you feel calm and able to see the pattern forming ahead of us.

There will be times when our channels of communication may become temporarily disrupted, but we will never be fully displaced from each other. I am the aspect of you which knows this is not displacement but new placement. I will always recognise when a situation or set of circumstances is no longer serving us; and that it is time for it to be replaced with a new situation which will better serve us on the road ahead.

When you find yourself challenged by being displaced from your comfort zone, whether it is in the form of a relationship that has ended, a job you valued which is no longer available to you, or you lose a place you think of as home (to name just a few) it is important to remember the following:

you and I are both children of the universe, and we are indivisible. Our strength is in our unity and our power to communicate with each other across different levels of consciousness. You can never truly be displaced, only moved on to the next stage of this journey in order to more fully complete the path of your soul – my path which I walk with your help.

If you can find it within yourself to remember your true nature, you will recall that you have always been and will always be as lovable and worthy as any soul on this planet. It is a paradox of living as a human being, that while the human and soul aspects are intertwined, the human condition can create an illusion in the mind that you are "bad" "guilty" or "unworthy".   This is compounded when your human mind believes the illusion and you find yourself acting in accordance with it. When you stop and look more closely you will see it for what it is, and will remember that it is within your power to be the best you can be, even in different places and different circumstances through the course of your life.   The choice is yours. Continue to believe the illusion or remember who you truly are, and dispel it. If you look inward rather than outward, with complete trust in me you will discover me, completely at ease ready to remind you who you are. This is when I can help you see what is ahead of you more clearly, rather than dragging you backward into unhealthy yearnings for a position you once had, but which no longer serves you.

When you experience this sense of being spun around that displacement can cause, you will need to recover your equilibrium. This when you will often find that you are facing a different direction than the one you faced before the displacement began. You may also realise that you now see a door you were unable to see from your previous position. This door may be in the form of an opportunity, an idea, or a new insight, but it is a door which you were unable to see before your experience of displacement occurred. You will begin to realise that where you are facing now is more appropriate to where you wish to go next. If the door you see is to your left then left is the direction to take, and if the door is to your right then that is where you need to go.

Even if you do not see the logic of the direction to be taken at this time, the important thing to remember is that you could not previously see this door at all. The experience which made you feel as if you had been displaced, abandoned, or rejected has opened your eyes to new avenues on this path of your soul. Of course you may find more than one door in front of you and then you will need to make a choice. So you see that not only has this displacement experience provided you with new avenues, it has provided you with new choices and better vision regarding the road ahead

There is also the possibility that you do not yet see a door at all. This is when patience and fortitude are important, and the realisation that if there is no door visible to you at this point, you simply need to quietly and without fear keep yourself open to seeing the new door when it appears. For when the time is right it will surely appear, even if it takes longer than you expect. If it seems as if the door is not appearing sit quietly and reach out for me to remind you of what I have just told you, that when the time is right the door will appear. I may also need to remind you that the door might be quite a different one to that which you have in mind.

So when you are experiencing these feelings of displacement, remember to stop and reassess your situation, so that you are able to move with the changes that have occurred in your life, and recall the words I have spoken on the subject of "Change" When it seems you are in a position or situation that feels wrong or out of place, check for circumstances that may have altered without you having noticed, and know that you are now in the right place for your situation at this new moment in time.

If you discover that you truly feel this is not the right place, even just in the here and now, recognise it as a stepping stone, and allow a little time to see when and where you can move on and find another position that will best suit your new situation. Even in this "place between" there will be lessons to be learned and progress to be made.

Wherever you find yourself in this life, and however unfamiliar or out of place you feel, you are exactly where you need to be to experience the challenges of this path of the soul, for I am with you at all times and wherever you are. Whilst you live this life, you and I will never be displaced from each other. I am a part of you that will always have an eternal place in the plan of the universe, in this life and in lives yet to come.

Embrace this experience that you may have seen as

displacement, and welcome with open arms the next part of the journey and the new opportunities and insights it will bring to you.

Concerning Love - Chapter Four

For Love Does Not Lay Down Conditions

When I speak on the subject of conditions, I am speaking of conditions human beings place on the love they give to each other. You will know of this, for it is likely that at some time in this life you will have been offered love with conditions attached. There is the condition that says "I will love you if you love me too", or the condition that says "I will love you if you become the person I think you should be". Then there is the love that is offered for being compliant and subservient or as a reward for many different things. You will know in your heart of hearts that love which is offered in such a way is not the true essence of love. For real love will be given to you whether or not you comply with one condition or another, and it will be given to you whether or not you return that love.

There are many kinds of genuine and sincere love: the love for your parents, or your children, love of your friends, love of your fellow human beings in many ways, and even love that does not focus on another human being. The love I wish to speak about first is the love shared between two adults, the kind of love often described as romantic love. For when children reach adulthood, this is usually the kind of love that plays a major part in their experience of life.

When this kind of love grows it is often described as "falling in love", and this is a good description. For when romantic love takes hold, the ability to see your way forward is often lost in the enchantment it causes, and you may stumble along blindly wrapped in the enchantment. This is a kind of love to which the expression "love is blind" would apply. It is a kind of love that often blinds one human being to the human frailties of another, and when the enchantment begins to fade, those frailties become apparent. This is when human beings often feel they have been deceived by the other, when in truth they were blinded by their own romantic vision of them. It is in the accepting by each of the other's frailties that really powerful and deep love is enabled to grow, and this can be so whether it is love of a romantic nature or one of the many other kinds of love there are.

Whether you have found a loving partner for life or just a short space of time, it is likely you will have encountered the feelings it stirred within your heart as you travelled through the teenage years of your life. You may still be recall those emotions that arose within you, even if you are not sharing a romantic love at this time in your life.

By now you will be aware that the experience of love can present you with many lessons. You can learn that to love is painful when it is given and not returned in the way you had hoped or expected. Perhaps the love you have given has not been returned at all, or perhaps you have been fortunate and experienced the miracle of love given to you without condition or limitation.

Because of the irrational and instinctive way human beings experience romantic love, it is likely that at some stage in your life you may offer your love to another human being and find that it has been declined. Alternatively you may find it is accepted and subsequently cast aside when you least expect. If this occurs it is a natural human response to withdraw and to close the heart. The pain experienced in these circumstances is often rooted in the ego and the expectation of a return on an investment of love you have given. Yes, you have given your love, but it has been given with a condition that the love is returned for ever more. It is at such times you may need to accept that this other person has been unable to fulfil the conditions you have placed on the love you gave to them, and as a result they withdrew.

Know that when love is offered to you conditionally, you will need to decide whether you wish to enter into a "loving" relationship with conditions attached, even before it has had time to develop fully. There are no conditions placed on a real deep and lasting love. It is given from the heart for its own sake, for love does not lay down conditions. It is reciprocated naturally between two people who each care more for the welfare of the other than they do for their own.

If you reflect on the encounters you have had with romantic love or those you have seen played out between others, you will know it is difficult for human beings to accept gracefully and without emotional pain that their path ahead will not be with the one they had hoped it to be. It is because of this that the person in a relationship who first confirms the feelings between the two of them are not mutual is often seen as "the villain of the piece". The other person who had not gained awareness that all was not well is seen as the victim. However, when you draw on your inner wisdom you can let go without pain, for to pretend falsely that love exists where it does not is to live a lie, and no truly loving relationship can be built upon a lie.

Imagine now the scene of two young lovers, one clings tightly to the other who is clearly in turmoil and searching for a way to detach from them. Those who observe will feel sympathy for the person who clings but will know from an objective viewpoint that whilst the clinging continues, the pain cannot end. Even when the physical clinging has ended, there is often a tendency within the human emotions to move forward into new relationships still clinging to pain and doubt around the honesty of another, brought forward from their previous relationship. This is when a human being is bringing conditions into their new relationship. These may be conditions that the other should never leave them as they feel their previous partner has done, or that this new partner should become subject to their will so they can retain control in this new relationship. These conditions are put in place as a subconscious safety net, which it is hoped will prevent an unhappy outcome to the new relationship.

If you find yourself in this situation, remember such conditions do not strengthen a relationship; they create barriers which become like a ball and chain dragging the relationship down and preventing it from making progress and developing healthily. You cannot look to others to remove the ball and chain of your conditions, and they cannot expect you to deal with theirs. For when you carry these obstacles into a loving relationship they are based in fear, a fear that you may be taken advantage of or that you will be abandoned. Ill treatment can only happen if you allow it to, and you can be abandoned only if you choose to see a parting of the ways as abandonment. Your fears can only be released if you are prepared to release them and to trust that everyone is not out to hurt you.

These things I speak of are clearly in relation to the emotion of love between two people and do not relate to the physical and practical issues of any relationship or friendship which such circumstances often give rise to. These are a separate issue and one more related to compassion which is another aspect of love. However, be assured that when you place conditions on a new relationship which are based on old pain, such conditions will not prevent new pain occurring; they will surely invite it.

Even in other kinds of loving relationships, there can be a tendency to place conditions on the love given. Children will often say they no longer love their parents when they are subject to discipline or required to make a sacrifice of some kind. However, as children they are undergoing a process of mental and emotional development and are still learning from the adults around them from whom they take their example. In addition, adult human beings sometimes place conditions on the love they offer to their children, only giving that love freely when the child reciprocates the effort and sacrifice they as parents have put into the relationship. In doing so they forget that they brought the child into this world and therefore have a responsibility to care for them until they are able to be self sufficient.

There is no place for conditions in the love from a parent to their child. Do not confuse this with a need for loving discipline and sensible ground rules, for this is a powerful form of love which teaches the child how to become a loving and respectful adult, and it can at times be uncomfortable for both parent and child in the process.

There is a tendency that comes into play in many different kinds of relationship, and this is when one person feels the other has failed to fulfil the conditions they have placed on the relationship. This is so even though that person may believe their love is unconditional. When this occurs, one or the other individual within the relationship will either as a child or as an adult be unable to resists saying to the other "after all I have done for you". This phrase carries an implied statement that there have been conditions placed on whatever has been done in the name of love – or friendship, which is an associate of love.

The only requirement in any loving relationship is mutual respect and caring for each other and this is not a condition but an indication that love truly is present.

Concerning Love - Chapter Five

Where Torment Can Flourish

When you look at the word "torment" you see the first three letters of the word "torque" which relates to the action of twisting, and the first four letters of the word "mental" which relates to the mind. It makes sense then that the experience of torment could be seen as a process of mental twisting. There are many individuals who have experienced torment and who would agree they have felt as if their mind has been painfully twisted by a situation or by the words or actions of another. An example of this link to twisting can be seen in the frequently used expressions – "I need to straighten this out" and "I need to straighten my head out".

The mental and emotional pain you suffer in life can be as a result of some cruelty inflicted upon you by another or simply from some unintentional or accidental occurrence. Torment can arise whether it is caused by a physical act or a form of communication, but whichever of these it is there will be pain of some sort. However, there will be times when the mental or emotional pain you experience is of your own creation. When you misinterpret the words or actions of another or they misinterpret yours, you may find yourself with a twisted perception of the situation or relationship. If you are suffering such torment, you will need to untwist your thoughts and feelings and let go of your suffering, in order to find peace once again.

An aspect of this which can be difficult to come to terms with is that no matter what your perception or understanding of that situation is, you cannot always rely on someone you may perceive to be 'in the wrong' to "make it right". When this arises between two people or two groups, each will firmly believe they are either the 'injured party" or they are justified in what the "other side" sees as an offence or an attack by them. As human beings usually only say or do what they believe to be the right thing it follows they will be reluctant to apologise for torment their words or actions may have caused, much less to admit that they have been in the wrong.

Torment is strongly governed by perspective, for each person or group can often only see a situation from within the limitation of their own viewpoint. It will take the ability to put yourself in the shoes of another, in order to consider the possibility that you may have said or done something which is hurtful to them and why this may be so. What is hurtful to one person is insignificant to another and the reverse applies.

The irony in relation to the pain of torment is that it is frequently experienced in the context of what should be a happy and loving relationship, and the added irony is that human beings often inflict emotional cruelty on those they profess to love the most. This can be due to a mistaken belief that if they do so the other person will come to love them or perhaps to love them more.
Because of this they sometimes act out an illusion and pretend to be uncaring, in the hope that they will appear

strong, and the other person will accordingly be more attracted to them. It may give them a sense of power and control, but this kind of power is unhealthy. These types of behaviour are often described as "mind games".

However, there are many ways that human beings set up the conditions where torment can flourish within the heart and mind of another and it is often done in the name of love. There are times when there has been no intention to cause torment and matters can be clarified and then resolved happily. But torment will at times arise from the pain of confusion or misunderstanding in relation to words, actions or situations.

Whether you suffer torment from your own error or the error of another, letting go is necessary. For if you are suffering torment as a result of something said or done by someone you care for, it is necessary to let go of your pain in order to see your way forward clearly. However, if someone has intentionally caused you pain, it is necessary to step back so that you can see this is not the relationship you perceived it to be, and to know whether or not it is time to move on, in order to find someone who loves you without the mental and emotional games that cause such torment. Alternatively, if you and another or others are able to resolve your differences, such a situation may turn out to be a catalyst which leads to honesty and mutual respect in the relationship, whatever its nature.

There are times when torment is present in many of life's relationships, and always it is necessary to step away, detach, and untwist the distorted thought form in order to be free from it. This is when it will no longer hold power over you. In doing so you will find the clarity with which to make your decisions about the road ahead, whether it is to stay within the relationship in question and reach a better understanding or to bid farewell and allow yourself and another each to walk the path ahead with the benefit of lessons learned.

When you learn how to detach from words and actions so they do not cause you to suffer torment, you can begin to find peace of mind. It is possible to learn and grow from your painful experiences, and find a good outcome from something that has caused such pain, even if that pain has in truth been self inflicted. Life brings less emotional and mental pain and suffering when instead of accepting it into your consciousness, you are able to lovingly step back from it so that you can perceive more clearly the inner anguish that makes one human being offer pain to another.

Such progress on the path of the Soul can be a steep learning curve. However, you will experience less suffering if you can find the strength to allow others to follow their personal learning curve without succumbing to the temptation to become judgemental. For this is when the urge arises to "teach someone a lesson" and that is usually revenge disguised as justice. So remember that when you feel someone has caused you torment, this will undoubtedly have occurred because you have unwittingly entered into an agreement with them to accept it and in so doing you have given to them a degree of your personal power.

When you become aware that torment is present in your consciousness, or even that it is imminent, remember to turn and face it and allow yourself to seek out the lesson it is bringing to you. Then quietly take control of your power, and lovingly step away to allow the other to fulfil their own experience without projecting their pain on to you. It is not unkind or uncaring to decline when you are offered pain by another in order to reduce their own burden of pain or to increase their own sense of self worth. For when someone seeks an increased sense of self worth at the expense of someone else's peace of mind, they have lessons still to learn.

If you find yourself in a state of torment, remember that I am the anchor you can hold onto and I can help to bring you back to a calmer and more reasoned state of mind, whatever the cause of your anguish may have been. Go to the quiet space inside of yourself at such times, and know that this is where you will find me within that calm and ordered place deep in your consciousness, away from the torment and the twisting. I will be waiting for you to ask how you can learn from your experience of torment, and then let go of it. This is when you can reach a more loving and gentle state of thinking and feeling, which is healthier for you and for everyone around you.

So do not flee from your torment, take a moment to open yourself to the experience it brings, and then to close your eyes and imagine that you have a length of fine cord tied around your head and knotted at the centre of your forehead. Reach up to the cord and slowly but steadily untie the knot and release yourself from the barrier it was creating to your ability to think clearly. Now you have untwisted the shape of that knot and released the blockage in the cord, you are free to let it drop or put it to a useful purpose then walk away. Any way of thinking or feeling which has intentionally (or unintentionally) become twisted will in time return to its natural shape and balance, if it is released with love

Concerning Love - Chapter Six

Now Let Us Speak of Towers and Turrets

Now let us speak of towers and turrets and perhaps conjure up for you images of those places in life that you see as safe and protected.

When you were a child you will have read of towers and turrets in fairytales. Princes rescued princesses from towers they were imprisoned in. Turrets gave concealment and protection to soldiers guarding those towers. One is a place where you may be locked away by force, and the other a place where you may go by choice for your own protection.

Whether you are a "prince" or a "princess", if you have suffered torment or painful emotions in matters of love, it is not unusual to begin building your own emotional towers and turrets. First you start the process of locking away your heart so that you are unable to give away your love, and this is usually (but not always) done in an unconscious way. Often it is an instinctive reaction to ensure that your heart and emotions will be protected from further pain when love you give is unrequited, or you feel it has been dishonoured.

This process usually takes place slowly and steadily over time, and with each subsequent event you experience that becomes emotionally painful the tower is made higher, and the windows of the turret through which you can see the world, (and through which the world can see you) become narrower.

In creating such towers and turrets around your heart to protect yourself, you are also creating a fortress in which to lock away the love you may at some time in the future wish to give. But, when that time comes you discover your self- imposed prison is preventing your love from being released into the world and fully expressed. Then you may realise there is another process taking place and you eventually come to see you have created a prison from which you are unable to escape, and this is the prison which isolates you from receiving the love you would welcome and even yearn for.

When this occurs, you will slowly become aware that the towers and turrets built around your emotions have become an impenetrable prison, and the longer you allow them to remain in place the more difficult it will be to escape from your high and sturdy tower, or to see out of your narrow turret window. Nevertheless, in order to free yourself so that you can give and receive love when you truly wish to, this escape from the prison of your towers and turrets and to freedom is essential.

Where unconditional love is concerned there is no need for towers and turrets, and yet you may become so afraid of pain that you are in danger of retreating into such emotional devices, which you perceive as your protection but which will become your prison. This is when you will discover you are incapable of giving or receiving love and your life is in danger of becoming a mere shadow of itself

Towers and turrets like the ones in the fairy tales of your childhood are structures not often seen in today's world, and so those you may see in the world around you are likely to be ruins which remains from a time long ago. They are usually dark empty and forbidding, even though they will in the past have been powerful fortresses, built on hills to withstand all approach from unwanted visitors. However, now all you see are these ruins, empty, dark, and lifeless.

If you surround your heart with a protective tower in order to avoid being hurt it will eventually become just such a ruin, devoid of life and love and happiness. To the world you may appear normal and free, but within your heart you will be gazing out through your turret windows locked away in a prison of your own creation. You will see that it would be wise therefore to avoid such emotional prisons.

When you give or receive love it does not mean you must be imprisoned by that love, for then it is not love at all. You can still give and receive love without the need to retreat into your very own tower that is impenetrable at all times, and peering out into the world from your narrow turret opening, which prevents you from seeing the world clearly.

Remember when love you give is rejected, this is not a rejection of the person you are, only of the love you have offered When this happens, if you are able to resist building a fortress around your heart, you will eventually become aware that the path of true love still awaits you, it simply awaits you in a different direction. Be aware that such emotional structures built around the heart are infinitely more difficult to dismantle than they ever were to build. When you know who you are and you know your true worth, you will have no need for such emotional towers and turrets. You will be strong enough to flourish without the need to create a self imposed prison.

If you have already found yourself in such a prison, there will be a need for you to make strong your connection with me, for I am able to help you begin the work of dismantling your prison walls, thereby allowing the pain to heal and helping you to give and receive love without fear once again. As we work together to dismantle those walls that have formed your inner prison, we will do so one brick at a time – sometimes slowly, but always thoroughly.

It is important to remember that you can open your heart and free yourself to give and receive love whenever you choose. There is no need to fear giving love just because it may be rejected or not returned in a like manner. If the love you give is unrequited, you will know it is time to move on.

The love you have in your heart does not have a limit; it will not run dry unless you allow yourself to believe the illusion that it may do so. You can give infinite amounts of love to infinite amounts of people if you so wish, and always I will be there to guide your emotions and your reactions and remind you that the ability to give genuine love does not need to have such a limit. As you live this life you are free to decide whether love offered to you is genuine or something that you feel in your heart is a facade under the guise of love. The choice is always available to you and to every human being. It is not necessary to be suspicious of all love because you have had one or more unhappy experiences in this area of your life. The most important love you will ever feel is genuine love for yourself. Until you are able to love and accept yourself you will be unable to fully give to - or receive from others, the love that can enhance and enrich your life.

When you know who you truly are, then you will know you are as worthy of your own love as you are of the love of anyone around you. This does not mean you need to constantly strive for some state of absolute perfection in order to be worthy of love from yourself or from another. It simply means you have begun to understand that every human being alive on this beautiful planet is subject to the frailties of the human condition.

This is not called "the school of life" without good reason. For all souls and their human counterparts have not come here to be *perfect* we have come here to *experience,* to learn, to grow, and to return home wiser and stronger. The path to perfection lies within those imperfections that give to you your very human experiences.

Do not make the mistake of thinking that pain and misunderstanding must be avoided at all costs. It is in the experiencing of pain and the work of learning to understand and to let go of such pain that you will create the building blocks which form the path ahead of you in life, the path of the soul we walk together.

Concerning Love - Chapter Seven

Tales of Wonderful Golden Spires

Having used the example of towers and turrets remembered from your childhood stories, I wish now to use another example of a more positive nature. Just as you recalled the towers and turrets from your childhood stories, you will also recall tales of wonderful golden spires. These were places to seek out and in which to find your very own "happy ever after". A spire is, of course, a tall pointed tower reaching up into the sky, and to *aspire* is to reach upward for fulfilment of your desires or ambitions. It is easy to see the connection between these two and why they were found in such stories. To reach out for your strongest aspirations is often described as "reaching for the sky".

When you think of castles with these golden spires soaring up into the heavens, you may believe they only belong in those magical stories set way back in the mists of time, a beautiful dream, a romantic image, but still - only an illusion. This is where you will have read about the handsome prince vowing undying love for his beautiful princess, and his princess returning that love, after which they ride off into the sunset and find their own happy ever after.

Human beings in today's world of modern technology and fast-paced insular living often believe that such love and happy ever after only exist in those tales from their childhood. Perhaps belief in this kind of 'happy ever after' has been whisked away with the speed at which so much is achieved and completed by human beings in today's world. But quantity is not the same as quality and a thing of great value takes time to create. It cannot be hurried and still be precious. So it is with relationships and love between two human beings.

Do not make the mistake of assuming this kind of love no longer exists in today's world, just because so many human beings do not allow the time in their busy lives for it to be found and then nurtured. Nowadays there is a tendency not to allow time to see whether the flower of deep and long lasting love will bloom, and so it may help you to remember and keep in mind the image of the golden spire to remind you to hold on to your aspirations, where love is concerned.

This undying love exists, but first you need to believe deep within your heart that this is so, as does the other human being with whom you may be developing a relationship. Only then will you be able to perceive the staircase which will lead you to the top of your own golden spire, and help you to grasp the flower of true and everlasting love that blooms at the very top. This love is all around you. It is a love you may find when you are young, and even sometimes when you are not so young. However, there are considerations to be made by all concerned, and it will be easier to make these when you understand that love is not a gift from a fairy godmother. It is something you and your beloved create between you from the depths of yours hearts and yours souls. When you understand these things there are no barriers to keep you from finding true love. But just as in the fairy tales of your childhood you will need to keep to the right path of integrity honesty and trust in order to hold on to that love.

Each human being is unique, and sees, hears, feels and experiences from their own perspective. Relationships falter when human beings begin to cause pain to each other, considering only their own perspective and dismissing all other viewpoints as "wrong". There are many things to consider as you walk your path through life and its relationships, and they are like the pieces of a jigsaw puzzle which when kept together and cared for will provide the complete picture and total understanding.

When you practice patience with each other you will allow time for understanding to be reached. When you practice tolerance with each other, you will create an endless cycle of tolerance from one to the other, for patience and tolerance extinguish the fires of anger and bitterness and allow love to breathe.

If you offer your love and it is not accepted immediately, store it in your heart so that it can be offered to another when the circumstances or the individual are more open to the love you have to give. Do not store bitterness and resentment with that love, for they will eat away at its beautiful centre and when you come to let it out of your heart in the future, you will discover that it has become a hollow shell which looks like love but has no warmth, patience, or tolerance, only fear, anger, and selfishness at its centre.

The metaphor I use of those magnificent golden spires from your childhood can be created by you in what you see as real life. Undying love and the acts of devotion which express such love arise from real love. They do not arise from a romantic illusion, but from a love that cares more for another than it does for itself, and a love that seeks to discover how much it can give to its beloved not how much it can take. When two people in a relationship think only of how they can express their love for the other then both of them will continue to receive such love, for if this is the case then it can be no other way.

However, love has many different faces and can be found in many different ways. It is a paradox of life that if you wish to find love then give away as much of it as you can find in your heart. When you give love from your heart without conditions or expectation of return, it will always eventually return to fill your heart with joy. For as you give love it grows and blossoms and expands until it finds its way back to you like a magical web of kindness and good will.

But love like many other aspects of this path of the soul is spread from age to age and from life to life. When you begin to feel you are giving love out and never receiving back your "fair" return of love, you will find it comes when you least expect it to, and from where you would never have believed it could come. It may even be a love that has travelled forward with you into this life from a previous life which eventually finds you just when you had begun to lose your hope.

Remember, you need not wait for someone else to create

this love in your life, for you have the power to do so. The greater joy of love is always in the giving rather than receiving. To feel you have created joy and peace or have eased pain with the love you have given, is to have climbed the staircase and reached the pinnacle of that golden spire, which contains your wholeness and the fulfilment of your aspirations where love is concerned.

Do not confine your understanding of what love is within a narrow definition or category or you will stifle its very existence, and face insurmountable challenges in reaching the prize at the top of that golden spire of your dreams.

Concerning Love - Chapter Eight

Always Offer Respect to Each Other

Each and every human being on planet earth has a need to know they are loved, and they usually like to know that the love they offer is valued by others. It is true that love takes many forms, for it is not just the love of a parent for a child or the love that lovers feel for each other. Love can be experienced and offered in so many ways.

Neither is love restricted to that which flows between human beings. It is more than possible to love animals and birds, or you can love the beautiful planet you live on, and you can even find yourself with a feeling that you believe to be love in relation to inanimate objects.

There is, however, a difference here, for love is a living thing and can only be offered to or shared with another living thing. When you believe you love a *thing*, what you are really feeling is an affection or fondness, a sense of attraction or pleasantness around the object which arouses the feeling you perceive to be love.

For whomsoever or whatsoever you feel the emotion of love stirring within your heart, there is a vital quality that should always be present. This quality is respect, and it is not restricted to loving relationships or experiences. Unlike love, respect can be shown to things, and such respect is an acknowledgement of the work, passion and skill that may have been invested in creating that thing.

You will be aware that when you find someone to love, or even to be friends with, it can take a little time to be sure of your feelings, and theirs. Sometimes when a relationship begins, it is difficult to trust that the love or friendship offered is genuine. This can take time, but that time should be respected if the relationship is to be a good and sound one. Whatever your doubts about yourself or others and the feelings that exist between you, I would remind you again that we are all children of the universe, and should always offer respect to each other. Whenever you choose to offer respect, or fail to offer respect you are offering, or failing to do so to yourself.

If you have allowed sufficient time for a relationship or friendship to develop, then one of you realises that the two of you are not compatible after all, and there needs to be a parting of the ways, do continue to treat them with respect. This applies whether you are friends, lovers, colleagues, or even acquaintances, and even if they cannot bring themselves to be respectful to you. Whilst it is not always easy to be respectful to another where there is mistrust or misunderstanding, and the other is not respectful to you, remember that whenever you give respect you become worthy of respect.

It is often overlooked that the greatest respect you can pay to another person is to be honest and to express to them the truth of what you think and feel. This does not mean you need to be cruel, unfair or ill mannered, simply that you should keep in mind the longer you are dishonest the more pain you are storing up for them and for yourself.

When considering the nature of respect it is as well to be aware that this concept of respect is not limited to categories or classes. As human beings none of you are greater or lesser than each other; you are simply dealing with your challenges in different ways. When human beings achieve their aspirations and climb to the heights of those aspirations they deserve recognition for their efforts to do so. However as a human being they deserve respect no more or less than any other human being.

On planet Earth there has grown a practice for offering *greater* respect to people in the public eye, or people who reach the top of their field. It is sad that these individuals often eagerly grasp at the respect afforded to them and lose sight of the fact that it is as important for them to show respect to the simple and unacknowledged people they encounter in their daily life as it is for them to demand respect from others. Respect is earned, and when it has to be commanded from another it is not true respect. It is a fear based behaviour which has the "other" believing they are a lesser person than those who they believe they respect, but in reality who they are idolising. To idolise is to worship or adore, to venerate and to place a high status upon.

This state of being may give the appearance of respect, but in truth that is simply a side effect of a syndrome that sees you or another placing yourselves lower in value as a human being, than the object of your adulation.

Such individuals often begin to take for granted that they

will be treated as higher beings by others, and expect them to be submissive to their demands and wishes. In doing so they have lost the ability to simply respect another human being. This lack of respect has become so prevalent in life on earth at this time that it has found its way into many if not all walks of life. It has even been given a name which is "abuse or "denial of human rights".

Whilst respect is a 'human right' it is also the right of each living thing, whether human or not. It is also something which can be earned, even if it is in acknowledgement of the respect given to others. The truly *soulful* human being practices respect for others as a natural way of being, and is usually rewarded with respect in return. However, there will inevitably be times in life when individuals or groups disagree or decide to part ways. This is when the principle of respect is more important than ever. If you must disagree or cause a parting of the ways at some point in this life, it is likely to be because you know it is the proper course of action. The manner in which you do so is a measure of how much you have learned on this journey through human life.

This does not mean you should fail to be honest with each other. Remember that respectful honesty will be of more value to both of you, than will either of you failing to acknowledge the other has the strength to deal with honesty or a parting of the ways. To disrespect because you have not been afforded respect is not worthy of you or your soul path through this life. Those who fail to offer respect to you are creating their own paths, and it will be for them to deal with the consequences in due course.

Always be respectful even in the midst of conflict and misunderstanding. For it will help both of us (you and I) to learn and grow and to be worthy of respect in return, even if it is not from the person or group you are offering respect to at a particular time in life.

Concerning Love - Chapter Nine

In Practicing Acceptance

Learning to accept people for who they really are, and not who you or anyone else may imagine or wish them to be, can be one of life's challenges. There are times when it becomes difficult to love (or even like) someone without trying to change them into the person you think they should be, or without placing judgments on them.

Before you can genuinely accept anyone else, you need first to accept yourself. Many people find self acceptance more difficult than acceptance of others. However, without self acceptance what is usually felt for others can be fear, awe, and a sense of wanting to be that other person or even yearning to have what they have. This can be seen as acceptance, but beneath the surface if there is no self acceptance there is unlikely to be acceptance of others, simply for what and who they are.

The perceived acceptance is often based on an image of someone that has been intentionally created or a celebrity status that has been sought and achieved by them. This persona is often far removed from who the person truly is, and yet large numbers of people willingly accept these manufactured characters. It is sad to see that such manufactured characters, while seemingly attractive on the surface, are disconnected from the guidance and wisdom of their soul.

It may feel easy to accept someone on the basis of the false premise of who they appear to be. Conversely, it can be difficult to accept someone for who they really are, and this can also apply to the self. When you find it difficult to accept yourself purely and simply for who and what you are, (to use a human expression "warts and all") this difficulty will in all likelihood stem from who or what you have been conditioned to believe you should be. Often your image of who you should be will be similar to many of the manufactured characters I have spoken of, and who, it is good to remember, are not real people.

All human beings have several roles in life as a natural and normal state of affairs. There are the roles you have in your family such as son or daughter, father or mother, sister or brother, and so on. Then there are the roles you have in the world around you as you progress through life. There are roles in your work and your friendships and roles in respect of others you meet on the path. As human beings, you all play roles in the lives of each other as well as in your own life. As each human being plays out their various roles in life they will come to realise that different aspects of their character are needed for the different roles.

You will encounter this with those who you come into contact with and they will do likewise with you. As a result they (and you) will find that some aspects are easier to be accepting of than others. You will discover this applies to the events, circumstances, and situations in your life also. When you find certain aspects of an individual, a group, or even a situation unacceptable, there is a danger of viewing the whole person or situation from the perspective of that particular aspect. This then creates the potential for dismissing all aspects as unacceptable. It is vital to keep sight of the fact that everyone walking their path through life on planet Earth has imperfections, for that is the nature of this life. If all was totally perfect, there would be no work to do, no life to live, no lessons to learn and grow from.

In today's world there is a powerful element of conditioning which urges everyone to strive for perfection in what they do and who they are. Of course this view of perfection depends on who is doing the urging, and so no matter how you may strive to be perfect, you will never be perfect in the eyes of everyone. When you realise this and know that everyone views life and the world around them from their own perspective, you are getting closer to self acceptance. You will begin to understand that all you can do is live to the highest ideals of love and compassion you find possible to attain. In doing this you will be achieving more than you realise. In this blueprint from which to live your life you will find self acceptance, and it is from this place you will begin to understand that each and every soul on the planet is working towards their own goals of perfection. Just as you and they do so, whatever you all achieve will not be seen as perfection by all. Just like you, they may not achieve the ideal they strive for in each and every aspect of themselves.

When you are able to accept that everyone has their strengths and weaknesses, and that this applies to you too, you will be able to more easily accept other people, things, and situations into your life. In practicing acceptance life becomes more of a journey and less of a battle, and you will find yourself beginning to see more clearly the positive and beautiful aspects in other people, and in the world around you. This is not to say there is nothing which is unacceptable, for human beings sometimes lose their way and forget their divine nature. This is when they are subject to causing pain through cruelty or lack of consideration for others or their surroundings.

Any way of thinking or acting that causes unnecessary pain is unacceptable if it is intentional or can be avoided. However, when something or somebody allows themselves to quite simply be naturally who they are, you will find they are kinder and more loving. Whenever a human being turns to their soul for guidance it will point them in the direction of acceptance of others and of themselves.

This does not mean you need to suffer abuse as a result of someone's imperfections, rather, that if they cannot be prevented from treating you badly then it may be time to walk away. For if you do so you are practicing acceptance that you have a situation which is not yours to change. If all of us were to change everyone we met who was different from us, the beauty of every one's uniqueness and originality would be lost, and the world would be filled with "copies".

If you are finding acceptance of someone difficult, and feel the need to change them into a version of themselves which is more acceptable to you, remember that someone somewhere may look at you and decide you need to change so you will fit their idea of whom or how you should be. It does not feel good from this perspective does it?

When you can begin to accept with compassion the imperfections in yourself and others, you will find you are also gaining acceptance from those others, simply for who you are. In the meantime you will continue, each of you along your own path, toward self acceptance and the closest to perfection that you can achieve.

Concerning Love - Chapter Ten

Re-discover Your Peaceful Heart

When you know you are loved and value this gift of love, it can bring a sense of calm and peacefulness deep within your heart. It is, however, good to be aware that if your heart was permanently peaceful and never touched by other emotions it would mean that you are only half alive.

The fear, sadness, and anger you feel at times in your life are what help you to identify the peaceful heart when you experience it again. They are simply part of the seeming "duality" of life as a human being. When you realise this you will also be aware that your peaceful heart will eventually be a part of your experience again if you really wish it to, and when this occurs it will bring increased balance into your life. When you are in a state of turmoil and feel your peaceful heart may be lost forever, if you desire its return in a truly genuine and heartfelt way the turmoil and "heart break" will pass.

It may seem strange to think that anyone would not wish a state of turmoil or unrest to pass, but sometimes as human beings you can become so familiar with your state of unhappiness that it begins to feel as though it is a normal way of being. To let it go and seek your former state of peace may seem dangerous like stepping into the unknown. If this occurs it means that you have given control of your emotions to your mind. When the mind alone is in control without its healthy heart connection there can be no peace within your heart.

The mind is generally seen as the right place from which to make your decisions and choices in life, and your heart centre (or what is sometimes mistakenly described as the emotions) is often considered to be foolish and unreliable. This is a misleading viewpoint, for when you allow your mind to truly listen to your heart you will find that it is taking you to a place that will bring you to a peaceful state of being.

Whilst the mind and heart are both important in helping you to walk your path through life, it is important that they work in harmony each with the other. When they become separated and out of balance one or the other will become overly powerful. This is when it is difficult to see and understand clearly what is going on within and around you.

A person working only from the head (or the mind) will be just as out of balance as someone working only from their heart, and it is this imbalance that has given rise to the belief that to work from the heart is foolish. This perception really refers to working from a heart that is totally out of balance with the mind. Because of this you may at times be reminded not to let your heart rule your head and this is good advice. Just as good would be to not let your head rule your heart, because either of these choices means your head and heart are out of harmony with each other.

It is important that your head and heart communicate

so that your head can hear the wisdom of your heart and make its decisions accordingly. Someone working only from the head will lack compassion, tolerance, gentleness, and love in their way of functioning. If they were to work only from the heart, they may have these qualities but would have no ability to be guided in how to use them wisely and in a practical way. The peaceful heart is able to remain so much more peaceful when you allow it to draw on the strength of your mind, and your mind will be stronger when you allow it to access the peace that lies deep within all hearts.

As you begin to consider this connection between head and heart, you will come to realise that when your heart is filled with love both given and received, this is when it is in its most peaceful state. When your mind is filled with compassion and tolerance, it is in harmony with your heart. When you remember this, you will live surrounded by the turbulence and turmoil of the world around you and yet still live with a peaceful heart.

To keep your connection with your own peaceful heart, sit quietly for a moment or two and imagine a fine line of iridescent golden light flowing between the centre of your head and the centre of your heart.

As you watch this line of pure energy flowing between the two, become aware that this is the energy of love, both mental and emotional, and it is always quietly keeping the balance between head and heart to keep your mind healthy and reasoned and the heart filled with peace.

When life becomes confusing and you are uncertain whether you should listen to your heart or your head, watch this line of constant and pure loving energy running between them to remind yourself that out of the turbulence and turmoil, you can always rediscover your peaceful heart if you allow that line to remain unbroken.

Concerning Love - Chapter Eleven

This is the Heart of the Matter

During childhood you will have looked to your mother figure for the love that sustained you and gave you a feeling of safety and self-worth. The basis of how you love will be rooted in her love for you, and how you learned to return that love. This is the heart of the matter where love is concerned.

You will know that this influence has been powerful in your life. As you have grown older, many of the decisions you made and directions you followed in your loving relationships, will have been guided by the teachings of your mother figure. You will see I say "mother figure" and not simply "mother" for the person who you have seen as your mother while growing from childhood to adulthood, may not have been seen as your real mother namely not your biological mother. Your mother figure can be your biological mother, your adoptive mother, or a woman who has taken on the role of your mother in one way or another.

There are various reasons why this other mother might be in your life. This can be as a result of the physical death of your biological mother during childbirth or childhood, breakdown of the relationship between your parents where your father has been granted custody of you, or simply a mother who has been unable to care for you due to ill health or for other reasons.

Those reasons why you might not have the presence, support, and guidance of your biological mother throughout your childhood can be numerous and complex, but they usually result in one or a series of substitute mother figures taking over your care.

Sadly there are parts of the world where a child who loses their biological mother will suffer desperately as a result. Life on planet earth is something of a lottery in this respect, and if you are fortunate enough to live in an environment where there is a support network in such situations, a substitute mother will step in and care for you. No matter whom that mother figure is and whether or not she is your biological mother, she will of course be a human being endeavouring to complete her own soul path. Her experiences with the child or children under her care will be a part of this path. It is possible therefore that life will have the the potential to be fraught with less than ideal situations and circumstances.

In an ideal childhood, your mother will love you deeply and as unconditionally as it is humanly possible for her to do; sustaining you and keeping you safe, providing food, clothing, and shelter. She will ensure that you are educated and have the best chances and opportunities in life she can provide, and she will do this from a place of love. She will be someone who you know without question will always be there for you whatever happens, and will always be on your side ready to defend you support you and protect you from harm, no matter whether that harm is physical, emotional or mental.

There are powerful lessons to be found when you receive this kind of care from your mother for she is providing a role model for you to follow in living your own life as an adult. This is so whether you are male or female, mother or father. So it should be borne in mind that whilst I speak of "mother love" you may have spent your formative years in the care of your father or father figure with no mother figure present. The same principles apply here and if this is the case for you then where I use the term "mother" I will be describing also what may have unfolded in your relationship with your father or father figure.

Although it is a generalisation, it is true to say most human beings live their lives in a similar pattern to that of their parents, for this is the most significant example they have been given throughout their formative and impressionable years.

However, in the course of their own soul path, the person who raises you may be unable to offer the unconditional love usually associated with the relationship between parent and child. Unfortunately when this is the case, the lack of love is often perpetuated through several generations. This may be because a mother (or father) has never been given loving examples and experiences from their own mother, and as a result they have no understanding of how important this loving support is to a growing child. Perhaps they simply believe that the lack of love from their mother is a normal way to raise a child. This may change only when a soul is born into the family line which is strong enough to guide its human counterpart so they are able to understand and break free of the destructive patterning.

A parent may be deeply loving or someone who has learned as a child that to give and receive love brings only pain when that love is unrequited or betrayed. As a result they teach this principle to their own child or children, who grow up believing that to love brings pain. It is therefore seen as something they need to avoid and protect themselves from. If this is the case then the child can continue the negative and unloving way of raising their children, or they can learn from the painful experience of feeling unloved, unsupported, and unguided in their childhood years. So, alternatively, they can break the cycle and take from their parents a lesson just as strong and powerful as the message that is given by loving parents.

For just as a child learns how to both give and take love from their loving parents, another child can learn that the ways of his or her parents bring pain and unhappiness and they can begin to open up their heart to find the love they have been deprived of; and in finding that love learn to give it back.

Such lessons are learned from the day you are born and may remain with you for the rest of your life. The choice is yours as to which lesson you learn. Were you taught not to give and receive love because it would bring pain, or to give and receive love because it is essential to your soul and to your wellbeing and happiness? If it was the first of these, then use it to avoid the mistakes your parents may have made in their lives and on their respective soul paths. If it is the second then you have learned what is at the heart of the matter where love is concerned.

Concerning Love - Chapter Twelve

A True Conqueror is Strong Yet Gentle

In matters of romantic love you hear of men making a "conquest" when they gain the love of a woman they pursue. It is a view of men which shows them representing the Yang energy of the universe, going forward and taking what they desire, whether it is power over a woman or some other kind of power.

In the past it was accepted that men would be the dominant figures in loving relationships, and it is still this way in many parts of the world. The positive aspect of this is that such men will provide for and protect the women they love. However, there is a negative aspect which comes into play when their will is imposed upon their beloved against her own wishes. When this is the case there is usually restriction of freedom for those women, and it may not only be their movements and major decisions that become limited.

This usually arises because the man sees the woman as a possession to do with as he wishes, rather than someone to cherish and love. He will make decisions for her about even the smallest details of her life, and even govern how she thinks and perceives the world around her, from which she may in any event be isolated.

Traditionally men have been portrayed as having within

them the energy of action and moving forward, of taking what they choose to. This is usually how the most famous conquerors in history ruled their vast empires, and they saw their conquests with women in the same way. However, a true conqueror is strong yet gentle, showing his skills strengths and power, whilst retaining qualities of humility and benevolence.

If you look back to the ancient past it was a time when men wore armour of steel to protect them when fighting battles. It is not difficult to see that in putting on that armour they hoped to convince their enemies they were invincible. To go out into battle without protection would seem foolish to say the least, because they knew their life could be in danger. But, eventually these brave conquerors would begin to identify with the image of themselves encased in steel and completely unapproachable, and they believed that this was who they were in all aspects of their life. For inside that armour they felt safe and protected from harm.

So this character became a cultural stereotype of a man who was distant and unapproachable in other aspects of his life also. He might spend years fighting battles without coming into contact with anyone apart from other soldiers. There would be no place or time for loving gentleness, no opportunity to take off the armour and let down the defences. When he returned from battle he would continue to be the conqueror because that was the role he understood, having played it for so long. As a result he would become deprived of love and tenderness by his own actions. The man became indistinguishable from the armour he wore. Because he had been isolated behind that armour for so long, he would believe it to be the normal and natural way to behave in everyday life.

There are many human beings who have been raised from childhood with a need to protect themselves from harm. Sometimes the harm would be physical, and at other times it would be mental or emotional. But whatever form of pain there was a need to hide from; the appropriate armour would be put in place. Such human beings go out into the world as if they are fighting battles to survive and they offer no chink in their armour through which love can penetrate. If they are successful in protecting their hearts as well as their very survival, they will perceive themselves to be conquerors.

The world is a far different place now than when those knights in armour fought their battles, but there are still battlefields to be conquered, and now it is not just men who fight the battles, for often women are fighting alongside them.

These examples of the perceived conqueror can apply to both men and women in today's world, for you may also have encountered women who put on their symbolic armour with which to face the world in order that they are protected from harm. This kind of armour is invisible to the human eye, but it is just as difficult to penetrate as those metal suits of olden days. Alternatively as you read these words you may recognize yourself as the person behind the armour whatever your reasons may be.

It will be invaluable to be aware at all times, that it is possible to be strong and overcome challenges and painful situations in life, without the need to hide behind armour that isolates you not only from the world you fear will give you pain, but also from your own feelings. When this kind of defence system is in place life can become a lonely place bereft of love and affection, and any conquest that is made becomes a hollow and painful abyss. It is a place inhabited by fear and disconnection from the soul. If there was an opportunity to speak, the soul would remind those who are in such fear, that love is stronger than their fears and will always be the conqueror in the end.

Never mistake a human being who appears open and loving, gentle and kind to be someone who is weak and vulnerable. Likewise never mistake someone who is totally self contained and apparently well protected to be strong and invincible with no need for the love of anyone. The armour is a disguise, an illusion, for the man with a kind word and a gentle hand who needs no armour to know his strength is a conqueror in the true sense of the word.

A woman who is unafraid to show her loving vulnerable and receptive aspects because she knows that being alive makes it worth the risk, will conquer far more than the distant aloof woman who repels all attempts to get close to her. It is important to remember that it is only when you have overcome your fears and discovered your inner strength that you will become a real conqueror.

Those who are conquerors in every sense have both the strength of the warrior when taking what they know to be the right path and protecting what is precious to them, and the soft gentle and loving heart when it is needed. Remember fear destroys – it is love that conquers.

Concerning Love - Chapter Thirteen

The Eternal Search for Happiness

Happiness is often seen as a destination, or some future state of being that requires certain criteria to be fulfilled so that it can be present, but true happiness is not something to be provided by a situation, person, or material thing.

If you were to travel planet earth asking the question "what would make you happy?" You would probably be amazed at some of the answers you received. You would also be amazed at how wide a range of answers there would be. But what many of those answers may have in common is the underlying message that the person in question is not already happy. You will no doubt be familiar with and may have used yourself, the expression which begins, "I will be happy when…."

These answers will range from when someone meets the love of their life, gets a job, can pay their bills or goes on an awaited holiday, to when they have a new car – or house, are able to alter their appearance or they are rid of some situation they find uncomfortable. There are many more answers to this question, but the common thread from a human viewpoint has a tendency to be that happiness will be found in some change that is awaited or just out of reach.

An even deeper underlying thread to this perspective is the belief by most people that happiness is something they will need to earn by fulfilling some condition or by being worthy of it. If you believe that you do not deserve happiness without fulfilling certain criteria, then you are on your way to losing touch with this wonderful state of being.

Then there is the belief that you may finally have achieved a state of happiness, but you fear it can be snatched from you at any moment. This fear usually stems from a perception that you may have fallen below the standard required to be allowed to keep your happiness in some way you were unaware of.

The eternal search for happiness us woven through the lives of all human beings, and they will at various times find themselves respectively happy or unhappy. This is not because happiness comes and goes it is because you perceive this to be so. For you can choose to be happy at any time in any situation. This does not mean there are no situations which lend themselves to a temporary loss of happiness as a predominant state of being, for this is part of the soul path and the lessons to be learned as we walk it together. It also does not mean that the loss will become permanent unless you decide to make it so.

Happiness is many things to many people and can come into your life in many ways. There is bliss, ecstasy, joy, delight, elation, rapture and on and on. However, these other words tend to describe a more extreme and fleeting experience which is amazing whilst it lasts, but can leave you feeling worse than you felt before it came to you.

This is because you believed it was something which should remain uninterrupted for the rest of your life.

Happiness is not a prize won by a select few, or gained by scoring points. It is the right of everyone, and you will find and keep it more easily when you understand it is like a beautiful butterfly, remaining just out of reach whilst you pursue it and resting gently on your shoulder when you sit quietly and wait. While you are waiting it would help you to remember that you could be waiting for something that already exists inside of you and is simply waiting for you to give it expression.

There is no necessity for great life events or major acquisition of material things; quite simply the joy of being alive can bring a happiness that will never leave you. Always in this life there are things around you if you will only look, that are reminders of how much happiness you could be experiencing if you were able to stop putting labels on it. For just like the butterfly you allow to gently settle on your shoulder and remain as long as it wishes, happiness will find you if you allow it do so without conditions or limitations as to its nature.

If you are able to simply *be* happy without some requirement having been met and to appreciate the smallest and simplest things in your everyday life, knowing these things may not be granted to everyone around you, then you are on your way to finding a more lasting state of happiness. When this occurs you will find different kinds of happiness appearing in your life when you least expect them to and from where you least expect.

Remember, where there is a situation you believe has caused your happiness that may be transient, this does not mean you need to be unhappy when that situation has changed or ended. Simply acknowledge another form of happiness in your life and focus on that. For when you limit your perception of happiness it is like keeping that butterfly captive within a net, so that it cannot be touched or be free to express its beauty, and eventually it will wither away and die.

What you focus on you will give power to, and when you yearn to reach a *place* where you believe your happiness lies, you are giving power to a perceived lack of happiness in your life rather than the place where it lies, which is of course deep within yourself. Learn to release that happiness from within you by experiencing the simplest and most innocent things in life and allow those bigger, bolder forms of happiness to settle on your shoulder in their own time just like the butterfly.

There is an obvious but frequently overlooked way of experiencing happiness and that is to give it to someone else. In any well balanced human being there is no greater happiness than knowing they have been the cause of someone else's happiness, and so the happiness begins to spread like seeds that are carried on the wind which then fall to ground and produce new flowers.

When you can recognize happiness in another and feel happiness in your own heart because of that, you are becoming infected in the most beautiful way. As your happiness grows it will reach out around you and touch others, often without their realising what is causing their happiness. Those who have found the secret of happiness which lies naturally within them, will then free that happiness to radiate from them, and so propagate it on to someone else who can continue the process.

You will undoubtedly know someone somewhere who is a naturally happy person. They seem to have no need to have a reason to be happy for they have found the secret of experiencing their own happiness from the smallest of things. Such people are precious for they do indeed propagate their happiness on to those around them, who invariably feel better after having been in their company for even a short period of time.

Look within for your butterfly of happiness perhaps released by the laughter of a child, a small kindness offered, the wonders of nature, or beauty in its many forms from the magnificent to the simple, and let it fly out into the world to help others release their inner butterfly of happiness.

Concerning Love - Chapter Fourteen

Healing is Not What Someone "Does"

How would you define "healing"? A simple answer would be to say that healing is love. But there is more to healing than this one word conveys. Whenever one human being opens their heart to another with a wish to ease their pain, healing is being offered. The gentle kiss from a mother to a child who is hurting from a fall, the warm hug for someone who is in grief or distress, or the listening ear for someone who needs to express their pain, all of these are forms of healing.

To be healed is to be made whole again, in any part of you. This is true no matter how great or small that part of you is. Healing is to be released from disease, pain, or suffering whether permanently or temporarily. The effects of healing are simple and often overlooked and yet they can be life changing.

An act of healing in whatever manner is an act of love, an act of re-creation. This can be from someone who has medical expertise or simply from an act of kindness, but always at the root of true healing is love for your fellow human beings and other beings. Remember this: a desire to ease the pain of another, extending from the heart, a smile, a touch, a word, will have a healing effect. You may not always find this easy to do, but the wonderful truth is, that in healing others, you hold the miracle of the universe in your hands and heart, and you also heal yourself if only in some small way. So if you feel some part of you is in need of healing now, offer a gentle touch, a kind word, or generous action to someone else, for your own pain will remind you how good it must feel for them and in doing so you will feel the energy of healing gently touching you also.

In today's world you will see around you major leaps forward in the arena of science. These will be in relation to the health and wellbeing of human beings and other species. Many of these developments are within the realm of surgical procedure which focuses on repair of your physical aspects when they become damaged or diseased. Others are by way of pharmaceutical solutions which do not intrude on the body in the way that surgery does, which is to directly damage in order to repair.

However, many of the pharmaceutical remedies available today can harm as well as cure. The medical world carries out checks and balances and makes a decision whether the help that such remedies can offer outweighs the harm they may or may not cause in the process. Each person must make their own decision about whether they wish to incur the risks involved in order to gain the relief they seek, and often the relief far outweighs the disadvantages. But this is not the whole story when you are considering the concept of healing. Even those who make the decision to undergo some of the rigorous procedures they believe will cure them; often get the relief they are seeking, but find there is so much more of their being that has been affected by their illness or injury.

It is often said that anyone can be a Healer and this is true, just as anyone can become an Artist, a Musician, an Engineer, or any of the many other activities that can be carried out by members of the human race, so long as they are physically able to do so. But – just as some will be Artists and others will be Engineers, many will not. Even so, some of those who make the decision to acquire a particular skill or art will excel and others will be moderately skilled or able, and the difference will be found in the level of passion they have in relation to their chosen field or activity. In order to follow any path and to fulfil that path well there must be a deeply felt passion to do what the path requires of you. Healing is a powerful example of this rule, and as in other walks of life there will be those who offer healing to others without having this deeply felt passion.

However, this passionate desire to heal the pain of others in some way is essential for good healing to take place. The statement "intention is all" has great meaning where healing is concerned. For healing is not what someone does it is what someone allows to happen and for the intention to allow it to be of value in a healing way, it must involve love. I am not speaking of sentimentality here, but real pure simple and uncomplicated love that all human beings are capable of feeling for each other and for living beings of other species.

The human body has its own inner healing mechanism that requires no external or internal intrusion. This is a natural process which when viewed from the perspective of science can seem miraculous. Have you ever cut yourself and with the exception of sticking on a plaster to prevent dirt or infection finding its way into the body through the cut, you have done nothing more to help it heal. Yet within a short space of time the skin begins to heal and in most cases there is no sign of the cut once it has had sufficient time to heal naturally. When a bacteria or virus invades a human being medicine steps in to rid the system of that invasion. It is true to say that the process is speeded up, but with certain exceptions left to its own healing mechanism the body will create the necessary defences to return it to good health. However, what I am describing here is a process of cure which is of course related to a specific part or aspect of the physical system.

Because humans are often disconnected from the wholeness of their being they focus only on the tangible physical or mental aspects or parts they can see and touch and therefore address only those parts. Accordingly they may be cured but they may not necessarily be healed. Healing is to curing as spirituality is to religion. It is so much deeper, wider, and far reaching. It does not limit its effect to a specific physical aspect or symptom. It flows like a river through the whole being, addressing whatever needs to be addressed and finding those parts that are often at the root of the problem and the true cause of a symptom.

When one human being offers true healing to another, they do not distinguish between apparent cause and real cause. They allow the energy of love to flow through them and into the other. They do not instruct the energy what to do for the other, they simply ask for healing to take place where it is needed, and to do so by going to the most urgently needed source of a problem first and foremost. For healing to be completed it is necessary for it to be offered from the heart and soul to another other heart and soul, for this is where the wisdom around what is needed lies.

A parent often knows what is best for their child, and the child often cannot see that this is so until much later in their life. Likewise the soul knows what is best for its human counterpart long before that human counterpart realises where the real problem lies. The important thing to remember about healing is that it is not something to be done it is something to be allowed to happen.

Book Three
Concerning Peace

The thoughts expressed here are concerning matters of conflict or confrontation which may disturb your peace of mind or tranquillity.

Some of the questions dealt with concern how to find peace more easily, when it may have been disturbed by events or situations arising in this life.

Concerning Peace - Chapter One

Sorrow is a Natural Part of Life

I have said that in this life you are likely to spend large amounts of time and energy seeking out happiness. But how will you be able to identify the state of happiness if you have never experienced the state of Sorrow?

In life there is always the seeming duality, and yet in essence there is only love and absence of love. All things in life that seem opposite are simply at a different point on the same scale. For instance if you consider hot and cold they are simply temperatures on a scale that moves from excessive warmth to undetectable presence of warmth. If you consider darkness and light it is again simply a scale that measures light up to an infinite degree – beyond a level the human eye can perceive or tolerate; and when you move down the scale, you will be going from light you can perceive to a level of light you cannot perceive that you call darkness.

Those things that give you a happy or joyful feeling are filled with the essence of love, and those that make you experience sorrow are an indication that love is reduced to a level so low it seems to be absent. You may see sorrow as simply the absence of happiness, and yet it is so much more. For sorrow has its very own place on the scale that measures love and the absence of love, just as happiness does.

When you are experiencing sorrow it can seem as if the tide of happiness has ebbed from your being, leaving you empty and lacking purpose. You may become submerged in your sea of sorrow and forget to come up for air. But, sorrow and happiness will ebb and flow in your life just as the tides of the oceans ebb and flow, moving along that scale from one point to the other.

Remember this flow of what you call sorrow takes place when you feel a sense of lack. This may be a lack of kindness or abundance. It may be a lack of things that are material or the lack of someone in your life whose presence you have cherished, and when they are no longer present you experience feelings of sorrow. It is threatening to your peace of mind when you allow the experiences of happiness and sorrow to be controlled by influences outside of you.

In this life on planet earth nothing is forever; not family relationships, not friendships, not jobs nor places to live. For when the body dies any of these that remain are left behind as I move on and your consciousness moves on with me. On that new journey we will carry the memories and the love, letting go of sorrow and many other human emotions.

Human beings generally do their best to avoid experiencing sorrow, and this is understandable as it is not a pleasant human experiences. Nevertheless, it is an indicator that your life is not stagnant and that energy is continuing to flow up and down those different scales from one point to another within the one main scale.

How else can you gain experience from this life or understand the experiences of those around you and whom you meet along the way?

When you experience sorrow you are being given a powerful reminder of how beautiful and valuable it is to both give and receive love and to lose and then regain peace. At such times you will be glad of someone who can love you sufficiently to take the time to understand your sorrow, and who will walk with you until you find the path back to peace and happiness. To experience sorrow does of course mean that you have temporarily forgotten who you really are and what you are really capable of. It is an indication that you believe you need other things and other people in order to be happy and free from this experience of sorrow.

To run away from sorrow is not a solution. When you find yourself in this experience of sorrow, turn and look it straight in the eye and be reminded that it is a temporary experience; one that has been caused by your sense of dependency on one thing or another. I am not suggesting you become remote and isolated from the world around you, so that you fail to make connections with others that are precious and filled with happiness.

Such connections human beings make with each other are filled with the essence of love, whether it is seen as love or not. But because they are external to your own being they are inevitably subject to change. They do however build up the self-worth of those who have made the connection, and in turn those human beings find themselves building up the self worth of others with whom they in turn make connections.

A sense of having value can come from skills acquired or wisdom gained, but your value does not come from any of these things; it comes from deep within you and it arrived in this life at the same time as you did. It is an integral part of you, and a loss of friendship or loving relationship, a job, an enjoyable activity, or a place to live, is not what makes you of less value. It is in the core of your being in your very creation and the natural aspects that make you who you are. No loss or absence, no change in circumstance, nor situation encountered, will reduce you sufficiently for you to be overcome with sorrow, unless you forget who you are and allow it to influence your thoughts.

When you can go into the silence and be at peace alone even for a little while, you are reducing your vulnerability to sorrow being caused by one external situation or another in your life. It is of course only in the experiencing of sorrow, and recovering your equilibrium and self worth sufficiently to be able to let it go, that you will reach the point where sorrow is not controlling you.

I would reiterate that this thing called sorrow is a natural part of the human experience, and when you allow yourself to understand it more fully and to understand what has truly caused you to feel sorrowful, you will have greater clarity regarding its place in your life; and this will help you to open yourself again to the experience of happiness.

You are always surrounded by the love and support of the

universe, and supported too by me your soul. I quietly draw to you the return of happiness into your life from the depths of your being. If you can pause and find my guidance in the many ways I offer it, you will find you are more able to make a conscious decision to dry your tears. Remember that while sorrow may come again, it can also depart just like those ocean tides which ebb and flow.

There is no obligation to feel sorrow because you believe it is appropriate or acceptable to others. When you know that a time has passed in which it is appropriate to experience and express your sorrow, then the period of sorrow will have been honoured.

This is when you can again accept happiness into your life without the need for guilt or regret. I have said that sorrow is a natural part of life, but it need not cloud your future happiness, for it is also a natural part of life to let it go when the time for sorrow has passed.

If you find yourself with a feeling that you are drowning in your sorrow, just close your eyes. Imagine yourself surrounded by beautiful spheres of light like a magical tide of rainbow coloured bubbles, lifting you above the dark cloud of sorrow and bearing you upward and back into the light of happiness. Feel it washing away the sorrow and leaving you refreshed and ready for your next experiences on this path of your soul.

While this may seem a fanciful way to deal with such a heavy and dark state of being, you will find when you practice the mindfulness of which I have already spoken, such a visualisation process will become a powerful tool in your journey toward releasing sorrow and rediscovering your peace.

Concerning Peace - Chapter Two

To Help You with Your Searching

In this life you will find yourself searching for different things and for various reasons. Your search may be for a set of keys you have mislaid, a telephone number to enable you to phone someone, directions to take you from one place to another, It might perhaps be a virtual search for a file or a website address in your computer that will provide the information you seek.

When you carry out a search of any description you are looking for a solution of some kind. Your solution could be as simple as those mentioned above or as profound as the answer to a question that has the potential to change your life. Whenever you are searching you will usually know precisely what you are searching for, and will have some idea where to look for it.

If your search is for a physical or material item, then you are attempting to locate the place it is in, either from the memory of where you last had it or from your own logical deductions as to where it will be found. However, if it is knowledge or information you are seeking this is a different kind of search, albeit with the same need for an idea of the general direction you need to look in. When searching for a physical or material item, you may become impatient and expect to find it quickly without too much trouble. This could be because you have had it in your possession at an earlier time, and what you are really trying to do is to remember where you left it. Although this can be a frustrating exercise you will, given a little time, usually recall where it is. Perhaps you will simply find it by a process of eliminating all of the places it is not, until you arrive at the correct one.

Then there is the kind of search that is deeper and more life changing. In this kind of searching you will be looking for information or answers that can help you to reach what you believe to be the right decision. But it is sometimes difficult to know for certain when a decision is the right one. It may be the right one at that point in your life, and then things change and it no longer feels right. As a result you believe you made the wrong decision when you actually made the right decision at the time you made it. This decision has given you the experience you needed and brought you to a place where you can gain the ability to reach a new decision more appropriate to your present needs.

Just as when I spoke of the mysteries of this life, your searching will often meet with a dead-end or cul de sac, and there will be frustration and possibly anger. If this is the case, remember, in this kind of searching you will find what you need when you truly need to find it.

You may be familiar with the expression, "as one door closes another one opens" but do you realise there is more than one way of interpreting it? You may believe it to mean, as one door closes behind you another opens to lead you on, but it may also mean a door you hope to go through closes to you, and another will open somewhere else entirely. If you feel you have searched sufficiently only to come up against a dead-end (or closed door) do not waste your time banging on that closed door, search again for the other door. This is the one you will know to be the *right* door, from somewhere in the deeper levels of your consciousness.

It may seem that in all of these words there is nothing to help you with a search you are carrying out right now, and in which you may not yet have arrived at a solution. But, consider what I have said about banging on closed doors. It may help you to look at your search from a different perspective, and find the patience to await the appearance of the door that feels *right*.

The practical searches I spoke of initially are usually resolved in time and often quite quickly. However, there is the kind of search that is anything but practical in the usual sense of the word. It is a sense of searching but without any certainty about what you are seeking. This is more of a deeply felt urge or need and it can become all consuming. When you reach a point in life where you are uncertain precisely what it is you seek, you will find I am speaking to you, because I have important knowledge or information to convey to you.

How you hear me will depend upon whether you have allowed me to retreat into the recesses of your mind, or we have become closely connected. If it is the first of these my voice may sound as soft as a sigh or as subtle as the wind murmuring through the trees. You may not perceive a distinct message reaching you at all, simply a sense that there is something you need to find. If this is where we are on our path through this life you will need to find for a little while that quiet place I have spoken of so often in sharing these thoughts with you. Move away from the noise and chatter of the world around you so that you may hear me speaking. When you, look inward in the silence, to the deeper part of your awareness, you will find it easier to listen carefully and my guidance will be clearer to you.

Remember, I speak to you in symbols, signs, occurrences, and events, or in the unexpected; in what is often called coincidence. When you learn to read the language of your soul – my language - you will know that I speak to you through the words of a song, an opportunity arising, someone you meet, a passing comment; the signs are endless.   When you realise this, the soft sigh or the murmuring of the wind will become a symbol so clear that it is like a bell ringing out in the silence of the night, reminding you what it is you seek and how to find it. I may even be pointing out that you are searching in the wrong direction.

If we are already walking this path together you and I, hand in hand heart in heart, you will have less difficulty in identifying and understanding the guidance I offer to help you with your searching. For you will know that my guidance comes in those many different ways I have mentioned, and you will find it in the world around you, in what you see hear and encounter. If you do so, you will be alert and aware ready to see the signposts I offer, each one taking you a step further in your journey of searching.

In the deepest and most profound searching you will carry out, the most rewarding solutions will always come from within where I await your call for help.

Concerning Peace - Chapter Three

Enchantment Is a Form of Illusion

You will no doubt have discovered by now that there are many things in life that have the power to enchant you, without you even realising you have become enchanted. Such things can be worldly possessions with which you are fascinated and absorbed, to the point where you lose your objectivity about them. They may also be experiences which you have become attached to so they become an obsession or what is often called "addiction".

You will believe you cannot live without them and this is part of the enchantment. If it is a physical addiction to certain substances or forms of food and drink (not uncommon in today's world) it can be a truly difficult enchantment to break. You may therefore need to seek outside help from someone who is free from the enchantment, but who also understands the nature of your personal addiction.

In order to end an enchantment you will first need to be aware that you have become enchanted; and then to know what caused you to be drawn into this enchantment. Until such time as you identify and acknowledge the enchantment and its cause, it is unlikely you will find the means to end it. Enchantment is a form of illusion, because it convinces you that something is actually other than its true reality.

When a person or a thing has an ugly appearance it will be repellent. If an enchantment is to be effective there needs to be a degree of attraction, and this is usually achieved by creating the illusion of attractiveness, or that there will be some pleasure or benefit to be gained. A common example of this is where drugs or alcohol initially give a wonderful state of bliss and pleasure. Then, if you become subject to this kind of enchantment, as the addiction grows, the pleasure decreases and the sense of need increases to an unmanageable level. This is where you can lose sight of the fact that you are enchanted and believe this enchantment is actually supporting you and helping you to continue to live without pain.   You will be unable to see that the enchantment is in fact causing you pain. Only when you are able to see what the cause of your pain is can you begin to break free from the enchantment.

On the other hand, enchantment often takes place within relationships, and this kind of enchantment can be more subtle and difficult to recognise. It is said that love is blind, because it can seem to cause a blind-belief in another person and all they say or do. Unfortunately this kind of enchantment will also blind you to the truth of whether a person you care for is sincere and whether or not their words and actions come from a loving heart.

If you have become enchanted in this way you may become so enchanted that *you* become the obstacle to being freed from your enchantment. For you will often be so completely drawn into this belief about another that nothing and no one will be able to show you the truth of the matter. When this occurs it is likely that you will have chosen to believe a version that is not real, of who this other person is and the depth of their feelings for you. It may be what you would wish to be the case rather than the truth. This can be the cause of your enchantment rather than a web of deception woven around you by another. When this is the case, freedom from your enchantment lies within your own hands.

If you find yourself in a relationship you sense is losing its way, and its quality of caring and peacefulness is in decline, you may come to the conclusion that this other person has painted a picture of who they are that is not true. While your conclusion may be correct, it may in fact be as I have mentioned above, namely that you have taken part in a self deception, painting your own picture of who you would wish them to be. If the deception has not been by you then you are starting the process of becoming disenchanted. If the deception has been of your own making, you will simply experience feelings of disillusionment but remain enchanted. The reason for this is that you have not found the real source within you of the enchantment.

If the enchantment has indeed come from the deception of another then action may be needed to ascertain what deception has taken place. However, if there has been a form of self deception or co-operation with the other in the deception, then it is time to turn and look inward to that part of you that is not blinded by denial, judgement, or fear. Step back from these and let them go, for they too are a part of the enchantment, whatever form it has taken.

Replace them with honesty, acceptance, and your own

strength and courage that are always here within you. For what is of greatest value in life cannot be bought, sold, or stolen from you; it is a part of you.

When you can do this you will see whether a situation or relationship is actual and genuine or has a future. Alternatively you will see whether it has become an enchantment in which you are blinded to the truth. Remember well that the truth can set you free to find a real and genuine peace. Go to this place of peace within you, where fear does not blur your view and your clarity is always undimmed. Look bravely for the signs of enchantment and then look even further past its illusion. You will see that you are not being served by such a situation.

There will be times when this will not be easy, for you may be faced with another who continues to maintain the illusion of the enchantment, and in doing so they will cause you to doubt yourself. But, remember the reason you are seeking your lost peace; because what you felt was bringing you fulfilment has begun to bring you to a place of doubt and discomfort, a place of loneliness and often despair.

So do not be deterred from your search for the truth and a return to peace. Soon you will begin to realise that to liberate yourself from such an enchantment will not see you becoming reduced or weakened, it will awaken within you the strength that you have lost sight of that is always here within you.

When you begin to recognise the illusionary nature of

enchantment, you are allowing me to guide you and you are on your way to freedom and peace of mind.

Concerning Peace -Chapter Four

Your Key to Detachment

When you seek freedom from pain and a path toward fulfilment, you can become attached to things people or situations, believing they will remove your pain and show you the way forward to peace. In a world of so many things to become attached to it can be difficult to avoid doing so. However, it is good to remember that while attachment is a normal part of human life, it can at times be a bedfellow of enchantment and in time this more aggressive and less healthy form of attachment can start to make you feel imprisoned, rather than voluntarily attached in a comfortable way. Then the attachment becomes like a sticking plaster refusing to be peeled from your skin, and seeming to become part of you.

If you discover that an attachment of any kind is holding you back or causing you pain, finding a peaceful and pain free form of detachment does not necessarily require extreme measures. There may be no need to flee into the wilderness to escape and find detachment from it, although this might at first seem easier than the pain of your attachment.

Many attachments in life that so imprison you, are self created. If you look within you will know this is so. In addition you will find that the key to detachment and release is found even deeper within your own heart. When you understand that your worth is not measured from outside, but at the level of your soul without the need for support from damaging attachments, this is when you will find your key to detachment.

I have said that in the course of your path through life within the human condition, there may be times when you will experience self doubt and lose peace of mind and faith in your own worth. When you lose your self esteem you are likely to seek ways of regaining a sense of your place in the world and your value to those around you. Remember what I have said on the subject of torment and how it is most often a result of a misunderstanding. If you stop and reflect even for a moment, you may see the possible connections between the concepts of torment and attachment; and the experience of lack of self worth and self confidence.

To lose a sense of being of any value, or even of what you believe to be sufficient or adequate value in this world around you, can cause feelings of torment. You may search desperately for something that will help you feel again that sense of value or attractiveness to others. This is when attachment often occurs. In becoming attached to something you see as attractive or powerful, you may believe you will take on these qualities as a result of your attachment to them.

In what is seen as the civilized world today, the media perpetuates the myth, that your value as a member of the human race can be increased or enhanced if you buy this item or that. You may even find yourself being persuaded to take part in one activity or another often at great cost to yourself, all in the belief that you will become happier, healthier, more attractive or more desirable. But this false image placed on materialistic values is hollow and has nothing to do with your value as a human being. It simply creates attachments that you may believe will bring you a sense of peace and fulfilment or status within the human race.

The quest for eternal youth is a good example of this kind of attachment. It is clear that in terms of the human body there is an optimum time when it is at its strongest, healthiest, and in deeply primal ways most attractive. This has a purpose that serves the continuation of the species, but is not a measure of the value of one human being or another. All human beings irrespective of character or morals will live through this process of reaching their strongest and most vital time in life, before they begin to age and suffer the slow degeneration of the body into old age and subsequent death of that body.

This attachment to the idea that human beings will find self-worth and peace of mind through the processes of putting on a mask of artificially perpetuated beauty or youth; or attaching themselves to what they may describe as a beautiful way of life; will eventually become painful to sustain.

Often a human being will arrive at a point where they understand that beauty truly is in the eye of the beholder, and furthermore that beauty is to be found within, and is not just a surface effect. You will without doubt know at least one person who does not fit the image projected by the media of this world as beautiful or even attractive to look at, and yet you are aware that they give out a beautiful energy and they are attractive to those they come into contact with.

That elusive quality that makes them so comes from what they have understood; namely that it is not necessary to attach themselves to anything or anyone in order to be of worth and attractive to others. They have simply realised that a love of life and of their fellow men and women is much more attractive. They have detached from all that would imprison them, and keep them unhealthily attached to the belief that they need this or that to be a worthwhile human being. They have learned that fulfilment comes in the giving – or detaching – rather than becoming attached because of a sense of need or inadequacy. At the same time they understand that in the giving or detaching they are still firmly connected to the world they live in.

So do not misunderstand my words and detach yourself from life in the world around you, for this is not detachment but isolation. The key is in accepting yourself for who you are and doing the best you can to be an honest and caring individual, connecting with your fellow men and women and even other species and nature itself. This simple approach to life is all that is needed. Remember connection is not attachment it is a healthy giving and taking of energy, done freely and without the need to reinforce your own self image and the belief that this or that will make you a better person.

If you search within yourself honestly, you will discover

that in your respect for others you have found respect for yourself. In finding your self-respect, you will have gained peace of mind and detachment from all that would imprison you or that does not serve you or anyone else.

Concerning Peace - Chapter Five

Dreams Are a Quiet Reminder

When you sleep you dream, and some of these dreams will be your mind's "housekeeping" process enabling you to wake mentally refreshed. Each night as you sleep, you will dream on average between three and five times, and these dreams are essential to your wellbeing. In addition, during your waking hours it is likely that at times you will have day-dreams.

You may dismiss the sleeping dreams as a form of imagination and the day-dreams as wishful thinking, and on some occasions this might be correct. However, to take away your dreams would be to take away your hopes, your plans and your sense of direction. For this is where your plans and goals (large or small) begin.

The greater universe and I whisper to you with ancient wisdom in your waking and sleeping dreams, guiding you toward fulfilment of your potential and completion of your soul path through this life. When I speak of the universe and I whisper to you, I am not speaking of the kind of conversation you would have with another person. For as I have already said we speak in symbols, knowing that it is important you find your own path ahead and reach your own decisions, rather than being specifically commanded what direction to take or which choice to make.

You may recall my thoughts about the process of sleep, and how it is quite simply a time when a different aspect of your consciousness is at work. This is you functioning at a different level to the one you are at each day in the course of your life. Dreams usually take place when you are sleeping, for this is when it is possible to access your deeper consciousness and allow it to permeate your everyday levels of thinking and understanding, thus conveying what needs to be conveyed. Those dreams that may simply be completing a process of organising and filing the mental record of your activities from the day behind you are a normal process of the human brain. However, there are also dreams that are experienced at a level beyond your everyday brain activity, for they come from the realms of the higher mind or inner awareness. These are dreams you will remember much more clearly and usually for much longer, sometimes for years or even for the rest of your life.

On waking from such dreams, you may often feel as if they have not been a dream at all. It may seem that you have experienced them in a way you would describe as "real", and they may be puzzling or confusing if you attempt to make sense of them or rationalise them using your everyday logic. These dreams do not lie within the limits of logic or rationale, nor within the parameters of the everyday life you are living as a human on planet earth. They come from a truly deeper, wider, and higher level of your consciousness. For this is when your soul is communicating with you, reminding you of memories that will serve you in this life here and now, even though they may be memories from many lifetimes ago.

However, although I have said they do not lie within the limits of logic or rationale, such dreams are not always dreams of soul memory from the ancient past. Neither do they lie within the limits of what scientists would call Physics. They are communications that may come from both past and future.

You will probably have heard of or even know someone who has described a dream about events that occurred after the dream had been experienced. These are usually described as prophetic dreams, as they seem to prophesy future events. They are often dismissed by the more scientifically minded as coincidence or even fabrication. At the time of dreaming they made no sense because the event had not yet happened in what you might call *real time*, and they seem to have no relevance for the person who has dreamed about them.

Such dreams may be the universe or perhaps a particular soul not here on earth, endeavouring to convey some important information to the dreamer, because it may enable them to prevent a potential disaster caused by human error already made.

The languages of the soul and of the universe cannot be languages of human verbal communication. If this was so they would become limited to the language of the individual dreamer. Language as you know it is a very limited human construct, that often separates human beings rather than enabling them to communicate with each other. If human beings can misunderstand each other when they are supposedly speaking in a common language, how much greater could the misunderstanding or misinterpretation be when they are speaking in different languages? So dreams speak in the language of symbolism which is universal, for symbols are a powerful and yet greatly simplified way of communicating information that can be understood whatever the language of the reader.

Dreams are a quiet reminder of how much is possible, so rather than trying to work out exactly what your dream has said to you, consider what it may have reminded you of, or perhaps what it has suggested to you. This is where you will find the message your dream is bringing to you.

There is an aura of mysticism that surrounds the concept of dreaming, and this is because when you are dreaming you are in an altered state of consciousness. It is a time when your subconscious mind is alert to the messages of your dreams, for it understands the language of your dreams so much better than your everyday waking state of awareness. There may be times when you awake and are aware you have dreamed but are unable to recall the content or message of your dreams. If this is so there is no need to be concerned, for information received in this way will remain in your subconscious mind until the time is right. Then it will arise in your everyday awareness and be understood or more importantly be relevant or of use in your journey through this life.

Remember too those daydreams that seem to be just wishful thinking can be a forgotten dream rising up into your everyday awareness ready to be fulfilled. You might see these daydreams as "castles in the air" or something that can never exist in real life. However, when those thoughts begin to rise up into your awareness for your consideration there will be a reason. This may be to underline that the time for this daydream to come to fruition has not quite arrived; or it may be because the time is approaching and the concept finding its way into your awareness should be thought through more thoroughly if it is to become a reality. It can even be to alert you to the signs that will soon be presented to you in this everyday world, to show the way forward to making your dreams a reality.

It is for this reason that your dreams, waking or sleeping, should never be dismissed, without reflecting on whether they are indeed relevant to your life here and now, or whether you can allow them to *sleep* in your subconscious for a while longer, until you are certain that the time is now for you to understand them.

I have discussed here the different kinds of dreams, and the different reasons for you having dreamed them, but I would remind you that you should never disturb your peace of mind by striving to interpret a dream that is not ready to be interpreted. When the time is right it will become clear.

Concerning Peace - Chapter Six

Trust Me

The first form of trust I wish to speak of here is trust in the source of creation, the universe, whatever god you may worship, or whatever you wish to call the object of your trust or belief. This kind of trust is usually complete and unconditional. Here there is no requirement to offer proof that what you are placing your trust in is worthy of your continued belief in it. From a human perspective this kind of trust can be challenging. But this is a trust that is simply an unquestioning acceptance that what another has told you is true. Such acceptance comes from the fact that when you are taught to believe in something other-worldly, it will usually begin when you are very young. At this time of your life this information urging you to trust comes to you second-hand. It is brought to you by someone who is of this world, namely an adult who you are dependent upon for your survival, or who has a strong controlling position in your life. As a result you trust what is offered to you.

Sadly, this kind of trust can be required from you in the form of controlling how you live your life. It may tell you that this other-worldly form of power is all-knowing and all-seeing. You can have no secrets from it, and for a child this can be terrifying. Even more frightening from a child's perspective is the accompanying threat that any misdeed in the form of thought word or deed will be punished by this great and powerful being. You may also be given guidance on what may be considered "good" or "bad".

The trust aspect of this system lies in your belief as a child that adults know so much more than you do about absolutely everything; they would never lie to you. You will therefore believe that what they are teaching you to trust must be an absolute truth and you must at all costs follow the guidance that is given to you from their belief system; usually for fear of what will happen to you if you do not. The thing to remember about this is that the very same adults who are offering the information to you as absolute truth are doing so because they will usually have received it as children in just the same way and have continued to believe it implicitly. This is how the major religions in this world have grown, namely based on the complete trust their followers have in the teaching of their figureheads. This is because they trust that those figureheads are speaking on behalf of this great and all powerful other-worldly being around which the religion is structured.

This form of trust is better known as faith, although this word "faith" is at times also applied to other more earthly kinds of trust. However at an earthly level trust is more of an informed kind of faith, without illusion or self deception. It is usually based on the acceptance that everyone will make a mistake at one time or another in the course of this life, and the understanding that as a result of this, trust is not always upheld by the one who has been trusted.

There may be times in life when you are asked to give your trust without information that would guide you as to the wisdom of giving that trust. On these occasions the outcome may be that you discover your trust has been betrayed. There are at least two ways where betrayal of trust takes place. One is when someone in whom you have placed your trust, genuinely believes (or has trust) that the outcome will be as promised. In this kind of betrayal there are actually two betrayals taking place, that of yourself and that of this other person who has trusted another and truly believes they can fulfil your trust in them.

The second is when another person requests you to trust them knowing they will not be upholding the trust you have placed in them. A reason for this may be that they have the intention of using your trust to carry out a deception that will offer gain to them and loss to you. In the case of the intentional deceiver you will often be able to sense or recognise that they are not to be trusted. Nevertheless, there will still be times when you will be deceived so skilfully that you will only realise this is the case when it is too late to undo the deception As you go through life you will become more understanding of other human beings and develop the ability to sense or judge whether a person can be trusted. .

There will also be times in life when you are asked to give your trust and you realise at the outset there is no guarantee your trust will produce the promised outcome. It is in these circumstances that the real essence of trust reveals itself. For you are required to see the best in another knowing they may be unable to live up to your expectations.

Whatever kind of trust you give to another it is never wasted at the level of your soul path. For there are always lessons to be learned, even if you believe the result has not been a gain or the fruitful outcome you anticipated or were promised. When you trust and are betrayed for whatever reason you will have helped me in my mission to learn and grow from the experience; so the knowledge gained will be carried forward with us when we leave this life together.

I have spoken of what could be described as "blind faith" in a religious teaching, and you will need to make your own decisions in these matters. However, there are most definitely times on this path we walk together when you will need to trust completely, not knowing whether what you trust is sound and true or even whether it is what you would call *real*. This might be at a time when you become lost and feel vulnerable and alone, and feel as if you are drowning under the weight of circumstance. At such a time you may see (metaphorically speaking) a hand reaching out which offers to pull you from the "waves" that would take you under. You have no way of knowing whether this hand is actually reaching out to help you or to push you down beneath those waves, and it is in that moment you will truly be required to understand the meaning of trust. Remember this, whether you are raised up out of your desperate situation or pushed down to an even more uncomfortable level, you will have learned a deep soul lesson, and you will survive. The owner of the hand that has pushed you down will also have completed a soul lesson and perhaps one that will be even more painful for them in the long term than the experience you have had.

So when you are agonising over whether you should give your trust sit quietly and listen for my voice; this quiet but certain sense of *knowing* that helps you to decide whether or not it is a time to trust whatever the outcome may be.

Trust me, for I am the essence of your being, in the place where your deepest wisdom lives. We are as one, and it is not possible for us to deceive each other.

Concerning Peace - Chapter Seven

Use Well Those Times of Peaceful Waters

You could compare your path through life to sailing on the high seas. Here you are relaxing on a wonderfully smooth voyage; the sky is blue and the sun is shining. All around is calm and peaceful and the water looks delightfully inviting. You may even consider going for a swim in those wonderfully calm and peaceful waters.

Then suddenly the sky becomes grey and cloudy, obscuring the warm, soothing sunshine. A storm begins to rage seemingly out of nowhere, and rain drives down out of those heavy clouds. The sea around you that a moment ago was so very inviting and calm becomes turbulent, and you find yourself and your craft being tossed this way and that so violently, that you fear you may lose your balance and be thrown overboard into the now seething waters.

As you look at the waters around you an even greater fear arises. You begin to wonder whether it will not just be you who is thrown overboard; perhaps those you care about who are accompanying you on this journey will also be plunged into the deep. When this occurs you will no doubt be so busy fighting for your survival that you will not have time to see how the storm caught you unawares, nor what direction it came from. You may even feel unable to think how best to find your way out of the storm or even how you could have avoided it altogether.

There will be times when life's experiences are just like that storm. Everything is flowing along nicely, there are no signs of danger, adversity, or conflict, and suddenly you find yourself in the midst of a raging, seething situation. You feel completely vulnerable and stripped of all that you felt so sure of, or you are staring adversity in the face far too closely for it to be anything other than terrifying, or at the very least extremely uncomfortable. When this kind of storm-like situation occurs in your life it may come as suddenly and unexpectedly as the storm at sea, and just as in the storm at sea you will be busy fighting to regain your equilibrium. Your predominant thought may be about how to regain your sense of balance or control, in order to return to a state of peace or to salvage all that you fear you are losing.

After the storm subsides, often as suddenly as it arose, you may find yourself alone having lost all of the people who were around you when the storm broke. In the case of the storm at sea your craft may have sunk without trace, and you are adrift in the ocean without any way of knowing in what direction freedom and safety may lie. Alternatively you may not be alone but are finding that the instinct for survival at its most primal level has taken over hearts and minds, and all who have been engulfed by the storm are suddenly fighting each other for what they fear may be the only chance to survive and reach safety.

These words may cause you to look back on certain

situations that have arisen in the past and to understand more clearly my use of the storm as a metaphor for such situations. Remember too that this may also apply in the future yet to unfold, where you find yourself in the midst of a conflict or battle, which like the storm you did not see coming until it was too late to avoid it. It may not be a boat you have lost, but perhaps a job, or your home, or a loved one. It is often in such situations that human beings turn against each other and begin to find something or someone to blame for the disaster that is occurring around them.

Ask yourself now, whether this kind of response or action would make the situation disappear and return those involved to their own peaceful waters. You will know the answer is that it would not. It would simply cause even more damage than the original conflict alone could ever have done.

Perhaps you would be focussed exclusively on how you could avoid ever finding yourself directly in the path of such a storm or situation without any prior warning. So, will you then revert to a state of fleeing the scene of the disaster without taking the time to consider what has caused it in the first place? If you paused for just a moment or two you might consider whether the storm like situation was caused by your own negligence or that of someone else. Perhaps it was the result of a lack of consideration for the facts on someone's part. Maybe you would simply see it as bad luck in the form of what is often called coincidence.

When storms erupt in life, do not allow waves of panic to

engulf you, leading you to avoid future storms at all costs; for then you are avoiding life. Use the space of the peaceful waters that follow the storm or precede the next one, to understand the torrent and increase your strength and wisdom in preparation for future storms in life. Allow yourself to enjoy your new found peace and build on the knowledge you have gained in the turmoil of the storm.

I repeat, because it is important to remember this; to avoid storms at all costs is to avoid life. Each storm whether it reaches its full raging peak or is dealt with before it reaches that peak, will contain a lesson for us both at the deeper levels of our being. Remember to use well these periods of life that are filled with peace, to consider what lessons you have learned. Think how those lessons may be useful to you, if in the future those peaceful waters once again become angry, and you are facing a storm. This will apply whether it is a storm at sea or in your life.

As I have said to you so many times, life on planet earth is a series of lessons for us both. The knowledge we gain from those lessons will not only be useful for future occasions in this life, but will be taken with us when we depart and they will become a part of our soul wisdom as we move forward into future lives.

It is inevitable that if you have learned from the storm, when once again you find yourself in peaceful waters you will be changed, for that is the purpose of the storm. You may even feel like a completely different person.

When you see someone who seems to deal wisely with the storms that occur in their life, they will probably have learned on a previous soul voyage how valuable it is to use well those times of peaceful waters, and so be ready for the potential storm lessons ahead.

The knowledge I hold has come forward with me and can be imparted to you, if you will seek the silence in which you can hear my voice. This is when you too will have the ability to deal more wisely and peacefully with your own storms as you use those times of peaceful waters to hear my guidance.

Are you ready to ride the storms and gently float through the peaceful waters?

Concerning Peace - Chapter Eight

Let Us Go Into Retreat

When you are faced with confrontation your prime response may be to strenuously defend your position by going into an attacking stance. The reason for this is likely to be that you believe it is the most effective way to free yourself from what you believe you are facing. This would generally be seen as a normal response, for warriors defend themselves when doing battle with their enemies by charging forward and attacking. It is true there may be times in life when you see attack as the only form of defence, but the wisest solution to any conflict is usually found more easily in a peaceful atmosphere than it is in confrontation, and to find this atmosphere, it may be necessary to retreat.

When you speak of retreating do you perceive it to be "giving in to" or "escaping from" an aggressor?   You might even see it as a form of cowardice. But this act of retreating can simply mean you wish to retreat to a place where you are able to consider matters quietly and in more depth. There are times in life when it is clearly wiser to retreat from the field of conflict, so that each opponent allows the other to consider their intended decisions and actions in relation to the matters at issue When in such a situation you can achieve a swift aggressive and personal victory, or a wise victory that gives peace to all concerned. In choosing to retreat you will have time to decide which of these you truly want.

Retreat is often perceived to be taking flight from a field of battle, or walking away from everyone until you are in a place where they cannot find you. A classic image of this is to see someone disappearing over a hill, up a mountain, or into a cave, for these are often ways of retreating. You may indeed find your place of retreat is many miles from your usual environment and even situated within the centre of a culture that is completely different from that to which you are accustomed. But it is not always necessary to find a cave or a distant place to retreat to, for at times your retreat need only be within your heart and mind.

The decision to retreat is not just the wisest course of action when you are facing conflict. There are many situations in life that call for retreat, and sometimes there will be a need to physically remove yourself from the world around you and from all the aspects of your everyday life. On the other hand, you may simply need to find a temporary space within your heart and mind, focussed away from everything and everybody familiar to you, so that you can contemplate clearly and objectively what direction it is wise to follow.

This will be a mental and emotional retreat, which means that while you are physically present in your everyday world, you are in fact mentally and emotionally focussed inward, away from the bombardment of influences and distractions that are being directed toward you.

The tool of mindfulness is once again of great value under these circumstances. Simply step back mentally from whatever the situation of conflict is so you can contemplate what you intend to do next. This can be more successful in finding a solution, than it would be if you were to forge thoughtlessly into action you could regret.

When there is a need for retreat you could compare it to holding a telephone conversation in the middle of a crowded place, and needing to move away to somewhere quieter in order to hear the voice of the person on the other end of the line. However, the voice you are actually listening for here is your own inner wisdom, the voice that is guided by your own previous experiences. Remember those previous experiences are shared by us and they are strengthened by the experiences I have brought with me into the path of the soul we are walking here and now.

Another reason you may be in need of some form of retreat is simply to allow you to refresh, revitalise, or re-invigorate those energies within your system that have become depleted by the external demands life is constantly placing upon you. These demands may come in the form of physical exertion, mental activity or turmoil, and even emotional turmoil which has its source in the conflicting influences you come into contact with, sometimes on a daily basis.

There are many wise and expert individuals in this world, but if you always search outside of yourself when the wisdom you seek is of a deeply personal and spiritual nature, you may become confused and weary. For it can be difficult to distinguish who is offering true wisdom and who is simply offering their own perspective on the subject when you are considering all of those different opinions. The absolute wisdom of the universe itself is quietly waiting for the right questions to be asked in order to answer them. This wisdom lies within each and every soul and its human counterpart, or if you prefer within each and every human being and its soul counterpart. The clearest, calmest, and most obvious of answers begin to surface when you sit in retreat with me your spiritual connection to the universe.

I suggest that every so often you find for yourself a retreat that physically removes you from the hustle and bustle of the world. If this is not possible then remain physically present and simply slip into a small pocket of solitude within the recesses of your mind, one that is sufficient for you to listen to me; for the value of this cannot be overstated.

Within this kind of retreat – no matter how small or temporary – if you listen carefully the answers will come. There is no need for striving to find the answers; you simply need to have the right amount of trust, that enables you to know the answers will come across that space between us created by the quietness of your retreat.

When you have this trust in your own small act of retreat, you will ultimately find peace of heart and mind. Remember that such deep inner communication with me will not always provide instant or immediate answers, but the answers will be given when the time is right. So when you are troubled or confused let us go into retreat and speak to each other, so that we can together find your path to peace both inwardly and outwardly.

Concerning Peace - Chapter Nine

Meditation is a Powerful Tool

There are different perceptions of meditation, and one of these is as a non-thinking activity that removes your focus from the world around you, allowing an oasis of "no-thought". There is also a view that meditation is a process of concentrated and focussed thought. However, thoughts can easily become unfocussed, taking on a spiral quality and never seeming to get anywhere. Both may be correct in their own way, and yet the first of these seems to be the more generally accepted one.

Sometimes your life may be overcome with more thinking than you find comfortable. This is when it is time to mentally leave the everyday world behind for just a while, and find your own way of meditating. To be peaceful and still, detached from the merry-go-round of life, and enjoy your surroundings is a simple form of meditation.

A frequent response in today's busy world when asking someone if they meditate is "I would like to, and I have tried to, but I simply cannot seem to master the ability to do so." The main reason given is an inability to clear the mind completely, because random thoughts constantly intervene and prevent a sense of peace and calm being achieved. This occurs more often when endeavouring to practice the first type of meditation mentioned above, and aiming for a state of "no thought". Within the busyness of today's world a state of no thought can take time to perfect. Nevertheless when you use the word "try" in relation to meditation it is a contradiction in terms. Meditation is a practice that removes you from striving and endeavour. It is a deeply relaxing and releasing process, and to describe yourself as *trying* to meditate cannot truly be correct. If you find yourself so locked into the mental treadmill of today's world and you are unable to release your focus from it, this is when you are truly in need of meditation in your life.

It is said that a devotee of the spiritual life once asked his Master what he should do if he wished to find peace of mind. The advice he received was that he should meditate for twenty minutes each day. The devotee replied that he did not have twenty minutes a day to spare for meditation, to which his Master replied that he should meditate for forty minutes a day.

This exchange between the devotee and his Master illustrates the point that in relation to meditation it is of paramount importance to remove yourself if only for a short while, from the constant thinking and acting that fills the days of most people. When you say you have no time to do this, then you are saying there is no space anywhere in your life to relax and become calm.

If you wish to listen to music, watch a movie, play sport, take a trip, read a book, eat your meals, complete your daily routines, however trivial or mundane, you will need to make the space to be able to do so. It is therefore simply a matter of prioritising.

Consider for a moment that in each day there are 24 hours and therefore 1,440 minutes, of which you will in all probability spend 960 minutes (or 16 hours) sleeping, eating, and working; perhaps a little more or a little less. However, this means you will find you have around 480 minutes (or 8 hours) remaining in which to make a space of 20 minutes for meditation.

When I speak of making time for meditation it may sound like a duty, a chore, or an obligation, but when you make the space to watch your favourite movie or read a good book, do you consider this a duty or a chore? You will have likely chosen these other activities because they bring pleasure and help you to relax. When you are able to make space in your life for meditation and allow yourself to relax into it, this is when you will discover the wonderful benefits it can bring to your focus, clarity, and peace of mind.

It may help to be aware that whilst there is much written and taught about meditation, this guidance can sometimes be daunting for those unfamiliar with the concept. All that is necessary is to find the way that works for you, and this will be the right way.

It can be easier to begin with a meditation that allows you to find a process of thought you find pleasant and relaxing, and to remain within that process for a short period of time. This can be
with the guidance offered by the voice of another or a visual image that is pleasing to look at.

The state of peace and tranquillity that is such a benefit of meditation can be found in many different ways. For some it is found in being close to nature in the quiet of the forest or the solitude of the hills. It may be to watch the tide coming in or going out, or to gaze upon a beautiful work of art. There are too many ways of bringing peace to your spirit for me to mention here. But it is important that you remember it is not a test or a challenge. It is simply removing yourself from the tests and challenges of this life, so you can see the road ahead of you more clearly in order to deal with it more wisely.

When you have made friends with your own chosen method of meditation, it will be time to move forward and try other methods. Perhaps you will eventually reach that state of "no thought". This is what can really move you to the inner realms where we can commune, and you can turn to me for guidance and support.

Remember that meditation is a powerful tool when wishing to step back from the more challenging aspects of life on earth. It is a tool that can help you view this path of life we are walking together more objectively, and with greater clarity. A tool that can help you to make stronger your connection with me and all of the wisdom I hold.

If you have never meditated before or you have met with the obstacles to meditating I have mentioned, begin your new practice with just one minute to still your mind and body, and slowly increase that time until you begin to experience the amazing benefits of regular meditation.

Do remember though that this is not a chore nor an

obligation, it is something that in time you will look forward to and will enjoy making the time for, time when we can be together even if it is simply to be silent.

Concerning Peace - Chapter Ten

In the Silence of Your Heart and Mind

You will know from reading my thoughts on meditation that it is generally seen as a process of mentally leaving the outside world and going within. It is a unique experience for each individual, and you will find your own personal level of solitude and peace in your periods of meditation. This can be through something as simple as walking, or even just sitting in a favourite quiet place; in contemplating something you see as beautiful, or perhaps listening to music that reaches down so deeply into your being that *I* feel its beauty and am moved by it.

When considering meditation it is inevitable that the experience of being within a state of silence will come to mind. However, when you enter true and deep silence, a silence that fills your being, you will know without doubt that you have moved into a more profound level of spiritual peace.

This is a far deeper form of meditation, which could be described as transcendental. If you are uncertain what this means, it is quite simply a level of meditation in which your mind settles inwardly so much more deeply. You find yourself beyond thought and in the most silent and peaceful level of consciousness that you have ever experienced. In short, you have made a connection with your innermost self and in doing so you have made a connection with me your soul, for that is who I am.

When you sense that you your inner awareness is calling you and you are experiencing a need for the guidance it offers, this is a time to dive into a place of peace and solitude and to enter the silence. Allow yourself to detach from the outside influences and pressures of your life, and you will find you are able to find the silence calmly and in a totally unhurried way. In discovering the silence you will allow the answers you seek to find you, instead of striving to find your way to them past the busy world around you and through the barriers of logic or intellect Only in the quietest moments can my voice be heard clearly. It is not a physical sound vibration I speak of here, for you are in a place completely filled with silence.

My voice is heard in a hundred ways as you walk your path through life on earth. This planet you are living on is filled with noise. It is everywhere and in almost everything. If you find yourself in an industrial environment you will know only too well how much noise is produced by the heavy machinery, and sometimes even the light machinery. When it is suddenly switched off you are likely to find that the reduction in sound is so tangible you can almost hear the silence created.

On the other hand If you have ever sat in a modern office working with the technology of print and communication, and that of the virtual reality that is computerisation, you will know this technology does not make the powerful sounds emitted by the heavy machinery of industry. It does, however, make a continued and continuous sound. When you are subjected to this continued sound vibration you will eventually adjust your awareness so that you achieve a state of unconscious awareness of the sounds around you and fail to register them.

When the technology around you is switched to *standby*, even these lesser sounds are intruding upon the silence, without you being aware of it. When these small sounds are removed you will start to become aware of the benefits of silence. The difference as these sounds subside will often find you breathing a sigh of relief and allowing your mind and body to relax more.

It is difficult in today's world to find a place that is truly silent. For even if you move away from the noises of civilisation and go out into the wilds of nature, there will always be sounds around you. It may be the sound of your feet making contact with the ground beneath them, birds and small animals darting around above you in the trees, or the wind rustling through the leaves and moving the bushes as it passes through them.

True silence is so profound that it almost seems to be another kind of sound. However, it is actually a lack of sound vibration, a stillness and peace that is far beyond your normal everyday experience. It is beyond the level that you will normally perceive as silence, but what is in fact a very low level of sound vibration.

True and complete silence is a silence of the mind and the body that can be found when you are able to shift your consciousness to a place where those outer sounds

completely disappear. They are no longer intruding upon your experience or influencing your thoughts. This truly is a place of inner peace and tranquillity. It is a silence that can only be found by withdrawing from life in the usual sense and placing your conscious awareness into a state that could almost be described as suspended animation. You have simply placed your active outer awareness on pause as it were, and allowed your conscious awareness to take a step inward, while remaining a sentient and animate being full of life and vitality.

This is finding your own personal silence, where there is no tension, no stress, no anxiety, and no fear. There is no anger, frustration, resentment, or disappointment. There is no striving to succeed and no fear of failure. Here you are at peace here you are at home; quietly enjoying the silence that I bring you as a healing force.

Although this is the place where you can hear my voice you should remember that I have said my voice is not carried on the physical energy vibration of sound. It will come to you in a way that speaks to you often without words, but it will speak to you clearly and powerfully when you are able to truly enter the silence. So are you ready to experience the ultimate meditation that is connection with me your soul, in the silence of your heart and mind?

Concerning Peace - Chapter Eleven

If You Are Granted an Awakening

You will usually feel certain about whether you are asleep or awake in a physical sense. But there are kinds of awakening that you may be less certain about. For when you first experience these other awakenings, you may feel you do not understand what is taking place.

When you have mastered the art of stillness, meditation, relaxation, and entering the silence, you will become more acutely aware of so many things you had failed to notice previously. This awareness comes from deep within you, in that quiet still place where you may have heard a whisper which you could not quite identify, except to say that you knew without doubt it had something important to say to you.

If you feel such an awareness stirring within you now that makes you see everything in a more focussed and colourful way, your everyday consciousness is awakening to the presence of your higher consciousness and making a lifelong connection to it. For once you have awakened to this higher level of consciousness; you can no longer be unaware of it. While this may sound overwhelming or daunting, it is a powerfully beautiful event in this life of yours. This is a further step toward enlightenment and progress on the path of your soul, and so I recommend that you embrace it and hear its wisdom.

The wisdom I speak of is the wisdom of your soul - the wisdom of the universe, and the awareness you are experiencing is the sound of my voice - the voice of your soul, that you have previously been unable to hear. When this occurs you will find significant changes in your life and relationships beginning to take place. Although they may not be noticeable to others, you will find they have the power to significantly alter how you function at every level of your being.

If you take the time to consider what your new level of awakening is showing you, it can enrich your life and the lives of those around you. It will start to become apparent that you are so much more than you had thought yourself to be, and you will have a greater understanding around how powerful and infinite a being you truly are. Now you will see you are not simply a physical organism of flesh and blood, skin and bone, muscles, organs and other matter.   Your new awakening is reminding you that contrary to what you may have believed up to this time, you do not have a soul - or what you may describe as a spirit – your consciousness is in essence that soul or spirit which for the duration of this earthly life time has a body - your body.

You will begin to understand more clearly some of those things you have considered deeply and found too elusive to fathom. Suddenly your world will seem to be a more colourful and amazing place. You may feel you are living in a different dimension, and in a sense you are. But you are living in the same dimension with what you might call *added extras*. Other human beings may appear differently to you once you have awakened to the true nature of existence. For you will realise that although some of these other people have not yet awakened to this new knowledge you have gained, they too, are just as powerful and infinite as you are. They have simply not yet become aware of this, and so like you have once been, they will be *sleepwalking* through life, remaining within the limitations of their human condition.

Use your new found awareness with compassion, and never allow yourself to feel superior to those who have not yet experienced their own awakening. Remember always that they are just as beautiful and powerful as you. This simply may not be the right time for their awakening. Be aware also there will be human beings walking this earth who are vehicles for souls who have given themselves a greater challenge, that of remaining unseen and unheard by their human vehicle for the duration of this life.

When you were born into this life, you were the vehicle I had chosen with which to travel my path through this life. You will recall from my words on sleep that the memory of my previous soul path was then concealed from you, so that the purpose of this part of my path could successfully be fulfilled. Since then we will have slowly connected more strongly to each other with each new experience, and the veil between us has become thinner with each soul lesson learned. For some it will take a whole life time to attain full awareness of who they truly are, with the knowledge only becoming visible to them at the point of dying. For others the soul awareness comes quickly even in childhood. The time of the awakening is connected to the path chosen by the soul, and the experiences and lessons committed to for the duration of this life. It is in relation to this that I have counselled you to avoid any feelings of superiority in respect of those human beings who after many years of earth life appear to be totally unaware of, or disconnected from a sense of their soul or spirituality.

When any soul is incarnated into a human body it faces the challenge of learning its chosen lessons through the experiences of that human being. This often takes place without the awareness of their presence within by that human being for large parts of the path they walk together. With full soul knowledge there would be no lessons, no limitation, and no lack of understanding. Only with time and the completion of soul lessons does the soul become stronger and even wiser, and so in most cases it will begin to strengthen the awareness of the human being to its presence within them.

Therefore when you encounter someone who seems totally unspiritual, totally unaware of having a soul or of anyone else having a soul, and even strenuously denies the possibility that there is such a thing as a soul; take a step back and consider them with your new found awakening. To incarnate into this life and make a commitment before such incarnation that the life will be lived without the soul connection ever being apparent to the human vehicle of that soul, is infinitely more challenging to the soul, and of course to the human being.

Therefore when you find that you are being judgemental or dismissive of seemingly unspiritual or soulless people I ask you to pause. Now consider whether it is possible that the souls of such people are following a path of enormous challenge, in which the human has no inner compass of the soul to guide its thoughts, words, and actions? If this is so, then to complete a human life with love, compassion, tenderness, or any sense of self worth deep down inside will truly be a challenge of enormous proportions for the soul and its human vehicle. For they will never have the beautiful experience that is human to soul connectedness.

Those who you see as unkind or uncaring may be so as a result of their own soul's chosen lessons for the life they are living, or they may have come into this life to be an example to others of what a human being is not meant to be. They may even be an example that helps another human being to follow more strongly and connect more powerfully with their own soul and the guidance it can bring.

Therefore if you are granted an awakening to the presence of your soul within, know that it is a gift from your soul; an offering of the hand of friendship and of guidance and wisdom, with which you can help yourself on the path of this life and perhaps help your fellow beings on planet earth.

Concerning Peace - Chapter Twelve

And Here You Will Find Clarity

When you are trying to clarify something in your mind, it is often like walking through a series of doorways or openings. Each time you feel you are getting closer to clarity another door slams or an opening disappears before your eyes, and you are once again facing a blank wall or have a vague sense of uncertainty. No matter what direction you take the blockages persist, and you seem unable to be free of their masking and confusing effect.

Confusion can arise in a number of situations during the course of your life. This can be because you do not have sufficient information or knowledge to find your way through the fog of misunderstanding or misinformation; or that you have too much information for your mind to process simply and clearly. The world today is awash with information, and whole forests have been sacrificed to provide the paper on which this information is printed. Remember that each person who offers information to others so they may find clarity on a given subject is usually offering their own world view. This is not to say their view is wrong, just that it may not be what someone else needs in order to find their own clarity.

An important aspect of this search for clarity, is to have awareness that there is a difference between real clarity and following your impulses or whims, for this is effectively taking the easy way at any given moment in time. Impulsive feelings that are believed to be clarity are often accompanied by a sense of urgency and a feeling that this (whatever this is) must be done now, without further hesitation, no matter what those around you are saying. When a feeling of this nature arises it is usually based on a sense of neediness, or such a strong sense of desire that you are afraid any delay will deny you that which you desire. Then there are those feelings you may have in which there is a sense of fear and a need to make your decision quickly. You may feel you will miss an opportunity, or your moment will pass.

When feelings of this nature arise, human beings often find themselves believing their intuition is warning them about the danger of not making a decision here and now before it is too late. It is not uncommon for the human race to mistake their own deeply hidden fears for intuition, because the feelings that stem from those fears are so strong. If you find yourself in such a place remember what I have already said about *enchantment*. This was when I explained that when you become enchanted by something or someone you will find yourself believing what is being presented to you as the truth. You will usually do so because it is what you want to believe, or perhaps because it means that you will be able to fulfil a desire without having to be patient and wait for fulfilment of that desire.

Your intuition does not communicate by creating feelings of fear within you. It will raise feelings of certainty or of what we are discussing here, namely clarity. For instance, people often say they made a decision to take a detour or a different route to their destination. They then add "something said to me that I should do so", although they could not explain what it was or why. They do not usually say they knew if they continued the way they were going something horrible or horrific would happen to them, simply that the decision almost made itself. However, after having done so they discovered their way would have been blocked or indeed they may have been affected by some disaster or tragic event.

How many times in your life have you found yourself with a feeling that you know something, although when asked how you know you are unable to explain? You may find yourself simply saying "I don't know how I know – I just know!" This is when your intuition is speaking to you and the feeling of knowing is so strong; because when your allow yourself to hear the voice of your intuition it comes with great clarity.

Clarity is what the word suggests it is, for it is that moment when you see clearly what direction is the right one to take for your best and highest good – and for the best and highest good of others involved. If that clarity comes at a time when you are actively searching for it, you will find it is also accompanied by the clearing away of all the misunderstandings or illusions that have been preventing you from moving forward, leaving you feeling confident that your decision is the right one.

If you seek clarity on any issue now, step back from your confusion and your fears and any sense of urgency. Close your eyes and breathe quietly for a moment or two. Then gently let go of your judgements, prejudices, preconceptions, and fixed beliefs about others and the world around you. Open your eyes once again and look with the eyes of your soul. You will find things look different, brighter, sharper, and more beautiful, and now you are seeing with true clarity. For I do not judge or criticise I see simply what is and understand that we each see things from our own perspective and in our own way.

You will know that you have found true clarity when you are able to see things as they are and not simply as you would like them to be, or as you have allowed someone to persuade you they are. Clarity is not simply reaching the point where you make a decision whether it is this or that, yes or no; it is so much deeper. With clarity you see whether things really are as you have seen them or something else altogether. You will also see whether the things you find unacceptable can be changed, or even whether they should be changed.   For most of the decisions you make in life will affect others as well as yourself.

To see clearly (with clarity) is the ability to see without attachment or imprisonment to a cause, an idea, or another individual. It also means that you can see there may be options you had previously been unaware of or had not considered relevant. This is sometimes described as "thinking outside the box", and it is a good description. When you think outside the box you are rising above the "box" of your limitations to how you see and consider matters.

However, this does not mean that with clarity you should become cold or aloof, or abandon those who may be less than perfect. To see with clarity does not rob you of compassion, it does the opposite. For you are able to see clearly the best possible way of dealing with matters for all concerned. So when you find yourself confused and facing those closed doors and blank walls do not hammer on the doors or kick out at the walls.

It has been said that what you resist persists and this is a good description of how the human mind works. Therefore if you seek clarity connect your mind to your heart, to that deeper inner awareness that you may so often lose sight of in the noise of the world around you.

For when heart and mind are connected and thinking as one, you are acknowledging my wealth of knowledge and wisdom always here available to you, **and** *here you will find clarity.*

Concerning Peace - Chapter Thirteen

Forming a Framework of Contentment

If you wish to let go of a need or desire for something you know is unavailable, you may say to yourself that it does not matter when in fact it matters deeply. In doing this you are perhaps hoping to free yourself from the discontent or discomfort that makes you feel something is missing from your life, and you will be aware that contentment is the opposite of this feeling.

Contentment does not come because you have been granted your wishes. On the contrary it may be the peace of mind that comes from feeling you have given of your best rather than received. Genuine contentment relates to more than the gratification experienced from granting of your wishes. It comes from being at peace with what you have; not having what you believe will bring you peace.

You may be be familiar with the belief that you will find contentment when you have this or that, or you will be content when this experience you are having here and now is over and done with. Perhaps you find yourself believing you will find contentment when you move into your next experience, but only if it is the one you dictate it should be, and that it will unfold only in exactly the way you believe it should unfold.

If you find yourself yearning for this experience of

contentment, you may be surprised to discover that like happiness, rather than you finding contentment it will find you. It will do so when you are able to acknowledge the blessings already in your life and to focus upon them, rather than constantly yearning to be removed from whatever situation you find yourself in. To be content is to be at peace, and to be able to let go of the constant striving for more than you have, no matter how far you have travelled or how much you have achieved.

This does not mean it is wrong to make plans, or to have wishes or preferences. It is not wrong to see that you have the ability to improve your life and the lives of others, and it is not wrong to have the possessions that are a healthy part of life as a human being. There is no reason why you should not enjoy the good things in this life if they become available to you, or even to make the decision to work hard in order to attain or achieve them.

Life is made up of many different experiences for each person living here, and you will no doubt have had a number of those experiences already. Some of them may have left you feeling frustrated, disappointed, angry, resentful, or fearful; in fact feeling the opposite of contentment. Each person will find contentment in their own way. What fills one person with contentment makes another feel unfulfilled and frustrated. It is healthy for people to have different aspirations and ambitions, or hopes and desires. If everyone had precisely the same goals they believed would take them to a place of contentment the world would be like a machine, repetitive and without colour or character.

Still, while living within the human condition it is too easy to see many of your experiences as negative and as having no place or use in your life. However, as your connection with me grows stronger you will better understand the value of such experiences to both of us. You will realise they are treasures of learning that we will take home with us when this life is ended. But, they will only be treasures for us to take home if they have been recognised for what they are, namely lessons on the path of the soul.

There are of course also the numerous possessions that a human being can accumulate, and it is so very tempting to fall into the trap of believing they are the most important things in life. Humankind has evolved and developed many skills, and in doing so is able to make things of beauty; but the beauty is often what you might call skin deep or superficial.

In today's world there is widespread belief that your value and status can be measured by the monetary value of the assets you possess, but contentment will never come from the accumulation of these possessions. I do not say they cannot give pleasure or comfort, or that some of them are not sometimes essential to make life even moderately comfortable.

However, true contentment does not come from the enjoyment of physical comfort or a labour saving device. It does not come from having massive wealth or great power; it comes from a much deeper and simpler place within you.

Those with great wealth and power are often desperately seeking contentment, and make the mistake of striving for more wealth or greater power. In doing so they are usually moving further and further away from what would bring them to a state of contentment.

In your quietest moments and in your simplest activities is often where you will unexpectedly encounter contentment. It will quietly slip into your awareness when you are able to be grateful for the simple things in life like the beauties of nature, and the sudden realisation that you are free to enjoy them. Perhaps it will find you as you sink into a comfortable chair at the end of a busy day, or enjoy a soothing, warm drink. It will find you many times if you are able to love your life and your fellow beings deeply and sincerely without requiring anything in return.

For contentment is more often found in giving than in receiving, no matter how small and simple or great and materially valuable the giving is. It waits quietly for you, and appears most often unexpectedly when you are able to lay down your desires. This is when you can find joy and peace in what is in your life here and now, without constantly yearning for more or better, or feeling deprived or under privileged.

When there is no longer the tension or unease you will inevitably experience from your continuous yearnings, you will find you can sit comfortably and at peace; contented in the knowledge that there is no need for the rushing round trying to "achieve", no need for searching for solutions, or material gain. You will begin to enjoy the simple pleasures that require no company nor any complicated preparation or resources.

In short, when you can do this and be contented with your own company or just to have those you love around you, this is when you are creating an opening for contentment to find you, often without being aware that it is happening, until that moment when you find yourself giving a gentle sigh of contentment. The wonder of this is that whilst you begin to let go of the striving and material yearnings, they will start to become fulfilled, for as with all energy, like attracts like, and your contentment will attract ever increasing levels of itself and so it grows and grows.

You are where you are meant to be, and your value comes from within, where our connection grows stronger as your contentment grows. As you increase your awareness of the small blessings in your life you are forming a framework of contentment that will increasingly fill your life.

Concerning Peace - Chapter Fourteen

For Destiny to be Fulfilled

Have you encountered the saying, "you must do this it is your destiny", perhaps in a book you read or in a film or play you saw? This expression often appears to be a command that closes the door to what someone is currently doing with their life, or even to something they are planning to do in the future. Suddenly the character involved has been imprisoned on a path they have not chosen but feel compelled to follow. For they see the concept of destiny being one where there is no freedom of choice. They firmly believe that if someone tells them it is their destiny to follow a particular path, they will be unable to escape from that path. It suddenly does not matter whether they would have chosen the path in question, or if it would be their free choice to take the route they are being commanded to take.

It is such a pity that as you walk the path of your soul through this life, you should be given this impression of what destiny is. If you were to look in a dictionary for the meaning of this word "destiny" you may find it described thus; a predetermined, usually inevitable or irresistible, course of events.

You will see examples such as:
She was unable to control her own destiny
or

He was a tragic victim of destiny.

These descriptions and definitions and the examples of how destiny is understood to work, give the distinct impression that "destiny" removes control from you as a human being, and directs your life in a way that you are forced to follow whether you wish to or not. This is all very misleading, for definitions of this word often speak of an inevitable or irresistible course of events. This can lead you to believe that destiny is linked only to a specific course of events, or a path or route followed.

Many human beings spend considerable amounts of time and energy trying to reach one target or another. This may be political power, the accumulation of great wealth, success in their chosen field of endeavour and on and on. In doing so they lose sight of the fact that it is not the destination (note the link to the word destiny) that is the point of the whole thing. No; it is the route followed that is the life experience and the path of the soul, where the soul lessons and growth of both your human and soul aspects occur. They are the route to and a part of your destiny, or to put it another way your destination.

Have you ever completed a journey from one place to another on a regular basis, and found that on a particular occasion your route is blocked or there is a delay? If you know the area well you will probably take an alternative route, but you will still arrive at the same destination. It is the nature of destiny that you have free will in this human life to choose the route of your path through it from birth to its ending. But the destination you arrive at when your life is completed is where you were destined to reach before you were born into the human condition.

The pathways to your destiny are numerous, but they will always take you to where you are destined to be in one way or another. There are those who will say "I am meant to do this" or "I feel that I have to do this", these are not usually empty words justifying a course of action. When this happens they are being given guidance on the path they wished to follow in order to reach their destiny, a path they chose before they entered into the human condition.

While the paths are various, some will of course be more practical or suitable, or give the lessons and the experiences that your soul has come to earth to gain. So in a way you could say there are what humans would call *right* paths and *wrong* paths. Nevertheless whatever path you follow you will reach your intended destination (i.e., destiny) at the end of this path you call life. Whether you will have fulfilled all the required experiences or learned the lessons I have chosen you for, in order to help me learn is another story.

It is often the case that an individual is offered a particular opportunity or route to follow in life, and they decline and take an alternative path. They are subsequently surprised to find that the route they have chosen has eventually brought them back around to place them where they would have been if they had made the other choice. This is when a soul has found a way to communicate with its human counterpart. In so doing it has clarified (remember my thoughts on clarity) that an alternative route to the one they were planning will provide a soul path experience already chosen for this life. If the destination at the end of that part of the life journey is a welcome and acceptable one for the human being that is a bonus.

On the other hand, it might be that an individual will choose a path or route for a particular period of their life, then circumstance removes its availability to them and they find they have to take another route. You will know from the stories of others that when this occurs they often say the "missed opportunity" or the removal of something they would have wanted, was the best thing that ever happened to them. This, again, is the soul path experience working as planned for this life time and the human – soul partnership.

Remember the riches are to be found in the journey. When a temporary destination is arrived at during the course of this life and it feels good, then you know that part of the journey you have just completed has done its job for the growth of your soul. If you wish to know the path in life that will bring you those all-important soul experiences and the one that will bring you the most fulfilment, then sit quietly for a while and ask yourself. You will find the answer does not lie in the mind of someone else, but deep within you, where I await your call. There may at first seem to be no answer at all, for destiny is often best fulfilled by simply going with the flow of life, and allowing your destiny to find you. If this is the case, to battle against the flow will simply exhaust you, until your energy is so depleted you will have nothing left with which to continue the next part of the journey.

It is often at this point when you surrender to the flow of life, and to the power of the universe, that you find yourself on the path that is precisely the one to follow if you are to walk the path of your soul. No matter what path you take, at its end is your destiny, the one chosen before starting this life, which will take *us* back home where *we* can become whole.

It is possible you may have heard there is an absolute need to follow your destiny, for if you fail to do so you will need to come back and follow it over again. What this refers to is that on occasion a human counterpart is unable to find their way to every part of the path their soul intended, and they leave this life with a part of the path incomplete. This does not mean that the whole lifetime must be lived again, but that the soul may need to fulfil that incomplete aspect in another incarnation.

So whilst doing battle with the direction in which life is leading you, be aware that those soul path experiences that need to be fulfilled, may just be in the direction you are so desperately trying to avoid. Your path through this life will often vary but destiny will always be achieved in one or more life-times; whatever is needed for destiny to be fulfilled will always be provided.

Book Four
Concerning Harmony

Here we are looking at issues around decision making or choices that may need to be made. These arise in many different aspects of your life, and between you and the different people you encounter.

These thoughts concern some of those issues and your quest to resolve the different situations and reconcile the various circumstances or events which may bring you into conflict with yourself and/or others.

It is a quest in which you will be seeking a natural state of harmony throughout your being.

Concerning Harmony - Chapter One

Feel the Treasures of Planet Earth

Earth is the planet you live on. It is the giver, supporter and protector of life, sustaining you throughout that life. This word "earth" is also the name for the soft brown soil that is home for seeds to grow into plants, flowers, trees, and the fruit and vegetables essential for your nutrition.

If you wish to use electricity without being harmed by its power, there is a need for it to be earthed. In order to keep strong your divine connection and to be healthy and balanced, you need to remain earthed. From this you will see how important even essential it is, to maintain a healthy connection to the earth beneath your feet, that is a part of this beautiful planet you rely on for your survival.

When you feel isolated or unsteady, you may reach out for something or someone familiar or strong to restore your balance, perhaps from whom or what you believe can offer you strength, support, or guidance; or even all three. At times like these the power and beauty of nature all around you should not be forgotten or underestimated. For planet earth has enormous stabilising power and significantly revitalising energy with which to restore your equilibrium and sense of wellbeing.

Within the greater universe planet earth has its own atmosphere that provides the air you breathe. In your immediate solar system it is the planet situated at exactly the right distance from your sun. This means there is enough sunlight to sustain life, but not so much that it will prevent life from thriving or even destroy it. This optimum exposure to the power of the sun creates the right elements to make physical life on earth possible. Without these things all of the life you see around you, including you and all other human beings, could not exist. So this beautiful planet you live on really is your life support system, as it is mine while I walk this journey of human life with you.

If you travel beyond the limits of the planet you will see that it is surrounded by a halo. If you asked a scientist what this is you would probably receive a scientific explanation, which would be "scientifically correct". However, when you think of planet earth and its life giving power, think of this beautiful halo and be reminded of its vibrancy and life, and of all the life sustained by this power.

When conditions on this planet cease to support human life, it will be time for me to leave and return home. When conditions within your human body cease to support your continued life, then it too will be time for me to leave and return home. It is important for both of us that you cherish your human body and use the resources planet earth provides to keep it healthy, in order that we may complete our planned path through this lifetime of yours. If you were to abuse your body or not to avail yourself of the nourishment and sustenance provided by this beautiful planet, know that you would be cutting short the journey it has been decided we will share.

When you feel confused or disorientated, or you feel a sense of weariness or depletion, remember the power of planet earth to refresh and revitalise you in a healthy and natural way. This beautiful planet does not only provide all of the ingredients you require to feed you and keep you healthy, it is also home to an abundance of natural resources that can restore well-being when it has been lost to you.

However, whilst these natural gifts can restore your physical health, it is also powerfully healing to simply connect directly with nature in the raw. The cities and the technology of mankind have given an abundance of good things, but they are also a source of ill health for many human beings. This ill health can be physical, emotional, or mental, as part of your human condition. Yet it can be soothed and rejuvenated by the sights and sounds of nature, in silent retreat from the man-made areas of the planet, and the harmful emissions and noises they may surround and invade you with.

You will have noticed that I say your ill health can be physical emotional or mental as part of your human condition, and I did not mention your spiritual aspect. This was no mistake on my part, for you will be aware that your spiritual aspect is inextricably linked to me – your soul. Nevertheless, while those unhealthy aspects of life can affect your physical being, they will inevitably be felt by me also. Know that they cannot destroy me, even though they will be felt by me as a part of our powerful connection and the path we walk together. But - if you choose to lead an unhealthy lifestyle, knowingly and intentionally rendering your body unable to continue living on this planet, then I will leave and will take with me only the part of your conscious journey that you have completed prior to the demise of your human body.

There may be a thousand other ways your life can be ended, at a time you would perceive as it having been cut short; and many of these will not be as a result of a conscious decision by you for this to happen. This is when the path of this life has been completed as far as possible at soul level, and it is time for us to leave the remains of your human body on planet earth, and return home together to continue my path into the future.

You will find that while there is no dire punishment following any decision you might make to end your life prematurely, (as is stated by many religions that believe you have intruded upon a divine plan for the path you would walk through this life). This life path of ours is not a strict dictate of any kind and the reasons for and results of such a decision are both something for us to discuss at another time.

I ask you now to stop whenever you have the opportunity, to sit quietly and to see, hear, *and feel the treasures of planet earth.* You may notice the blue of the sky and the green of things that grow in nature from out of the planet's surface. You may be enchanted by the sound of birdsong or the feel of the ocean washing over your feet. This may stir a sense of creativity within you and inspire you to produce images of those things that you see and hear around you.

Humanity is capable of creating much beauty, and that beauty in the form of art or creativity of other kinds, will in most instances be inspired by one or another beauty of the natural world; born out of the creative inspiration I have just described. However, there will also be beautiful creations that appear not to be of this world in any way, and these will be gifts to the world inspired by the soul of the human being who created them.

Whatever you choose to connect with, when you connect with nature, remember to listen and feel the many treasures of planet earth. Enjoy its beauty, absorb its strength, and feel yourself being healed, and in doing so you will be offering healing to me also, for which I thank you.

Concerning Harmony - Chapter Two

Music Goes Straight to the Heart and Soul

Music has been around you since the day you were born, and even earlier when you heard your mother's heart beat from within the womb. When Mothers hold infants close to them, that drum beat of the heart is familiar and comforting. It is not surprising therefore; that all music has a rhythm running through it, and the drum beat is a deeply primal music with which all human beings feel a sense of connection. Mothers sing to soothe their young to sleep or calm them, and lovers dedicate songs to their beloved. Indigenous tribes use drums to beat out the rhythm of the planet and of their own hearts, and workers often sing and drum together to summon up strength to work as one force, when great physical strength is needed.

Each culture or nationality in this world has developed a language of its own, and this is a wonderful tool for helping to connect to and communicate with those who speak the same language. However, you will need no reminder that one of the great barriers between human beings arises when two people who are trying to communicate with each other speak different languages. Different ways of communicating are sometimes found through body language or sign language using gestures or symbols. However, without a common use of words the messages can become distorted or misunderstood, and rather than resolve matters, additional problems are often created. However, there are no misinterpretations, no misunderstandings, no need to have knowledge of the language of the composer, when music is heard. For music goes straight to the heart and soul, by-passing the usual constricts of language.

The widely understood definition of music is an arrangement of notes forming a harmonious sound, which in turn can be pleasing, moving, stirring, or inspiring when listened to. So stop for a moment and decide what you perceive to be music. Now consider whether you feel music is missing from your life, and if so in what form it is absent.

The power of music can stir your emotions and inspire your mind. For music can simply be experienced, without the necessity of complex consideration or deep interpretation, when there are no words to interrupt the flow of its beauty. This type of music when created by human beings is played by groups ranging from just two or three people, to large orchestras made up of almost a hundred different musicians. Of course many musical performances, whether with musical instruments or with the human voice, are done as solos, namely one individual singing or playing alone.

You could fill a room with people none of whom speak the same language as any of the others, and yet if you were to play music to them they would understand its power and beauty. They would be moved to tears or filled with joy at the sound of the music, for music transcends the barriers of language and creates a universal language of its own.

Many people perceive that what I have described above is the only type of sound that can be described as music. However, there are other forms of music that do not fall within the above category, but which can have the same effect on the listener. The sounds of nature are frequently musical when listened to more fully, for they can bring a sense of peace and tranquillity and can be stunningly beautiful to the the individual listening to them. It can be most therapeutic to listen to the breeze rustling in the leaves of a tree or the sound of the ocean as the tide ebbs and flows. The sound of water in a small country stream rippling over the stones that lie on its bed, can often create the same effect as what is more commonly perceived to be music.

You will no doubt have heard beautiful solo performances of birds on the branch, offering arrangements of notes that are perhaps closest to what would be perceived as music. When you bring together some of the natural sounds I have mentioned, they can seem almost like an orchestral composition which stirs in the listener a great sense of peace and tranquillity.

There are of course other perceptions of this word music, often used to define sounds of many kinds that are pleasing to the ear. These can be identifiable, repetitive, and rhythmic sounds that give a sense of familiarity and reassurance. Then there are the sounds that tell you something you are eagerly awaiting is about to happen. People often use the expression "that is music to my ears" when they hear sounds like the post box opening as an awaited letter arrives. For you it could perhaps be the sound of a voice that tells you someone is home safe, or a machine beginning to work again when you feared it had been irreparably damaged.

So be aware of how many different sounds there are that may be *music* to your ears, for you to be soothed or reassured by, or simply to take pleasure from. Listen to the beat of your heart, or turn to nature to hear the melody of a rippling stream and the song of a bird. Music really does come in many forms, and each can bring joy or simply reassurance to the listener for whom it has meaning.

Listen to your own favourite sound – for every human being has at least one favourite that is music to their ears. Remember whatever your favourite sound is, it is reminding you of your ability to hear with your ears, and this is a blessing not granted to everyone.

Music of any kind is truly a blessing. It can heal you down to the depths of your soul. For when I hear music it reminds me that we are still here on planet earth continuing our path of the soul, that has so many lessons and joys to offer as we live this life together..

Concerning Harmony - Chapter Three

Give Some Joy to the World

Joy is a small word that describes a universal feeling, for joy can be experienced alone or with a multitude of others. Every human being has within them the capacity for joy. It is like a light shining in the darkness, and if it is completely absent from your life experience you may lose your vitality and sense of purpose.

If you become aware you have reached a point where there is no joy in your life, recall when you were a small child and how you felt when you would shout with joy. You are likely to realise that it was almost always the simplest thing like dancing in the rain or splashing in a puddle that gave you a moment of joy.

It is difficult to think of a visual image that portrays joy; for it often defies description or definition. However, you may find it helpful to think of a heart, although the heart I am referring to is the familiar heart shape which is such a widely recognised symbol of love and romance. This simple and symmetrical shape does not truly represent the physical heart, but rather is symbolic of your emotional heart centre. In doing this you may more easily be able to associate your thoughts with love, and of course joy, rather than thinking of the physical mechanical heart that sits within the human body.

You will hear many human beings declare their heart is filled with love, or they will state "I will love you with all of my heart"; they may even say something fills their heart with joy. These mental images and verbal expressions clearly establish the link between the physical organ that is their heart and the emotional heart centre, the latter of which is capable of experiencing loving and joyful feelings.

While the heart is powerfully associated with the emotion of joy, when people speak of feeling joyful they also use expressions such as "this lifts my spirits", or "that feeds my soul." For feelings of joy defy all efforts to describe them in any logical or rational way. These are feelings which are not just a part of the physical, emotional, or mental aspects of you, although all of those aspects can be affected when joy is present. No; joy is a feeling that reaches in through your heart centre to me, your soul, and then expands outward again to fill your whole being.

This may help to give you a sense of how joy would appear as a visual image; picture the heart-shaped outline that you will know so well, and then imagine it is filled with the sweeping and gloriously ever changing colours of the aurora borealis, or northern lights as they are more commonly known.

Joy is not quite the same as happiness or contentment, although it is of a similar nature insofar as it is a positive and pleasurable to experience. However, it is more related to what you might call bliss or delight. It is charged with a vibrant energy that fills you, motivates you, uplifts you, and makes you aware of your strengths rather than your weaknesses.

If you were to ask someone who has lived *or* is still living a life filled with poverty, oppression, or pain, what brings them joy, they would undoubtedly give you an answer as to what that is. It is unlikely they will say "what is joy?" for they are likely to be able to find within their memories, at least one moment of joy somewhere in the darkness of their life.

Consider those times in your own life when you have experienced a feeling of joy. For everyone in this life will have experienced joy at some time if only briefly or rarely and if you are fortunate you will have many joyful memories to draw upon. It is likely you will find when you recall such a time, even the memory of this sensation makes you feel temporarily more positive and uplifted. You may find yourself smiling as you bring the memory to mind.

Now try to recall some time in life when you offered joy to another. This may have been some small kindness or favour, perhaps simply passing on good news or offering reassurance in some way. When you did one or more of these things, you did it without any thought of payment or return; you simply did it because it felt like the right thing to do at the time. What it will also have felt like could perhaps best be described as *good*. In short, in *giving* joy you *received* it as well. Just like love, and happiness, and the many other positive emotions that human beings are capable of experiencing, joy increases as you give it away.

This principle of expansion does not of course apply when you give away a material item of some sort, for it is finite and of a physical nature. The laws of physics dictate that if you give something of this nature away to someone else then where it has been there will be a space or emptiness. However, human emotions, whatever their nature, are experiential rather than material. These are formless types of energy that defy the everyday laws of physics you will be familiar with. Whether these sensations are good or bad, filled with sorrow or with joy, they will return to the giver each time they are offered on to another. When you encounter joy in another even if you were not the one to help create it, the look of joy on their face or the sound of their joyful laughter will usually cause you to find yourself smiling as a natural reaction.

Joy can be experienced following a period of anticipation when the awaited occurrence arrives in someone's life, or it may arrive unexpectedly; and while the smiles of joy will be a little different for these two situations, each will nevertheless cause a temporary feeling of upliftment and joy in those who witness it. It may seem to be a paradox that when you do offer joy, love, compassion, and many more of these positive and wonderful gifts to others, they are going to return back to you; but you will sometimes find the feedback or return from these emotional offerings (whether it is positive or negative) is not always experienced by you immediately, or even in the near future.

Remember in all of this; those spiritual laws that govern life on planet earth and beyond. You will be familiar with the various natural laws at work on planet earth, for instance the law of gravity. This dictates that unless some external force is at work what goes up must come down. What you may not be as familiar with are the spiritual laws that govern attraction or resistance. One of these laws is the law of Karma, a much-misunderstood spiritual law. This is also known as the law of cause and effect, meaning that whatever you put out will come back to you. It is sometimes also described as the law of attraction, or to put it another way – like attracts like.

This principle is simple; if you wish to experience or attract joy in to your life, the most effective way to do so is to offer joy to others. That is not to say you should perform a mechanical exercise in which you offer joy specifically in order to receive or experience it. For this is working from an energy that is self motivated or needy, and because of this you will attract to yourself that same energy.

When you offer joy purely for the sensation of seeing joy in others without thought of yourself, you will attract real joy into your life. Are you ready to give some joy to the world?

Concerning Harmony - Chapter Four

The Essence of Hospitality

If you look at this word "hospitality", you will see that it also contains within it the word hospital. You will no doubt know the word hospital describes a place you may be taken to if you are ill or injured in order to be cared for. It is a place where you will be given the space and time to rest and recuperate; to be supported and assisted in the process of recovering good health.

You may be wondering what the connection is between a stay in a hospital and what you might understand to be hospitality. In a hospital, help will be given by experts with a high level of medical knowledge about your condition. However, it will also be necessary to treat you with hospitality – in other words - kindness, warmth, generosity and shelter, in order to help you return to full health. For all of the technical skills and medical knowledge will be less effective if these experts do not truly care whether you recover in all aspects of your being or if they are not supported by those who will offer you a degree of hospitality.

It is likely that only some members of your team of helpers will offer their expertise in treating your medical condition. Others will be helpful in ensuring you are fed and accommodated until such time as you are well enough to be self sufficient again. Remember though that there is an invisible component needed at such a time that is often overlooked, and it is the need for the gentle touch, the warm heart, and the kindness that is better known as hospitality. For without these things your medical condition will recover more slowly and less fully, and your whole being will have difficulty in revitalising itself following the trauma of your illness or injury.

The essence of hospitality is a warmth and generosity that comes from a kind heart and a benevolent spirit. It will usually come from someone who cares not only whether another lives or dies, but who cares as much about the quality of their life. Someone who has a heart truly filled with hospitality will also not distinguish whether their hospitality is to be offered to a human life or the life of some other species.

When disaster strikes, whether natural or accidental, there are usually those who are in dire need of both rescue and medical attention. There might also be those who are physically uninjured but traumatised by what has happened. In circumstances such as these there is an urgent need for hospitality in its broader sense. There may be a need for people who are qualified to deal with emergencies of this kind, or simply human beings who are concerned for the welfare of their fellow men and women. It is the latter of these kinds of rescuers who will be willing to offer hospitality in the ways I have already mentioned, by offering assistance, kindness, warmth, generosity and shelter.
Hospitality is often associated with the provision of food

and drink and a place to partake of these things. It is *not* often associated with a life-or-death situation. However, at some time in your life you will most likely have heard someone saying of another "I don't know what would have happened to me if they had not taken me in. They saved my life"

There will be times in this life when you and others may be in need of hospitality. This may be if you are on a long journey and need to pause for food and shelter. Perhaps you will have lost your way and need someone to guide you back onto the path you were following.

However, there are many ways of becoming lost in life and not all of these are from simply taking a wrong turning when travelling from one place to another. When members of the human race lose direction it can relate to a relationship, a career, a life plan, or simply a way of living. This life has various opportunities for you to lose your way and be in need of one form of hospitality or another. Without the intervention of someone who recognises you are lost and offers you the hand of hospitality, your life might indeed be lost.

The police officer or ambulance worker talking down someone, who is proposing to jump off a high building because their life has lost meaning, is offering the essence of hospitality. They remind the person who is so despairing that they and their life both have value, and they are welcome in this world. The adult who sees a child separated from their parents and unable to find their way back to them is offering hospitality when they assist them. When someone offers to help another find escape from a situation where they are being mistreated or neglected, they are also offering hospitality.

You will find hospitality comes from an open heart in many ways, even from those who are expert at offering that help in jobs or careers that specialise in working with those in need. Even so, the work they do is not often described as hospitality. For as I have mentioned, this is a word more often associated with the offering of food and drink or accommodation which has been paid for, as a catering service of one sort or another.

True hospitality is offered without any expectation of reward or return. You will find that amongst those who work in what is sometimes called the hospitality industry, there will be some who simply do the job they are paid for, nothing more, nothing less. Nevertheless, most people will know of someone who goes above and beyond what is required of them in accordance with the job they are paid for. This is the essence of hospitality, and at some stage in life when you find yourself in need of it, your need will be filled. Be aware though that these occasions will not always occur simultaneously; for there will be times when hospitality is needed and those in a position to offer it will turn their back.

If this happens to you, remember, the nature of life is such that when you fear you have no chance of receiving much needed hospitality it may be offered to you from a totally unexpected source. It is from such experiences that the often used expression "a friend in need is a friend indeed" has arisen, for this simply refers to those times of need when friendship (or hospitality) is so essential.

I have said it is likely that at some time in your life you will find yourself in need of some form of hospitality. If such a time occurs for you, whether it is because you are ill or simply in need of food or drink, shelter or support, remember it well if it is offered to you. Remember how good it feels, and ensure you will be there at a time when hospitality may be needed from you in some way.

When you do this you are working from your soul and being guided by your soul wisdom. The purpose of this life for both of us is never to turn our backs on those in need if we are able to offer hospitality.

Concerning Harmony - Chapter Five

When Attempting to Reach Agreement

People in different parts of the world shake hands to confirm agreement, and this symbolic clasping of hands is widely accepted and understood. But there are different kinds of handshake, and different cultures and belief systems who do not see the symbol of the handshake in this way. Agreement is usually when two people or more are as one mind, and it brings a smoothness and sense of harmony, or a feeling of rightness. For if you feel safe with someone you let down your barriers, open your mind, and allow an exchange of thoughts between the two of you. .

If you know someone well you will no doubt be familiar with their culture and their belief system. However, it can also be important for you to be familiar with their approach to life and their personality. If this person is from a culture the same as your own or has a similar way of looking at life, it is usually much easier to reach agreement about most things. When you come into contact with someone who is from a different culture, a different belief system, or just with different character traits and outlook on life, it can become more difficult to see the other's point of view. If each side takes the time to understand the other a little better they are more likely to allow for the differences that exist in how each of them perceives things. This ability to acknowledge and to some degree accept the differences between human beings is invaluable when attempting to reach agreement. When each of you feels able to make any form of compromise then the process of reaching agreement becomes even easier.

You will no doubt have had a disagreement with someone at some point in your life. They may have been someone who you liked and believed you would always be in agreement with. The disappointment of discovering your views are so different as to cause disagreement often causes a reaction that closes the mind. This occurs because there is a situation you would not have believed could ever exist, and you need time to process the thought. But, when I speak of agreement, I do not refer to one or the other side of any agreement sacrificing their views or beliefs entirely, for this is not agreement it is a defeat for one person or the other. Agreement is when an acceptable solution is reached that works for all concerned.

When your disagreement is with someone you care about or feel you would like if only this point of disagreement had not occurred, you may be more inclined to consider their point of view. You may be prepared to make some compromises in order to keep the friendship or acquaintance with this person. But, if the disagreement is with someone you have already decided you dislike, the likelihood of reaching agreement might be considerably reduced. When you are in a disagreement of this kind you may find yourself closing your mind, just when you most need to open it. A closed mind will not reach agreement, no matter how important it may be that agreement is reached. If this closed mind approach is taken up by both parties, it is likely the disagreement will fester and grow until it becomes far worse than it was at the outset.

The mind has an amazing ability to create stories, and often when this takes place the story that unfolds in your mind will be one which justifies how you feel or what you believe. It will usually be a story written by your ego, as the purpose of this story is of course to protect you and your viewpoint on any issue that arises. It is not a story designed to make you feel you may have been wrong or intolerant, or that you should reconsider the whole issue at hand. It is a story that reinforces your worth and your status, and does not include any suggestion that you may have been mistaken or have misunderstood anything. This is the story being written from within a closed mind. If this happens to you your mind will believe it is under siege and that your opinion or view, your perspective or status, are being undermined. It has therefore effectively pulled up the drawbridge and is ready to repel all suggestions that you may need to reconsider things.

Remember, what I describe here does not apply only to you; it is common to human beings from all walks of life and all cultures. It is true this state of mind may sometimes be needed in order to protect yourself from unfair criticism, conflict, or confrontation. Nevertheless, if this approach was taken in respect of all disagreements that arise, the world would eventually be comprised of individual human beings, each living in their own little world within a world. All the benefits and advantages, all the progress and evolution that comes out of compromise and co-ordination, out of tolerance and agreement reached through reasoning, would be lost. The world would be poorer for this, but each and every individual on the planet would be poorer for it too.

An important part of the soul path through life is to learn and grow, and the way that humanity does this is to share their viewpoints and knowledge gained by each of them, in the process of their individual soul paths. This is always more easily achieved by opening the mind and discovering that the differences between you and others are something which can enrich you rather than stifle you. You may see some differences that seem to be insurmountable, and so you give up and let your mind become closed and static. No learning takes place no progress is made.

Where there are two points of view which are completely different to each other, it is often the case that a small adjustment here or there in either of those viewpoints, can produce a third viewpoint that is a composite of the first two and that turns out to be a better way. This is because it contains the strong points of two approaches, often having had the weak points of each of them dispensed with. A closed mind does not just repel those things that are unwelcome or feared; it also repels those things that are of great value. Unless the mind is opened in order to fully consider an opposing viewpoint it cannot truly know whether it is indeed "wrong" or "right", so if you are in disagreement, open your mind calmly to the flow in and out of thought or opinion. Then you will consider the opposing thought more clearly, and know whether it is valid.

When you have done this, you may be more certain that your view is right. Still, perhaps no agreement can be reached because the two viewpoints are mutually exclusive and no middle ground exists. It may also be that you have gained the insight you needed, which was to be certain that your own viewpoint is valid; even if its validity is right for you but not for another. But, you will know without doubt that you have considered the matter fully and fairly. On the other hand, you may discover to your surprise that the two viewpoints are not as distant from each other as you initially thought them to be.

I believe it is appropriate here to quote another widely used expression that is relevant to this issue. "Never judge a man until you have walked a mile in his shoes"'. This expression is a reminder that before you pass judgement on an opinion, an approach, or an action which seems to be in conflict with your own, it would be wise to consider things from the viewpoint of the other. Only when you have done this can you truly know whether or not you can reach agreement.

When a solution seems impossible to reach, allow the vital time to take your conflict into the depths of your being and sit with it quietly. For you may just be able to connect with the counsel I can offer you as to what will be the best way forward. It requires wisdom and humility to acknowledge that a change of mind may be needed, or even to be certain that the right way forward is to continue with a viewpoint that you know in your heart is the right one. If we consider these things together we will both learn and grow. I am an open door waiting to allow your thoughts and concerns into my realm for consideration and ready also to pass through the door you may open so that you are able to consider mine.

Concerning Harmony - Chapter Six

True Charity is a Generosity of Spirit

The word "charity" has come to describe offering of voluntary gifts or monetary donations, for some worthy cause or person in need of help. More often than not these gifts or donations are offered for large groups of people who have been hit by natural disaster or tragedy of some kind.

When you think of receiving charity from another or others, it may bring forward within you a sense of shame or failure, perhaps a sense that you have reached a point so low you are dependent upon the charity of others. If you see charity in this way any need you have for it will be likely to bring feelings of helplessness or loss of control in respect of what goes on in your life. This is not surprising, as it is widely perceived that the person who pays for something is entitled to decide how it is used. Whatever *it* is and whether that person will be the one who uses it seems to be less important than the rights of the person with the means to pay.

If someone offers you a gift you are not likely to have these feelings of failure or loss of control. A gift is something given without any question of a return being required in any way. It is given freely to express love or friendship, perhaps sometimes to express gratitude. All the recipient usually feels is a sense of gratitude or of being fortunate enough to have received their gift. In addition the person offering the gift does not feel entitled to dictate how the gift should be used or have feelings of superiority over the person they have gifted.

For most human beings, life will be comprised of what they might call good times and bad times. These vary from person to person, from situation to situation, and from nation to nation, or even culture to culture. It is clear that what one person considers to be a need another simply sees as a preference, or indeed does not even see it as relevant. It can therefore become difficult to see clearly where there is a genuine need for what you might describe as charity.

There are of course situations in which it is obvious that charity in its usual sense may be required. Some of these I have mentioned already, and natural disasters or tragedies in families or individuals would fall within this category. These disasters or tragedies may have been anticipated but unavoidable, and the resulting loss or distress creates sympathy, which arouses charitable feelings in those who have not had to suffer their effects.

People make charitable donations for different reasons, and these may include compassion for those in need of charity, gratitude that they do not have such a need, empathy for the terrible experiences those in need are suffering; or even guilt that they have so much while others have so little. However, "charity" is not simply about offering charitable donations, for charity can be offered in the form of guidance, practical support, protection, kindness, friendship, and more.

Charity is woven into the nature of your being if you will only stop and seek it out. If you look within and cannot find it, you may discover a fear of lack or sense of need in your own life. This can be a feeling that ownership of what you have (whether financial or material possessions, or a comfortable and advantageous situation in life) is fragile and may be easily lost leaving you disadvantaged. Such fear is not natural to you; it is a conditioned response you have learned from others. If this is what you find when you look within, then seek out its source and release it to the universe for healing, so you feel able to give and receive charity in its many forms in a more natural and comfortable way.

There are certain cultures in this world which believe that if you love something dearly and someone else admires it, you should give it to them. This is a spiritual perspective and worthy of consideration. Nevertheless, when you reach the point in life where you own certain possessions that you believe you could not live without, perhaps you should ask yourself this question. "Do I own it or does it own me?" However, a system or culture which dictates that you own nothing, in a world that requires you to own certain things in order to live in even moderate comfort, is not realistic.

True charity is a generosity of spirit, in thought, word, and deed (and giving to others materially or otherwise) with no expectation of, or wish to, receive any return. This does not mean you need to give away everything you have until you too are in need of charity.

However, what you might call true charity could perhaps

be compared to the cornucopia, which was a horn written of in Greek mythology. Each time the horn gave away its bounty it was magically refilled. The cornucopia is often described as the "horn of plenty". So you can see the similarity between this cornucopia and your heart filled with charity toward others, for when this is the case your spirit is enriched, and the universe will always offer you enough for your needs if not for your "wants".

Do you know of the saying "Charity begins at home"? This originally referred to always fulfilling your responsibilities to your family first and foremost. Unfortunately, the expression has become distorted by many to be used in a more selfish or greedy way, namely that you should think always of yourself without ever thinking of others. In truth whenever you have charity within your heart then charity will always be "at home".

Charity does not mean you should not observe and fulfil your own needs, for you are a part of the circle of life and subject to the natural laws, just as are those you give to. But if you are to practise charity it is just as important to include in your awareness those who may be in need of help, and to consider honestly whether there is room in your life to give from what you have without causing undue hardship to you; for that would be solving a problem, only to create another.

Concerning Harmony -Chapter Seven

The Hand of Friendship

Another word for friend is ally, although this other word is often associated with political or military matters rather than in a personal sense. This is because an ally is considered to be a friend in times of conflict; but an ally is also someone who is "on your side" and so is also a kind of friend.

I have spoken of those who will be there for you in a time of need when we discussed hospitality. You may feel you know precisely who your friends are, and who amongst them have the appearance of being a friend but are really acquaintances. There is of course a significant difference between friends and acquaintances. You will encounter many acquaintances in life and although some will pass through your life fleetingly, others may be around for a very long time. However, those who remain in your life may not automatically become friends. You will also have colleagues in your workplace, some of whom may also be friends, but others are just people you get on well with and get to know quite well – or perhaps not.

It is a human trait to place those you get to know into groups. For instance, relatives, colleagues, neighbours, medical consultants, professionals who offer a service of one kind or another for payment, even friends of friends.

Most of these will not be seen as a friend; they will come into your life for a specific reason or purpose, and will only ever communicate with you in relation to that purpose. Many of those in the above categories may become friends in time, although you will also have friends who may not have been in any of these categories in the first instance.

You will be aware that a friend is someone to share good times with and who is happy for you when things go well; but a true friend is also someone who stands up for you when others are against you and when life becomes difficult. It is at times such as these that it becomes apparent how strong a friendship really is. You may see someone as a friend and believe you could rely upon them whatever situation you found yourself in. But the feeling of friendship that lies in the heart of a person will vary from deep friendship to the more casual kind.

If your friendship with another is the second of these you may find that just when you feel you really need their support they have created a distance between you. But – when you judge this kind of friend consider whether you have always been steadfast with other friends when the situation has been reversed. Even if you know that you have always been a good and dependable friend, you will not be able to guarantee that all of your friends will do the same for you. If this is so it may be necessary to acknowledge that the friendship was not what you believed it to be, and if this is unacceptable to you then perhaps you will naturally drift apart. On the other hand, when someone feels that a friend has let them down it can cause anger, and bitter words may be spoken.

Remember if you find yourself in this situation, while you may not approve of the action of a friend you can be honest with each other, and do your best to go your separate ways without anger and with a lesson learned about who your friends really are.

True friends may not always agree with each other, but they can respect each other's views and still continue to care for each other. This kind of friendship is able to withstand all of the challenges it is faced with. When you find such a friend in life you will most likely have found someone whom you are communicating with *soul to soul.*

However, where there is a soul connection, an indication of this is often that there seems to be a natural agreement about all of those things that really matter. For such souls are likely to have lived many lifetimes and learned much about what is important and what is not. This usually means there is little if any conflict in the friendship. In the right conditions and between the right people you will find that your souls do communicate, although not in the way human beings do. This is where the description of "Soul-mate" is often used.

You will need help on your voyage across the sea of life, and at times a helping hand when you fall overboard; for it is likely you will fall in one way or another and at one time or another. That hand will be the hand of friendship. When you feel as though you are in danger of drowning in the sea of life, or when you realise you have not been the best that you can be, that is when you will discover who your true friends (and soul-mates) are.

They will be those who have seen you at your best but also at your worst, and still they are steadfastly prepared to accept you without changing you and even to help you in working toward becoming the best you can be. They are those who will stay by your side until you are able to climb back on board. These are the people you will call a friend in a much more profound way. Often with friends like these you may feel you have walked the path of life together previously, and it may well be that your respective souls have done so.

It is easy to be friends when things are going well, but not so easy when things become tough or you encounter something on which there is strong disagreement. This brings to mind the concept of torment of which I have spoken earlier. Disagreement between friends, whether trivial or significant, is often due to misunderstanding or misinterpretation rather than intentional conflict or offence. That is not to say there will never quite simply be a difference in how friends view a situation, but many disagreements between friends can be resolved if each friend can find it within them to look at things from the same angle as the other.

In friendship you will defend a friend as you would yourself. You will draw strength and reassurance from each other and to be in each other's company will make you both happy. This is the gift of friendship, a solid relationship with each of you caring for the welfare of the other and holding each other in mutual respect and affection.

Concerning Harmony - Chapter Eight

The Search for Inner Calm

We have already looked at how some days you will feel good and others you may feel sad, angry, fearful or frustrated. You may look at those around you who appear calm, and wish you could find that quality within you. Perhaps you will think it is easy to see whether a person is calm, but what you see is often surface calm that masks a deep inner anguish.

Only when you are still and present in the moment for long enough will you be on the way to finding your own inner calm. For it is in the smooth undercurrent of your being, deep down below all of the irritations, helping to calm them from within so that you are able to deal with whatever arises. This is not the mask of calm you often see in others, but a quiet steady strength always there when it is needed. If you are feeling less than calm about life, connect with this strong, wise, peaceful calm that is deep within you, for it will remind you that this too will pass, and harmony will return to your life.

The search for inner calm is everywhere in this world, rather like the concept of happiness. Everyone chases after it but it seems to elude them. They eventually find it only to feel that it is immediately snatched away from them. Of course this is not what is really happening, for what is found and then seems to be snatched away is often just an illusion.

It is in fact sometimes difficult to distinguish between real inner calm and an appearance of inner calm. If you check the meaning of this word "calm", you will find words like tranquil, cool, still and composed are used. However, there is such an air of busyness that pervades the parts of planet earth where large populations of human beings are to be found; and the result of this is the conditions that prevail are not conducive to being calm, cool, tranquil or composed.

There is a description often used for the busy lifestyle pervading the towns and cities of the world, and it is used in such a way that speaks of people wanting to escape from it all. The description is "rat race", a phrase which refers to an existence where human beings strive to compete for wealth and power, and this would accurately describe large swathes of the *civilised* world.

This ethos becomes like an infection with each one desperately trying to do better than the others around them. But of course they are doomed to fail because for each one that rises to the next level and looks down on their competitors in the "race" there is another waiting in the wings to be the next "winner" or supreme expert.

You will notice I have referred to this expression "rat race" as describing something that people wish to escape from. It is interesting to consider that there is another expression which refers to this animal the rat, and this one speaks of rats leaving a sinking ship. The source of this second expression lies back in a time when rats were known to inhabit cargo ships carrying foodstuffs. This was a time when sailing was the main method of transporting goods from one country to another. If a ship was sinking the rats raced frantically to escape knowing they would drown if they did not. It is clear that this is an appropriate description for people desperate to escape a lifestyle in which they feel like they are drowning, but from which there is little chance of doing so.

If you can relate to this expression "rat race" and the feeling of wishing to get out or escape, you may believe the only way you can do this is to uproot yourself or your family and set up home far from the area where you have always lived, or where you earn the income that helps to supports all of you. It may even be that you love living within the hub of activity that is your town or city. Perhaps all of your leisure activities and interests are here, and you would miss them if you were to move away to somewhere quiet and remote. However, you perhaps also yearn for the quiet space in which to find your inner calm, feeling that the busy energy and sounds around you prevent you from achieving such a calm state of being.

There are two ways of achieving inner calm and they are both quite different. One of these is to physically remove yourself from your noisy and active environment, even temporarily as you would when you take a holiday. You may choose to stay in a peaceful village somewhere or even to find a place to stay up in the hills or in the depths of a forest. When you choose this way of finding your inner calm, you are assisting the process by controlling the environment in which you are situated. If this is a quiet woodland space or a remote hill or lake side, much of the city noise is immediately dispensed with. In this kind of environment you simply need to relax and breathe, listen to the sounds of nature, or to sound levels which, compared to your usual place seem almost like silence.

But then you return to city life and the demands of work or business; even the leisure pursuits you normally enjoy resume their place in the queue for your attention. You probably believed that because you had taken yourself away for a while, these demands for your attention and invasions of your inner calm would now be easy to cope with. However, everything returns to normal very quickly, and all of these things may begin to feel like a group of noisy children clamouring for your attention. Once again you may find yourself yearning for your place of peace and quiet. So while such trips away take you to a place where inner calm is more easily found, the effects are usually temporary.

A more lasting way of finding your inner calm, and more importantly keeping it close enough to reach out and touch whenever you need to, is to create it where you live in the midst of all the busyness of your everyday world. Contrary to popular opinion a meditative pose is not always needed for your inner calm to be found. In times of stress and turbulence if you will only take the time and space to connect with it, there deep inside of you is your state of inner calm.

Begin by taking a moment to be still and inwardly connect, instead of making your usual outward connection with all that is taking place around you. A deep breath, a moment's pause for thought to detach from your anger or frustration, and you are on your way to finding your own inner calm. First take your focus away from that which is causing you to feel a lack of calmness. Simply close your eyes and "watch" each in breath and each out breath, namely "watch" your breath entering and leaving your body at that point at the end of your nostrils, where the air is taken in and then expelled. You will soon find you cannot focus simultaneously on this mental activity and the aggravations and irritations you have been experiencing. You will start to become more mindful of what is happening in and to your body,

When you are in a state of tension, this is often indicated by increased heart rate and blood pressure, a tightening of the throat and chest, and other signs and symptoms. When you begin to watch the breath in this way you will become more aware of this and of how unpleasant or unwelcome those feelings are. As you continue to watch your breath in this focussed way you will begin to feel those sensations slowing down and eventually disappearing altogether. You may find yourself taking a long, deep breath, completely filling and then clearing your lungs. As you breathe out you may feel your shoulders soften slightly and your head and neck become less tight. When you do this you are usually clearing from your system the tension and the stress that was preventing you from accessing your inner calm.

I do not wish you to believe that meditation is not the way to find your inner calm. Meditation is indeed a powerful tool, in strengthening your inner awareness and helping you to find that calm and peaceful place within the centre of your being. However, if you attempt the short exercise I have described above even once or twice, you may find you are beginning to understand the basis of meditation.

If you then explore the different kinds of meditation available and find the one that is just right for you, your inner calm will have reached out from the centre of your being into your outer areas of tension, stress and anxiety, and begun to heal you from within.

Concerning Harmony - Chapter Nine

Seek Your Absolute Centre

If you place the centre-point of scales a fraction either way they will not weigh true; for they will be influenced by the side the centre-point has been moved toward by even the smallest amount. The centre-point must be perfectly equal in distance from each side, so it cannot be influenced more one way than the other.

When you need to find your own truth, seek *your* absolute centre. It is within the heart of your being and protected from being pulled one way or another. Your absolute centre is a place of peace and calm where conflict cannot reach and pressure cannot push. You might believe this is an unattainable state of being, and in one sense you may be right. For if you are constantly in contact with the many opposing opinions of others around you in this life, finding your centre can be difficult to achieve or attain.

It is true that in order to remain balanced it is necessary to consider all points of view and all options when it is time to make a decision about something important to you. To remain blinkered with a desire to see things only from your own perspective, will leave you with a severely limited view of the world and the issues you encounter on a daily basis. However, when it comes to making decisions in life, whether they are large or small, trivial or critically important, there are often more than one or two views of a situation to be considered.

There may be times when a number of options, opinions or viewpoints will need to be considered, in order to make your decision or choose your option. If you wish to make a wise choice and be fair to all concerned, then take your time and listen to each and everyone's views. Unfortunately when a human being holds a strong view (from their perspective of course), a view they truly believe to be the "right" view, they will have a tendency to argue their point in a way that is relative to the strength of their view. After all, they believe their view to be right.

If someone is trying to persuade you that their view is right it can be helpful in the first instance to consider how they have arrived at this conclusion. Ask yourself if they have become fully informed and therefore have strongly supported reasons for their view. You may discover they hold their view because it is beneficial to them; in other words they may stand to gain if a choice is made in line with their view. It can be difficult enough considering a well thought out argument by one other person. When there are several, each with a different view, it becomes almost impossible or at the very least time-intensive, and that time may not be available to you before your decision needs to be made.

In addition to the external decisions that become necessary on a regular basis, there are considerations you may need to make about how you feel, what you are experiencing, and whether you are happy with a whole range of things. But, life is often lived in an automatic way without time being allowed for the consideration and decision making. It can seem as if your path ahead is mapped out for you before you are even given the opportunity to consider or make decisions. So remember when you feel a sense of uncertainty, and the need to ponder on significant (or even insignificant things) in your life, something is urging you to stop and listen before moving forward.

As a child, decisions that are important have a tendency to be made on your behalf by an adult who is responsible for you. Shifting from that status quo to one where the decisions lie on your shoulders alone can be daunting, and there is a temptation to over-think things in the hope that you will not make a mistake. Over-thinking usually arises out of fear, and this fear is usually passed on to you from another or others, for quite often fear has been passed on to them. In this way large communities of people live in a state of fear that is so permanent in their lives they do not even realise it is present. The fear is usually underlying and unidentified, leaving those who carry it with them to feel it is wise to always take the safe and certain path ahead. But while the path may be safe, it is not necessarily the path that will lead you to where you want to go.

If you find yourself in this situation where you are bombarded by the views, opinions, and unsubstantiated fears of others, and you reach a point where your head is spinning and you feel unable to make a choice one way or another – stop; it is time to go into your centre.

At first you may not find this easy, for the world around you is constantly calling your name and offering you tempting, ready-made choices. Remember these choices are not your own, and until you are comfortable with them and know they match what is in your heart and mind, you are entitled to request the space to consider them before making your final decision. This principle applies to almost everything about which you need to make a choice or a change in your life.

When you first make the choice to suspend your decision until you have consulted with the deeper and wiser aspect of yourself, you may have difficulty in reaching inward and finding that aspect. If, however, you have already begun to strengthen the connection between us, you will be aware of my help in achieving this centred state of being. On the other hand, if travelling inward to your centre is a concept new to you, there is a possibility that it will take you a little time and practice before you reach the certain knowledge that the world has released its grip on your mental processes.

It is helpful when seeking your centre, to let go of all views and opinions directed toward you from the different people in your life, if only for a few moments – or even longer if needed. In this process of letting go, remember to include in your release the views and opinions of those you hear and see from a distance. For they too are able to affect your thought processes. Because they are physically distant you may believe their influence on your view is weaker, and there are times when this would be a mistake. When you can do this you will begin to think more clearly on matters you wish to resolve or make choices about.

In your place of complete centre you will start to know your own mind in the truest sense, perhaps for the first time, and you will find the answers to your most pressing questions are becoming easier to find. Remember that in searching for this centre of your being, it can help to temporarily find a quiet place where the calls upon you cannot disturb your tranquillity.

Close your eyes so the world around you no longer distracts your attention, and visualise a fine line of pure white light running between your heart and the centre of your forehead. If you recall my thoughts on finding your peaceful heart, you will know that this point in the centre of your forehead represents the place where your mental energy is at work, in both rational and intangible ways.

Your heart centre represents the place where your processes of compassion and emotion are at work. When these two become connected you are working in harmony with me – your soul. From this beautiful energy connection between these two you are using a power within you greater than logic or rationale can ever achieve.

When you can extend this process to include an extension of that line down to your solar plexus and to the core of your being, you are using an even more powerful aspect of your ability to connect with your soul. You may be aware of the expression "gut feeling". This expression is often used when human beings have a powerful sense of knowing or certainty they say is felt in the gut or the stomach area. This is the area of the Solar Plexus Chakra which is more commonly described as your "power centre" Decisions made from such a powerful sense of certainty achieved in this way are usually the best decisions. They are not as some believe impulsive decisions, but rather decisions made when you reach your centre and listen to its guidance.

So remember when you become confused and you need to know what life is really telling you about what needs to be changed; go quietly into the centre of your being and allow your thoughts to follow that line from the core of your being to your heart to your thinking mind. What follows the thinking mind or thought-processes is usually intention and then action.

You will find your choices and the paths you decide to follow so much more easily when you have found your absolute centre, and have made the connection between, and listened to, your emotional and thinking centre in place of the babble of conflicting views that may surround you on a daily basis.

Concerning Harmony - Chapter Ten

A Homecoming in the Deepest Sense

Home is the place you most often lay your head at night and fulfil your everyday needs. It is where you keep your belongings, and where you may feel you are most protected from the world when you feel vulnerable. However, many people change the place they call home a number of times during their lifetime, and you may already have done so at least once if not more. So is "home" a place in the physical sense, or is it something more related to your deeper feelings?

It has been said that "home is where the heart is". This seems to indicate that home is not one particular place; for it expresses the feeling of affinity or connectedness you may feel in many different places during your life. So when you speak of a homecoming what is this home that you are coming to?

You will know a homecoming can be to return to a place you call your own after a lengthy period of travelling, or simply after a hard day's work. Perhaps it is to return after a long trip away from your usual place of residence, when coming home is likely to be a welcome relief. Home is usually somewhere you can relax and simply be yourself. There is no need to create a good impression on anyone or to make an extra effort to be someone you are not. You are, in short, at home with yourself.

Some people remain in the home they have lived in since their childhood for the whole of their life. Others find a new home when they reach adulthood, and then again when they find a life partner and wish to settle down. Even those who have chosen to settle may move to a number of other homes during adulthood with the partner they have chosen, and you will see there is a parallel here with the expression I mentioned above. While A person may change the building they live in, they often do so with the same person; and that will be the person they feel closest and most intimately connected to.

However, everyone does not remain with the same partner for the rest of their life; they might change their partner once or several times. When this change of person with whom they wish to share their life closely takes place, they will invariably also change the building they live in, the one that is usually referred to as their home. This suggests the word *home* is something they see as whatever building they live in with the person they feel closest to, that is to say where their heart is.

Although what I am discussing here is home as a particular building, or somewhere you might reside with your family or the people in your life who you see as family, it is clear that both the concept of the building and the people considered as family (or close partner) may be various different places and people during the course of a lifetime. So what does this word *home* really mean and how do you know when you have achieved a homecoming? If you consider the feeling that you get when you return home, to the kind of home I have described here, you will probably describe it as relaxing, comfortable, and safe, providing you with all of your needs. However, there is another kind of homecoming to be found in life and it is often an experience rather than a place or a person. It is fair to say that your true home can simply be a place or even a situation that feels just right to you in a special way, although it can also be so much more.

There are some human beings who spend their whole lives searching for a place to call home. They move from one place of residence to another and from one country to another. They move from one job to another and even from one career to a completely different one; and yet, they fail to experience that sense of homecoming. One of the reasons for this is that they are searching in the wrong place. For when the search is external it is usually connected to acquisition or achievement, with each new acquisition or achievement failing to provide the experience of homecoming that is being sought.

If there is a subtle feeling within you that you have not yet found your experience of homecoming in the deepest sense, it may be time to step back for a little while, and take a break from your quest.

If you are with another person in a large building and you become separated, the first instinct is usually to begin searching for each other. However, the concept of a moving target being difficult to hit comes into play here. If both of you keep moving around looking for each other you will have much more difficulty in reconnecting than you would if one of you stayed in one place. For if one of you did so you would eventually be found by the other and the sense of relief is usually quite strong. The natural, safe, and comfortable experience that is homecoming is usually felt in the same way; except that what you have found may be an experience rather than a place or person. When you take the courageous step of taking no steps at all, this is when you are more likely to to discover that your homecoming has found you in a very special way.

So when you feel lost or fear you will never find your true homecoming, take that quiet break and allow it to find you. It will probably come from where you least expect, as many of life's most important discoveries often do. This will be so even if it is a place you have reached or a situation you have found yourself in. This feeling comes when you reach a milestone as you walk the path of your soul. It will be one of many homecomings on your path, and each one is waiting for you, each a homecoming in the deepest sense.

Concerning Harmony -Chapter Eleven

Floating With the Tide of the Universe

You may believe that floating is aimless, because the direction of movement cannot be controlled. However, floating is simply following a natural direction, and you will always reach a destination even if it is not a destination you had planned or anticipated.

I have spoken of the concept of trust and you will remember that to trust another can have a varied range of outcomes. This is because you will usually be placing your trust in another human being. The very fact of being human gives rise to the potential for error or misunderstanding. You will have heard others saying in defence of their actions (and perhaps have said this in defence of your own) "well I am only human". When this is heard it is generally understood that a person is pleading the case that they cannot be relied upon completely, because they are "only human" and to be "only human" means to be fallible.

Broadly speaking members of the human race accept that fellow humans may disappoint or let them down because of this fallibility that is common to all humans. This may seem like a very negative and perhaps unkind description of the human race, but this is not so; it is simply a reminder that fallibility is an important aspect of the human condition.

If you were infallible, I would achieve no growth, nor would I learn any lessons as a result of living within the human condition and walking this path of life with you. You may recall my thoughts on the concept of denial when I explained the need for a separation between your human mind and my soul memory that has wisdom beyond your understanding. It is because I have come here to be a part of you that it is necessary for my memories to be held in safekeeping, until this particular path through your life is complete. This enables me to gain the soul path experience I have committed to before this life of yours began. I am your soul, but you are my sensing, seeing, hearing, touching, guide through the experiences of this life. You are invaluable to me and my soul path.

Without your fallibility I would drift through this life as a soul with soul knowledge and wisdom, suspended inside of you but unable to experience in a tangible way, and learning nothing to add to my soul development. I would simply sit in the innermost recesses of your being awaiting the end of your life so that I could return home. What is more you could say I would be returning home empty handed. For as you live your life I would remain untouched by all those things I have come here for you to share with me; the doubts and fears, the joys and sorrows, and all that makes your life so rich and rewarding.

So - when your fallibility finds you searching around for help, or for guidance on a decision you need to make, think of me and what I am able to offer you, for although you cannot access my memories and wisdom completely, you can access my guidance. This will not make you infallible, but it can help to make your path ahead a little clearer.

It is at such times I can return the favour you have given to me by carrying me through this life and its experiences with you every step of the way. This you can do by taking those quiet moments I have spoken of so many times, and by listening for the sign that tells you I am speaking to you. You will find that when you can do this you will begin to discover the courage within you to recognise that there may be no immediate and specific answer to your question. If you listen carefully, you will hear me, whispering in your ear about the importance and benefits of floating with the tide of the universe.

If this seems like a crazy piece of advice remind yourself how well the tides of the universe continue to ebb and flow and for how long they have done so. You will see that this is a tide so big and so wise there are far less reliable ways of finding what would be the right decision. Float with the tide of the universe and of life for even a little while, and you may find you have reached a staging point along the way. This will take you where you need to go, or will at least move you closer to being able to make that all important decision.

You may find this concept of floating brings to mind a kind of aimlessness, and the opposite of being guided to the right place, thought, or action. However, consider the water lily; it is such a beautiful delicate and yet exotic flower, simple yet complex and with rich green leaves to complete its magnificence. This is a flower that spends all of its life floating on water. Of course it throws down roots into the depths of the water until it reaches the mud to obtain the nourishment it needs to feed itself and continue to grow. It does what all of life in nature does, which is to adapt, and it does this by drawing from mud what most plants obtain from soil.

In listening to my voice you are like the water lily, reaching into the depths past where most everyday searching is done on the surface of human life. When you are able to summon the courage – and the patience - to float with the tide of life, you are adapting the more usual ways of finding your guidance and reaching your intended destination.

Float with nature and allow the universe to guide you, and you will have found the gateway to your true soul path. The answers you find and the destinations you reach may be different to those you had in mind. You may at times doubt you have reached the right destination at all, and even have the sensation you might have had if you stepped on to the wrong bus or train by mistake.

However, in time you will find awareness that the "bus or train" you stepped onto in allowing yourself to float for just a little while carried you to the right place after all.

Concerning Harmony -Chapter Twelve

Speaking of Flying

We have just discussed the concept of floating and how you might usefully apply it in your life. You will recall that we talked about adapting and about reaching down into the depths for nourishment whilst still being able to float along with the tide of life. Of course when I spoke of floating I was not suggesting you find some body of water and lie on it in the hope that it will take you to the next point on your soul path through this life.

So now I wish to offer you my thoughts on flying, and again I am NOT suggesting that you physically launch yourself from a great height in the hope that you will have the same experience as the birds above you have each time they take to the air.

Most if not all human beings will at some time in their life have stood looking up into the sky watching birds soaring high above. As they observed the aerobatics of the birds they might have wished they could do the same. This is because watching those birds could have stirred within them a sense of wondering how it must feel to fly free, and to be released from the responsibilities and limitations of their everyday life. If you have ever done this you will understand clearly the feeling I am describing.

Of course in today's world human beings can fly, so long as they are inside some kind of aircraft. In addition they can only go where the aircraft will take them, and they must go when the aircraft is flying. You will know this is not the same as feeling the air on your face and watching the world below, as you move freely like those birds high above you do each day, moving to wherever you wish to go. So, how do you reconcile these two activities with each other in terms of living your life in a soul connected way?

Remember there is far more in this life than you are able to see with your physical vision. I often remind you that you will find me within the deeper aspects of you, and yet here I am speaking of flying which seems to be the opposite point of focus. They may seem so different, one closely linked to the earth and yet at the same time floating free, and the other seemingly detached completely from the earth.

Consider for a moment the planet you live on as you see it, and how the depths of the earth below you and the heights of the sky above you seem so very distant from each other. Now consider the vastness of creation and notice how much smaller the distance from the centre of the earth to the highest point of earth's atmosphere may now seem by comparison.

The human energy field is so much greater than the physical body seen by the human eye. It can also be contracted or expanded by conscious (and sometimes unconscious) intention. So where do the limits of you reach to? Are they from the centre point of your physical body to the surface of your skin? Or are they out there in what you see as the space around you, and – do they go deeper than the physical centre point of your human body? Furthermore, is it possible for them to go deeper than that? The answer to these questions lies somewhere in the latter of the two statements. Finding those depths and heights is something you can only do with an open mind.

If you have stood and watched the birds in the sky in the way I have described, you will have been aware of how wide a perspective they must have on the earth below. Of course in this modern age you understand this concept on an even greater scale, because of the evidence brought back to planet earth by those who have travelled outside its limits and into space.

But for a moment let us stay with planet earth, for that is the home for the path you and I have chosen to follow through this life. If you are in a city walking between tall buildings, or even inside one of them, you will see no further than the walls that surround you whether you are inside or outside. However, a bird high above those buildings can see an incredibly wider range of what is below it. If you were high enough up there in the sky you may even see all of the buildings in the city and the countryside beyond; every street and road and the fields and hills all around.

If you were searching for something what an advantage this would be, if you also had the ability to focus in and take your vision down to a particular area of that scene. If you begin to stretch the horizons of your thoughts and realise that thoughts are limitless you can see so much more.

When you close your eyes and shut out physical vision, this is when imagination begins to come into play. The word "imagination" is often used to describe something that does not exist. However, the human experience is unique and individual, while at the same time being global and universal. It is therefore an incomplete truth when you say that something does not exist, because it cannot be seen or touched by anyone other than the person experiencing it within their mind.

When I speak of these two apparently different concepts of floating and flying they are not so very different because they both release you from within your consciousness to travel in your mind outside of your physical or earthly limitations. You could say the human expression "thinking outside the box" is relevant here, for that is what you are doing when you travel from within your consciousness to those places you would find difficult to reach in a physical way.

If you feel weighed down by life and its experiences, close your eyes and let your thoughts take you wherever you wish to go. Imagine you are soaring above the world and feel the sense of freedom that comes with this. Know that you can fly as high or as far as you wish to find what you are seeking, whether it is some kind of freedom from the restrictions of everyday life, or the solution to something you perceive to be a problem. For you are safely travelling within your consciousness, and we both know that this is as vast as the universe itself.

When you can visualise this sensation of flying you will begin to fly through the various parts of your imagination, and new horizons will open up for you. Your thoughts become released from the box they are in and your potential is also released. What is rigid becomes flexible, and your perspective grows wider and wider. If you allow your mind to fly high enough the impossible begins to become possible.

Concerning Harmony -Chapter Thirteen

Processes of Completion

The last brush stroke of a painting or final stitch in a tapestry are actions of completion. But completion sometimes occurs naturally and with subtlety. It may even be such a slow process that you fail to notice it taking place. When you do see a completion, it may be the end of a stage toward something bigger, rather than what you would consider to be an absolute and final completion. So when you seek completion know that it is always completion of a part, and the process will continue even after you have left this life.

Nevertheless, each completion, however small, will have made its contribution to the universe. Each petal that forms on a flower, each drop of rain that falls within the shower, is a completion in its own right. So do not underestimate the process of completion however small, for each completion down to the most seemingly insignificant is part of the whole, and yet it also stands alone in its completeness. This is true whether it is the result of human endeavour or a miracle of nature.

Remember each moment you live has a completion of sorts, albeit a momentary and seemingly insignificant one. For this word completion relates to so many things in so many areas of life.

In today's society you are urged to finish what you start and this can be large or actually quite small in the bigger scheme of things. Sometimes things are quite easy to make progress with at the beginning, then, as they become more difficult the temptation arises to walk away without completion of your original plan. However, if you reach a point at which you no longer feel motivated to continue to what would generally be acknowledged as completion of the task, perhaps it is in fact your own personal completion.

Consider that it is possible the experience you came here to gain or the knowledge you came here to acquire only required you to have reached that point. There is such diversity in life on planet earth that almost everything from emotion, to knowledge, to experience, to aspiration, to size, or to quality, has a vast range of levels that can be considered completion.

Human beings are unique; and with certain exceptions in relation to mass production of material goods, so are most other things. So who is to say whether something or someone has reached their completion in any given thing, or perhaps to describe it another way a final and unsurpassable point.

Most things in this physical world you live in have a measurable limit. This can be a physical dimension, a set length of time, or an optimum point of achievement. Anything that falls short of those accepted limits is usually considered incomplete. But what if the job you took intending it to be for life lasted for only five years, or a year, or even a month? Will it always mean that you have failed in completing that job? Perhaps you decided to complete a University Degree that took four years to graduate from and then you decided after three years that the process was no longer teaching you anything of value to your own personal life plans or hopes? Would that mean that your education had failed to reach completion?

What if the book you began reading no longer held your attention after the first four or five chapters? Does this indicate you have failed to acquire the knowledge or enjoyment you had hoped to gain from reading the book? Finally I ask you what if the grand design you planned and began to work on eventually became a much more modest design, would you consider you had failed to achieve completion? If all of the set limits, parameters, and plans, were achieved or attained uniformly in accordance with what could only be described as *standard*, how mundane and unexciting life would be.

I have spoken earlier of how sad it would be for the world to lose the wonderful uniqueness of each and every human being. But this also applies to almost every other thing of any significance. It is clear from a mundane and practical level there are many things in life that it is necessary to standardise so that they can be relied upon. This will usually relate to things that need to fulfil a very specific and unvarying service or usefulness.

These will be things that you could describe as inanimate or lifeless. They are things that are often mechanical, moving, or even static parts of a greater whole. They have no will, no consciousness, no intention; they have simply been manufactured to perform a basic service.

Things that come into this kind of category will have a need for each one to be the same as the others to fulfil what is required of them, no more no less.

However, for all living things this does not apply. Would you say that a plant that has only four blooms is incomplete because the same type of plant next to it has ten blooms? I think you would not. Nor would you say that a tree that is several feet smaller than a tree of the same type is incomplete. No you would simply accept it as different and unique.

So let us go back to my earlier questions. The job you took that ended earlier than you expected perhaps took you to a point where a better job had now become available. This was a job far more suited to you and your enjoyment of your work. What is more the job you saw cut short gave you just the amount of experience you needed to take with you to this newer job. It may have been that the time you spent in the initial job allowed you to realise it was not what you had anticipate, and it was no longer suitable for you. Either way, you have seen completion of its intended purpose in your life.

I would also ask you to consider again the University Degree you saw as incomplete, the book you never finished reading, and the grand design that became a modest design. In each of these cases what you saw as incomplete was a completion of its own kind, for instance: The University Degree will have taught you something, and if nothing else it will have taught you what you did not wish to pursue that you previously thought you did: Therefore a Completion. You perhaps never finished the book because you had acquired the information or the knowledge that the book had come into your life to offer you: therefore a Completion. The grand design that became a more modest design taught you that bigger is not always better, and in working on it you had time to realise that there were other more compelling designs you wished to work on: therefore a Completion.

These you understand are quite simply examples of how what you see as incomplete, may quite possibly, and more than probably, be processes of completion that are a valuable part of your life experience. It would be wise to apply this principle to many other things you see around you in your life and in the lives of others both near and far.

Never overlook the importance of even the smallest forms of completion in your life. For each completion from a single stitch to a single brush stroke, and to a single brick in a wall, is still a completion.

Remember the words of Confucius who said "Each journey of one thousand miles begins with just one step" and know that each small individual completion is a step towards the biggest completion of all.

Concerning Harmony -Chapter Fourteen

Out There in the Heavens

When you look at the heavens, they may appear to be out of this world and in all that is beyond you. In their vastness and distance they remain shrouded in mystery. If you believe in a higher power you may believe that this higher power is somewhere in those heavens. You may even believe that the creator of the universe rules all that it surveys from these same distant heavens.

If you look into the heavens on a clear night you can see millions upon millions of stars and various different constellations, which are groups of stars. Now consider the galaxy that planet earth is situated in that is made up of one hundred billion stars, and it is not a particularly large galaxy. This may give you an idea of the vastness of those heavens.

Now think of the cells that make up your human body and the atoms that make up those cells. The number of atoms in your human body is almost too large to write down as it amounts to billions upon billions. From this you will realise how vast you may appear to smaller life forms. You will recall my thoughts on these comparisons when I shared with you my thoughts on the subject of the universe that the heavens are a part of.

If these thoughts make you feel small and insignificant, it

is good to remember that heaven and earth are both a part of the greater universe. The heavens are not some distant place, for you are a part of them and they are a part of you. Your feelings of separation come only from your logical mind. When, as a human being, you stand on planet earth and look out into those heavens, they may, as I have already mentioned, seem so very distant. However, while this planet you call home may seem to be isolated in space, the universe is filled with stars, surrounded by planets, and planets surrounded by their moons.

The heavens as a whole can actually appear to be crowded when you look at the images the scientists are now revealing that have come from what humans call outer space. But there is always enough room, and although it may seem distant, you are in the centre of all this existence and activity, truly an integral part of the heavens. In looking at these comparisons it is possible to see the contradiction in how small your planet is in relation to the heavens, and yet as I stated when I discussed the universe with you, how vast you are in comparison to so many other things on this planet.

Those on this planet who are at the forefront of the race for power and wealth are discovering that such power and wealth does not make them feel more important or significant but less so. In fact this lifestyle seems to drive the ability to achieve the goals they pursue further and further away. One of the reasons for this is that the search for power and wealth, or even striving to simply hold your current position in life can become so very time-and -energy-intensive. This means you become like an automaton with your head constantly looking down at the earth beneath your feet and never moving your gaze to the heavens.

When you read these words if you find yourself saying that you do not have time to stop and look up at the heavens, the need to do so has reached a critical point in your life. If you step back you may see that in always looking downward you find it reassuring to feel this small spectrum you are focussing on is something you can control. However, it is not really beneficial to you, because whilst you appear to be in control, your inner self is still doing battle with all of the stresses and strains of "keeping up", an activity that consumes large parts of the lives of so many human beings.
.

There is an irony here, for in the process of attempting to "keep up" you lose sight of the fact that those you are endeavouring to "keep up" with are doing exactly the same thing. For they believe that while they keep their focus on that small aspect of life they can control, they will never be seen as lacking or inadequate by their fellow human beings. Of course all of this striving usually concerns acquiring abilities which are stressful to achieve, and which will lead them to the acquiring of material possessions that provide short-lived satisfaction, until a new and more desirable material possession becomes the new goal.

You may have heard the term "big fish in a little pond" and this of course describes how being in an environment that is comparatively small to you will make you feel comparatively large – and perhaps more important. But with a sense of importance also comes a sense of

responsibility or of being burdened

When you raise your eyes to the heavens you will be reminded how small many of your aims really are in the grand design. You will come to see that the constant striving for material goals can become like a ball and chain around your ankles. This does not mean that earthly dreams and aspirations are insignificant, simply that continuing to focus upon them to the exclusion of all else can make them appear larger and more significant than they are.

It is interesting to note that as this world gets louder, faster, and busier, human beings feel an increasing need to distance themselves from what is taking place around them. But where can they go to achieve that distance? The heavens seem too remote to be within reach for the average person. When you believe this you should remember that the heavens are not "up there" or "out there" they are here all around you, and you are situated right in the centre of them but also around them.

Consider for a moment where you would appear to be if you were transported to another galaxy or even just another planet within this solar system. The answer is of course that you would be somewhere "out there" in the heavens.

Book Five
Concerning Understanding

Finally we are discussing things in your life which may give rise to confusion or misunderstanding; for many of those issues you experience as a problem or difficulty may have arisen from a misunderstanding of one sort or another.

So here, we are considering those aspects of life that are often linked to this concept, and looking at how such misunderstandings may be avoided or resolved in order to attain understanding.

Concerning Understanding - Chapter One

Sowing Seeds of Thought

Sowing seeds in earth begins a process of growth. If you water those seeds you will eventually see new growth shooting out from the ground. Eventually, flowers, trees, vegetables, or other types of plants will start to grow and produce blooms or fruits of one kind or another. In the wild plant life grows naturally without you having to do anything. This may be as a result of a seed having been intentionally buried by some creature or unintentionally dropped on the ground and then trodden in. It could even have simply fallen from the tree or plant and naturally settled into the earth. Nothing grows from nothing; somewhere there will have been a seed sown in some way, and thus you see the result in the form of a tree or flowers, fruits or vegetables.

The kind of seeds I wish to speak about here are the ones human beings sow in the minds of each other; and they are seeds of thought. These seeds have an entirely different outcome, but they will nevertheless produce a result of some description. Where you would feed your plant seeds with water your thought seeds are fed by the focus of attention upon them.

A positive result of thought seeds is that they can be sown deliberately with good intention, and this can be surprisingly uplifting, affirming, or reassuring to the person who has had that thought seed planted in their consciousness. However, a negative result can be produced, when the intention behind the words or actions that have caused the seed to be sown is intentionally damaging or harmful.

Then again, you can also sow the seed of an idea in someone's mind and not even know you have done so. This unconscious sowing of thought seeds is widespread amongst the human race, when words are spoken without considering what their effect will be on those who hear them;. and just like those intentional thought seeds it can be amazingly helpful, or just the opposite.

When you comment about a person in their presence (which is of course a verbally expressed thought seed) your comment then becomes a seed sown in their consciousness. If the comment is about something important to the person, they will usually feed it with the focus of their attention. It is in the nature of humans to expand and add to what they hear from others in line with their own world view, or self view. In this way they are nurturing and increasing the essence of what you have originally said to them.

If the person is not present, then it can - like a seed in nature carried on the wind – be carried to them by way of being repeated by another. You will know from experience when something is spoken and then repeated by someone else, the second person will speak from their own perspective. This means it will in all likelihood be altered from the original statement, albeit in a minor or subtle way. Unfortunately with each repetition the original meaning is shifted slightly, until eventually it becomes a different statement or expression of thought altogether.

This kind of thought seed can be most damaging, and one reason for this is that when human beings speak they accompany their words with different tones and different facial expressions. Indeed, they often use completely different body language from other human beings. As a result, some of the true meaning of what was originally expressed has been lost in translation each time it was passed from one person to another. For when you verbalise your seeds of thought from within your head it is not just words that you convey, but also meaning.

An example of this could be the simple phrase or question "are you leaving?" These three words can mean *I'm checking whether you are leaving, or, I'm expressing concern or disbelief that you are leaving;* it could even mean *please don't leave.* This example shows how differently the same words can be interpreted by the person they are spoken to, and how much power the spoken word can have.

So you see how powerful those seeds of thought you plant in someone's mind can be when you speak them. You can even plant a seed of thought with your actions rather than your words. However the seed is planted, when the person in whose mind it has been planted begins to consider, reflect, interpret, and so on, they are effectively watering it with the focus of their attention, and making it more powerful.

Consider for a moment a seed of thought that has been planted in your mind at some time in your life. Perhaps seeds have been sown that you dismissed and thought no more of. If this is what you did then the thought will disappear into the recesses of your memory within your subconscious mind storage space, and there will be no discernible outcome. However, if you see what has been said as important, you will find yourself returning your attention to it, probably more than once. Each time you do so the feeling attaching to what has been expressed is likely to become stronger. So you can see that when expressing an angry thought or one that is resentful, insulting, demeaning, and so on, it can become negatively charged if it is then considered and re-considered by the listener.

But – it is not all bad news when it comes to seeds of thought. It would serve you well to remember that sowing seeds of thought that are life enhancing, enriching, encouraging, uplifting and so on can be just as powerful in a positive way. When you sow a seed of thought expressing what you believe can be achieved, or reminding someone of their finer qualities, this too can be watered with the focus of the listener's attention.

Remember also that a seed of thought does not even need to be spoken aloud to have power. If you perceive something in a certain way and then continue to feed that perception in your mind it will without doubt become more and more powerful. As I have already mentioned, if this is a negative perception or understanding then the more you feed it with your attention the more negatively powerful it will become. This can happen even without someone speaking to you and this is self-sowing of thought seeds.

Another way of describing thought seeds is to describe them as ideas or concepts. We have looked at the danger of sowing negative thought seeds in the mind of another or others, and even of sowing them in your own mind, so now I want to remind you of something equally important and this is how powerful positive thinking can be.

Positive thinking is quite simply nurturing, and feeding a positive thought, idea or concept, with the focus of your attention. The laws of the universe are powerful in their way of dealing with both positive and negative; so if you nurture an idea or thought about yourself or another you give it power. If you express that positive thought to another you are using an extra watering can to water the seed.

When it comes to a belief that something wonderful can be achieved if enough people believe it can be achieved, then the watering and feeding process relating to that seed of thought or belief becomes so powerful it is almost impossible for it to fail to materialise. Even if just one person believes powerfully enough and focusses on (feeds and waters) the idea that it can be achieved, sometimes unbelievable things can be done. Some of the most amazing feats have been completed by the simple planting of a seed of thought, which was then fed and watered until it became strong enough to manifest physically or materially.

In nature Seeds grow in darkness and under cover of the

earth. When they are becoming so powerfully advanced that the product of that seed breaks free and shoots through the surface of the earth, you see what they have produced. Consider this and choose carefully those seeds of thought you sow in the minds of others, and even those you allow to grow in your own mind.

Keep in mind that while the seed is growing within the mind unnoticed and unseen, a powerful process is taking place. When the product of that process becomes visible it is already strong.

Remember - from tiny acorns mighty oak trees grow.

Concerning Understanding - Chapter Two

The Roots of your soul

I have just discussed with you those thoughts that are encouraged to grow in the mind, using seeds as a metaphor. Now I wish to discuss the subject of roots, again recruiting the help of nature to discuss your *roots*.

I mentioned earlier, that when a seed is in the ground it starts its path toward the light by pushing shoots upward out of the seed case to find their way toward daylight, and the other nutrition it needs. However, that is only half the story, for it also pushes roots downward. With these two actions the seed makes its connection with the earth and also with the life-giving daylight above. This creates a balance between darkness and light, enabling both to work together to help the seed fulfil its potential.

Darkness is often seen as negative, but while seeds grow in darkness before breaking through to the daylight, roots remain in darkness and continue to take sustenance from the earth. In this rich darkness of the earth those roots help the plant to grow toward the light. Much of life develops and achieves enormous growth in the dark, at first unseen and often unknown. It is therefore important that you maintain a good connection with the earth you live upon through your roots.

In human beings roots are formed in a slightly different

way. As an unborn child, you will have grown largely unseen and in the darkness of your mother's womb before emerging into the daylight to continue your life on planet earth. This is when you became physically detached from the placenta, which by way of the umbilical cord enabled you to draw nourishment from your mother's body. This connection through the umbilical cord is similar to the way in which the roots of plants draw nourishment from the earth they are surrounded by. You could say that in a physical sense the umbilical cord was your first experience of having a root. It is clear that roots give a stable connection to the source of nourishment that enables new life to grow to a stage where it can survive and thrive.

Nevertheless, there are also roots in life that provide support and stabilise, but which you are not physically connected to unlike the time spent in your mother's womb. What you might call your roots are usually things you would associate with your background or beginnings, and in this way there are similarities to the roots I have spoken of.

In nature, plants remain connected to their roots for all of their natural life, and they continue to maintain their connection with the earth and draw nourishment from it through their root system; for it is unusual for a plant to have a single root. There is usually a main or primary root which then branches out into secondary roots. This formation creates a wider and more stable supportive base for the plant life to grow from.

A fully mature tree that grows from a single trunk has

spreading branches at its top, and it is clear that it must take a powerfully stable base to prevent the tree from falling over, or becoming detached from its source of nourishment within the earth. From this you can see the importance of the branching of the root system which is able to draw more nourishment and stabilise the tree.

This illustrates the importance of one of the least noticeable aspects of life, namely roots. There are many different kinds of roots in life; and when you use the word *roots*, you maybe referring to your history or beginnings. These will be the roots that connect you to family members who you began life with, and whose circle of support and protection you would usually grow within.

A human being can sometimes begin their life by following a particular path or culture and then change direction part of the way through that life. Most people in the *changed* life they have chosen will see them in a way that relates to that new part of their life, but it could be said that their roots stretch back to that earlier and different part of their life. So your roots can be associated with many things that exist or take place in your early life. This can include your country or nationality, your career path or religion, your family, your friends, and so on.

Your roots can be related to your biological family in which you have physical connections in terms of genes, parents, physical similarities, or perhaps some other connection. They may be connected to the place where you lived in your early life, or the friends you made during that time. Whatever the connection is it will serve a purpose in your life however far you stray from it.

There are times when an individual is unable to feel a sense of connection with the circumstances or people that you would normally describe as being a part of their roots. When this occurs they often take action that is described as *uprooting*, and they move to another place, another job, or even another family relationship or friendship.

Sometimes such an uprooting occurs as a result of prevailing circumstances, rather than being a matter of choice. When you are uprooted in any way that has not been of your own choosing you can feel like a plant would be if it was simply pulled out of the earth that feeds it and thrown to one side. It would wilt and die without the nourishment and stability it once had.

It is true that a plant can wither and die if it is torn from its roots, but it is good to remember also what any gardener will tell you. When done correctly a plant may be uprooted and carefully placed in another location or environment, where, after a little adjustment, it will continue to grow healthily, establishing new roots from which to find its stability and nourishment.

As a human being you have other abilities with which to survive and even flourish. You are able to uproot and create new roots, but also to return to your original roots and reconnect with them, alternatively or in parallel. You will often hear people refer to having a second home or a second family, and this is a description that shows the human capacity to change the nature of its roots, or to have more than one root system to draw from at any given time.

If you begin to feel you have lost purpose or direction in life, look to where you feel your roots are buried. Then return to, and reconnect with, the roots most closely related to healing your sense of loss or detachment from your source and your strength. Remember always that when you put down roots you are choosing what will nourish you and help you grow and become stronger. So choose those roots that will serve this purpose in your life in the healthiest and wisest way, and connect with the nourishment they can provide you with.

I have spoken here of physical and human roots as well as the roots of plant life as a comparison. However, remember you have roots that reach so much further back than this life you are living here and now. These are my roots, the roots of your soul, for my beginnings stretch back through the mists of time and space. These roots can nourish and strengthen you, stabilise and guide you, if you will just make stronger your connection to me.

Feel your soul roots stretching back through the ancient past and know that they have eternal strength available to you whenever you most need it.

Concerning Understanding - Chapter Three

Nurturing is a Gift to the World

You will know that in addition to roots, nurturing also provides what is needed to promote healthy growth. In the fields of horticulture and agriculture it is necessary for nurturing to take place. Gardeners nurture the plants in their gardens, and farmers nurture their crops so they grow to a healthy maturity. This is an aspect of nurturing that ensures the food those crops produce will nurture the physical health of those who in due course will consume the food.

If the farmer has integrity he or she will nurture the animals in their care, even though they may be breeding the animals so that their bodies will in due course also be used for food. Human beings have differing perceptions on the subject of killing animals to consume their flesh for nourishment; some believe it is unacceptable and cruel to do so. However, others believe that this process is a natural part of what is described as "the food chain", just as different animals kill each other for food.

This is not a subject for this discussion on nurturing, but one that I may explore with you in the future. I am simply providing an example here of what nurturing produces.

Nurturing is offered by loving parents to their children, and as a result those children grow from tiny defenceless and dependent infants to fully formed and mature adults. This nurturing of a child can also come in more than one form and different parents will offer varying levels of nurturing to their children. This is as it should be, for parents and children are each of them quite unique, as is their need for nurturing. If the child suffers from some physical weakness the parents will need to address this and ensure that nurturing is provided by way of the correct physical nourishment. If this proves to be insufficient, the parents will most likely seek outside help from the medical profession to ensure the necessary nurturing is received. In the case of an emotionally vulnerable child, good parents will nurture this aspect of them so they become strong enough to go out into the world without their emotions overwhelming them

When the child grows old enough to attend school and then university they will receive other forms of nurturing from their teachers and tutors. These individuals will guide them and offer the knowledge they require to complete their education. If you are to become stronger and wiser it is vital to benefit from being nurtured in one way or another, but the need to be nurtured is not limited to the frail or the weak, the young or the immature. It is a far deeper and wider part of the basis of all life.

When a soul makes the decision to come to planet earth and to incarnate within a physical human body and mind, it does so because it has chosen to work within the structure of that human being, in order to learn and grow. Therefore, if that human being's physical body and intellectual mind had already completed all processes of growth and learning, the soul would have no reason to join forces with it for that very purpose. This is the purpose of this life we are living together you and I, which is to learn and grow. When you learn and grow I share the experience with you and I learn and grow also. This is the process of the path of the soul.

I am consciousness and my state of consciousness may be wiser and more mature than you as a human being can understand. However, my consciousness does have a capacity for growth and learning, and only from living the experiences that offer this process can I fulfil my path. It may help you to understand this concept if you consider that I (your soul) am completing a university degree. Each incarnation I fulfil, or to put it another way, each lifetime I share with a human being, will complete for me a part of that university degree course.

In turn as your humanity completes its lifetime, it in turn joins with me and becomes a part of the soul that I am. Your physical body may be returned to the earth in other forms, but as I have already said to you, your conscious aspect lives on in me and becomes a part of the family of conscious experience that is me.

You will from the above that for the process of growth and learning to take place there needs to be support, and that support needs to be provided in all aspects of life so that the person you are can learn and grow, and so I can absorb your growth and learning into my consciousness. This is the process of nurturing and it is essential to all of life. It is an ongoing part of the growth and learning of both humans and souls; and it is vital to receive nurturing if you are to grow to maturity and thereby complete the path that is your human life but also the path of my soul.

It is the continued cycle of sharing of knowledge that is the essence of nurturing, and that helps all souls and humans complete this soul path experience. For as you do so, I grow in strength and wisdom from your experiences. When you are nurtured you acquire the strength and knowledge with which to nurture others when the time is right, and so the cycle of nurturing continues for all future soul paths to be completed.

Be aware that if you give the gift of nurturing to others, it is a gift to you also. For the miracle of offering nurturing to another is that you become for a while less self involved and more aware of your universal nature. This is when your eyes are opened to a deeper understanding of many things.

There is always a need for those of you who can nurture to do so, for in doing this you also unconsciously help yourself. Nurturing is a gift to the world of two stronger wiser human beings, the nurturer and the nurtured.

Concerning Understanding - Chapter Four

Other Kinds of Communication

To pass information from one person to another or to many others is to communicate. When you wish to learn, or increase your knowledge, you will usually communicate with those you believe have the information you seek. The information may be communicated to you through the written or spoken word, and each of these has its own particular strength in communicating information. You can do so when you are present together, or through the various ways of communication that are now available across long or short distances.

Sometimes information needs to be absorbed slowly in stages to be of use to you, so you are able to learn it fully and recall it at will in the future if a need arises. At other times information needs to be provided quickly even urgently without a delay. This can be because the information is being communicated to you while you are actively completing some job or task, or because you are moving as you listen or watch for the information to be communicated to you.

This is the kind of information that is immediate and intended to guide you forward to a necessary action that must be done without delay. This immediate form of communication is usually necessary when using machinery and in particular when driving a vehicle of some sort. In this situation you require the communication to be made without it interrupting what you are doing, and so a different kind of communication is needed. This is when symbols are invaluable, for they communicate information in a condensed and easy to recognise form. Road traffic signs are a good example of this kind of communication.

However, there are other kinds of communication that relate to peoples' energy and this communication can sometimes be misunderstood. If a person is disappointed about something, or concerned about an outcome, they may unintentionally communicate a feeling of anger to you. On the other hand it may be you that misreads the energy they are giving out or the body language they are using with their spoken words.

It is widely believed that to give good eye contact indicates a person is being honest and open, and accordingly to avoid eye contact suggests some deception. This is often the case, but avoidance of eye contact may not always show an intention to withhold the truth. It can be a reluctance to see disapproval in the eyes of another about something that has been said or done, or even something that should have been said or done, but has not.

It is clear that where human beings are unfamiliar with each other, they may misread the efforts of the other to communicate. This is because they are attempting to communicate without each having an understanding of the various forms of communication that would normally be used by the other. As a result misunderstandings and misinterpretations arise. From the lack of familiarity also comes hesitation about what can comfortably be said to someone, and so communication becomes incomplete or distorted.

Nevertheless, it is often those who are closest to each other to the point of intimacy who have problems in communicating honestly and effectively. This is the other side of the coin in this issue, for those who are close and know each other well are able to "play" with their communications to achieve a desired result, using word and mind games to do so. They are in effect using what they know to be the vulnerabilities, likes, or dislikes of the other person to achieve the desired outcome. So you can see that this issue is filled with potential pitfalls when human beings are communicating with each other.

This brings me to yet another form of communication, namely inner communication, and this is connecting with your inner wisdom - my voice - the voice of your soul. I have spoken of communication being a useful way of passing information or wisdom from one person to another; and this is one way to access wisdom you seek. You will know by now that you each possess your own wealth of inner wisdom that resides in the consciousness of your soul. So if the information or wisdom you seek is deeply personal to you or of a spiritual nature, you may find your communication needs to be inward rather than reaching out into your everyday world.

It is here in that inward direction I will await your communication so that I can communicate with you in return. For you will not successfully communicate with me and the wisdom I can offer you in a crowded and bustling place or in a place filled with sound and colour. You will also know by now that our communication can be achieved when you go within to where the quietness of your being can be found. Let go of thoughts of seeking and striving and remember the butterfly I spoke of on the subject of happiness.

Sit quietly and gently let go of all of your fears and worries, let go of all of you desires and ambitions, let go of all of your anger and frustration, and simply be.

Quietly repeat the following words to yourself, breathing in harmony with each line; this will help you to open up the precious line of communication between us:

Be still and know that I am always with you

Be still and know that I am always

Be still and know that I am

Be still and know

Be still

BE

This is when your everyday consciousness will begin to form communication between your humanity and my soul essence. Once this communication is opened up it will never fail you. You may feel that you are waiting longer than you perceive to be reasonable or acceptable for your answers, but they will always come, even if they are not the answers you had expected to receive.

However, once you have enabled the channel of communication between us to open up, you will be able to return to it whenever you have a real need for its guidance. It may even be of assistance in guiding your future communications with others in your outer world.

Concerning Understanding - Chapter Five

A State of Balance

At times in life you may seek balance or what you might call stability. You may also feel you will have found this state of balance when you know where you stand and that things will not change. However, when you resist change you create a place for staleness rather than continued balance. It is the nature of life for change to take place, for without change there would be no life, just a snapshot of life at the point where change ceases to occur. While all around you moves forward and progresses, the point at which change is resisted very soon becomes a snapshot of the past until it becomes stale and stagnant and no longer relevant.

"But how" you might ask, "do I find a level of stability that helps me to feel safe?" I would answer that this word "balance" is often put into use where the word stability could just as easily be used. A definition of the word balance may offer words like poise, steadiness, and of course stability. However, it is interesting that if you check the word stability, while you will find words like steadiness, strength, and firmness, you will also find the word immovability.

While using a dictionary to discover what words really mean can be extremely helpful this is a perfect example of how it can also mislead. For if you consider a tightrope walker who needs perfect balance and stability you will be aware that he or she must also keep moving. Likewise, mountaineers must keep moving if they are to reach the peak of their mountain, and yet they too need perfect balance and stability to do so safely. What would happen to these two people if they reached a spot they felt was nicely comfortable and decided they would stay there and never move on? It is not difficult to see that they would both eventually fall to their death or die of starvation. I realise you may think this is an extreme example, but I have used it to remind you that to find balance is good and to find stability is also good; but these two states do not indicate that once you have found them you need go no further.

A state of balance enables you to explore your surroundings and reach out to those things that feel right for your progress or evolution. It enables you to do so without falling by the wayside. It prevents you from being drawn to the edge then further to a point that becomes dangerous.

Life on earth is largely considered to be an existence set within a state of duality. Everything seems to have an opposite, dark and light, cold and hot, happy and sad, angry and peaceful, strong and weak, and so on. However, I ask you to think a little further on this. Consider for a moment that all of these things are actually a part of the same concept. Cold is simply another place on a scale that measures heat. Darkness is another place on the scale that measures light and angry is just another place on the scale that measures peace.

All of these things we consider to be opposites are perhaps moving to a position on the scale where we can no longer perceive them. So we believe we are seeing a complete absence of, for instance, light or heat, strength or peace, when we are simply unable to register or measure what is taking place.

It is usually the case that with any of these things the area around the middle of the scale is the most comfortable for human beings to experience. Extremes can become most uncomfortable even dangerous or life threatening. So you will seek the comfortable place because it feels right. That place is your point of balance.

A helpful example of this is to picture a set of traditional weighing scales, a classic symbol for balance. You will usually find there is a strong steady base on which the scales are fixed, and yet the two sides of the scales used for weighing are able to freely swing up or down dependent upon where the weight is placed.

Visualise this image of the weighing scales swinging up and down until they find their place of perfect balance, where both sides of the scales are precisely matched, and you will see that there is a wonderful symmetry in balance. You could say that finding balance is like perfecting a dance sequence where you take a step or a number of steps and then pause. The pause will be perfectly in tune with the music you are dancing to, but then the music resumes and the dance continues until it reaches its natural and final conclusion.

Allow yourself to find this strong steady base in your life

while remembering that to have balance is not always to be static in one place, but to move evenly and healthily from one aspect of your life to another as you dance the path of your life to the music of your soul.

So if you feel that life has lost its sense of balance and you find yourself swinging out of control, remember, there is always time to pause before the next step, if it is important to do so, and to reweigh your options and check that the state of things is right for you, before resuming your dance in perfect balance.

Concerning Understanding - Chapter Six

When Choosing Directions

There are times when it may feel as if life is a constant search for direction, wondering what direction you should follow next and what would be the right choice for you to make so that you are faithful to your intended life path, which of course is also the path of your soul.

If you are looking for direction now or at any other time in your life, do not begin to agonise. For when you agonise you are following feelings of fear. These are usually fears that you may take the wrong direction, and fear of what will be the outcome if you do so. Such fears may have been passed on to you from a person or persons who are close to you and whose perspective on life you value or look up to. You therefore hope they will in turn value your choices and the directions you take.

Perhaps your fears have been passed on to you by someone who has a degree of control over what happens in your life, and therefore you would not wish to alienate them by taking a direction you fear they may disapprove of. You see that word "fear" is in there again.

On the other hand, your fears can stem from conditioning by your parents in childhood, for this is one of the strongest kinds of conditioning there is. When you are young and still learning about life and how to live it, your parents are usually the role model available to you.

Because they guide you and protect you, and because they provide for you, it is natural you will see them as wise, and knowing the right answers for any of your questions. For parents are important teachers in this life and teachers offer knowledge and information, so you may believe they also have the answers you seek when making decisions and choosing directions.

Parents are human like all other human beings, although if they have taken the time to study a subject they will no doubt have good knowledge of it and their help can be valuable. Teachers are also human, but they will have studied certain subjects in order to be able to teach others about them. They will not necessarily have the knowledge of everything you may feel you need guidance on.

So if you are seeking advice from others, there is the possibility that with the advice you are given you will also be given the fears present in those who advise you. To choose your directions in life from a base of fear around what may happen if you take another direction can be counterproductive.

You may remember when I spoke about solitude I cautioned you to check whether you were actually seeking solitude in a positive way or simply running away from something else. This same principle applies when you are choosing a direction in life. This is especially so when your choice of direction is made from a fear of what will happen if you make no choice at all.

If you are feeling forced into choosing a direction it may be wiser to resist such force and step backward even if it is only for a moment or two. This will allow you to take your bearings and be certain this is the direction you want and that feels right for you, not simply what you think will be approved of. When you have an important decision to make about what direction to take in your life it is important that the direction is right for you, and not one that may be right for someone else who is offering you advice.

When the need for such decisions arises it can be difficult, because all of the different things that have been said to you, or that you have read, watched, or listened to, may be spinning around in your thoughts. You will know if you have experienced this kind of indecision how the more you agonise the more you seem to keep on reaching a dead end in terms of finding a clear path forward.

Do not forget that I am always here within you, quietly ready to listen to your thoughts and your fears and help remind you to let go of those fears and turn to your own inner strength. Intuition can be a wonderful aid when choosing directions in life and it is too often ignored when it speaks; for it is the voice of the soul speaking and it will never mislead you. Remember your intuition will never stir fear in you, and if it seems you are receiving inner guidance that strikes fear into your heart, then dismiss that thought. The voice of your soul may, if it speaks clearly and you listen carefully, provide you with a sense of certainty but not of fear.

It is helpful if you are able to recognise which feelings of reservation come from a groundless fear or one passed on to you by someone else, rather than your own natural sense from within that this may not be the direction that will lead you where you wish to go. Just remember when you find yourself working from a base of fear, it does not matter whether that fear has been passed on to you by another or is simply a fear you have developed during the course of your life, it is unlikely to bring you to a satisfactory outcome.

If you are still beset by uncertainty, this is a good time to acknowledge the positive aspects of directions you may already have chosen in life – even if you feel there have also been negative aspects. Remember that both of these will serve you on the future path of your soul, even if the benefits are not immediately apparent.

When you are able to follow your own inner guidance and decide upon the direction you wish to take, you will then find increased certainty about the outcome of your chosen direction. It is possible when a change of direction is chosen in this way you may at some stage in the future reach a point where you feel it is no longer a direction that is right for you. As a result you may doubt your original choice and suspect that it was the wrong one, thus creating a nagging sense of doubt about your ability to make good choices.

If this occurs remember always that whatever direction is taken from a deep inner sense it will be the right one, for it will have provided you with some positive outcome or needed experience. This does not mean the direction will remain as the right one in perpetuity, only that it was right at the time of choosing.

If you find yourself feeling out of place or uncomfortable with a direction you are following then it is time for change. You and I both know the nature of this life is such that directions sometimes take a little time to change. If this direction you are following is a significant part of your life, then like a large ocean liner it will take some time to turn around and head in another direction. It may require some thought and some further consultation with your intuition.

You may find the experience of this direction will help you with your decision about a new direction. If it is important enough the direction can always be changed, even if it means there are sacrifices to be made in order to do so. You will know if you listen to my voice – your inner wisdom - that this is so.

If these words give you cause for concern about taking a wrong direction do not despair, for often when it is time to change direction again the opportunity to do so presents itself automatically. When this occurs you are likely to sense (even from only a moment of checking with your inner guidance) that this is an opportunity for change you should grasp with both hands.

So when it is time to choose a direction in life, whether it is a choice of job, home, relationship, or another kind of direction, simply make time to pause and consider each direction available to you one at a time. Then take note of how you feel about each one. Is it a sensation of lightness, or one of reservation?

My voice (your intuition) will guide you in the direction that is right for you.

Concerning Understanding - Chapter Seven

Growth Can Be Present in Many Ways

Where there is healthy life growth will take place; it is only the rate and direction of growth that may vary. Growth can be present in many ways. For instance it can be physical, or it can be a positive development of something less tangible. A friendship can grow, but so can hatred. So while growth is everywhere there are times when it is not for the good of planet earth or its inhabitants.

At birth human beings are tiny infants, unable to survive without care and support, but as life continues the size of the physical body grows and becomes more robust. However, as with many things in life the growth rate varies in terms of the various parts of the body, each one reaching maturity at its own rate, although the ears and nose sometimes appear to grow for the whole of this life.

All forms of life are comparatively small at birth, increasing in size until maturity is reached when the growth appears to stop. However, there is a continuing form of growth within each system which may expel old outworn cells and grow new ones. This maintains a healthy and continuing mature state of being in accordance with the natural life span.

There are of course other kinds of growth, some of which

will produce an increase in size and/or numbers of people, animals, buildings, towns, and countries. There may be growth of a type of manufactured item, and even of the number of factories that produce those items. Sometimes growth takes place in residential areas with greater numbers of houses being built, or in industrialisation. Some types of growth are not in size or numbers they are in strength, intelligence, wellbeing, and so on. The word growth is sometimes used to describe a diseased or destructive organism, but it can also describe the progress of something wonderful. So you can see that this word *growth* can have many meanings.

The kind of growth I wish to speak of here is the growing into full bloom of the human being, while again, at times, using nature as a metaphor. If you have read my words on seeds and roots you will know how important the background that creates growth is. You will also know that in order for healthy growth to take place the right conditions need to be in place.

In nature the different trees and flowers and all types of plant life have their own natural rate of growth and size at maturity. If they are in too small a space, their growth will be stunted and they will not grow to full size. They may even become distorted in their efforts to resist the limitation to their growth that they come up against. But there is another factor that is important in the process of growth and this is time. Each thing that grows will have its own natural and healthy period of time in which it reaches full bloom or full maturity. These two necessities for growth I have mentioned namely space and time, will also vary from life form to life form, just as the length of a life will vary from life form to life form.

You may also be aware that just as a space limitation will prevent healthy growth to full size, if the natural time for healthy growth is not given, or the growth rate is artificially accelerated, while growth will take place it will not be healthy growth. Where a life form of any kind is interfered with artificially its size may be reduced or made unnaturally large, and its length of life may also be reduced. Where animals are bred in an unnatural way their growth and length of life is often distorted and this applies to human beings too.

In order for a plant to grow there needs to be the right amount of time and space for the seed to break through the ground, and for the plant to spread its leaves and branches, and continue to grow at a healthy rate. There is artificial interference with growth in many areas of life in today's world, and the distortions and states of ill health that result from this interference are all around you.

In general, society now has a tendency to condition its members to strive for everything to be acquired more quickly, and this includes forms of human growth, and can relate to intelligence and skill, or those things often described as "success" and "beauty". But many of these forms of so called growth actually limit the potential of individuals, urging them to fit into a standardised norm of what *beauty* or *success* is. Sadly, this leaves the world with a lack of variety and the individuality and uniqueness that is natural to the human race. It is healthy to be aware of this conditioning and to resist the temptation to allow it to dictate how you look, feel, behave, and grow.

If you feel there is a need for growth in any area of your life, or you have a sense that growth is happening in some part of you, take the time to ascertain whether it feels healthy, comfortable, and natural. Then allow yourself the time to establish what kind of growth it is and what has stimulated its occurrence. Do not force the rate of growth, for it will become a distorted version of what it should naturally be.

This does not mean you cannot encourage growth and devote time and energy to its healthy progress. To do so is a form of nurturing, which I have already spoken of. It simply means you should follow your deeper feelings about how the process of growth feels, if you suspect that you or someone else is pushing it a little more than is healthy.

If it feels healthy then it will be healthy, but if you have any underlying feelings of discomfort around this rate of growth and how it is being achieved, then it is time to reconsider how you will continue to achieve growth that is healthy.

In this world of immediacy and instant gratification it is easy to lose heart when growth seems to be falling behind what is suggested to be the "normal" rate. However, the normal growth rate of one human being may not be the normal growth rate of another. The standardisation of such things has grown out of a need for power and control and the seeking of financial wealth.

When you can exercise patience and allow the natural time and space for your own growth and the growth of others even when the growth is not immediately apparent, the eventual maturity or blossoming will be healthier and more long lasting.

When the temptation to force growth begins to creep in to your decisions simply say to yourself: *"I will allow the growth in my life to progress at a pace that is natural to me, so that I may experience stronger healthier outcomes."*

Consider the length of time it takes an acorn to become a fully grown oak tree, and then one tree to become a forest. Remember always that when an unnatural rate of growth is forced, there may be a correspondingly fast pace of deterioration, or worse, for you may get an unstable, unhealthy, and even life threatening outcome.

Concerning Understanding - Chapter Eight

The Process of Flowering

When you look at a flower in bud you cannot see its beautiful shapes, colours, delicacy or flamboyance, for at this stage they are still tightly enclosed within that bud. This does not mean they are not there, waiting to open out and show themselves to the world. This will happen in good time, when their beauty can be contained within the bud no longer.

When you are considering how you perceive yourself, or perhaps more importantly how you may be perceived by others, you might not see that there could be parallels with a flower. Nevertheless, the same process is taking place in each human being on the planet as they grow through their childhood and adolescence into young adulthood, and then forward into full maturity.

I have used nature in a metaphorical way several times to help clarify the thoughts I have shared with you, and I wish to do so again. Even the subject of these particular thoughts concerns the process of flowering, which is probably something you associate with plant life.

Both humans and flowers begin as a seed, and, as I have already mentioned, they draw their nourishment from the earth or biological mother through their roots. Then eventually when they have grown sufficiently they break out into the world from the mother's womb or through the surface of the earth. However, even at this stage they are both extremely immature and fragile, and show little indication of what they may become when they are fully mature.

So let us look at how a flower grows from that tiny seed in the ground to what it will eventually become. When you first see the new shoots of the flower to be it will just be soft green growth, perhaps with some small leaves. But at this stage they are likely to be tightly furled together so that you cannot see any sign of a flower at all. Then the bud appears a firm round green shape, again with no indication of what is inside. Slowly the bud becomes larger and then softer and begins to unfold, until eventually you see the beautiful flower in full bloom. Each flower type will have its own range of colours and its own shape of bloom, as well as its own particular type of leaf. But what they all have in common is the beauty that unfolds from within. Some flowers are in full bloom by the end of winter and others by early spring. Yet others will bloom at times ranging from early through to late summer.

Now think of human beings. At the time of their birth they appear as small curled up little bundles of humanity. They rarely have hair and their muscles will not fully develop for quite a long time. But then they stretch out and begin to grow, each one uniquely different from the others.   Just as flowers have different shaped and coloured petals, human beings have different coloured hair, some of which will be absolutely straight, some wavy and yet others will produces masses of curls. Their eyes may be blue, grey, green or brown, and their skin may be white, brown, yellow, or black. Some human beings will be tall and others small; some will be rotund and others skinny. Some will have rounded features and others long straight angular features, and each of these is perfectly normal with its own special beauty.

So you see to compare the different kinds of human beings is a pointless exercise, unless you need to select someone to help you in a particular way and it is necessary to find someone who has the skills you will need. But remember my thoughts on the subject of nurturing; this will remind you that these human beings will grow so much more healthily to their full and beautiful flowering if they receive the necessary nurturing.

Finally, I want you to remember one of the most important aspects of human beauty. I speak here of inner beauty, of the character and personality, of the mind and the heart, in short, beauty of the soul or essence. This is the kind of beauty that is like the flower when it is held safely within the surrounding leaves of the bud. It is unseen until it comes to full flowering.

So when you suspect you have no inner beauty think of that bud and what is concealed inside away from the eyes of the world. Remember that it can only grow to full bloom if it is allowed the correct time and conditions. If you pull the bud open to discover the flower inside you will destroy it or distort it beyond its true shape.

You will recall that some flowers take longer than others

to reach full bloom, and human beings are no different. They are also no different insofar as they can be damaged if they are forced to open their inner beauty to the world before it is ready to emerge.

So when looking at another – or yourself – and thinking that you see no inner beauty, remember that the finest way to help that beauty emerge is to nurture it with love. In this way the miracle of unique magnificence within each one of you will be enabled to emerge and show its stunning beauty to the world, just like those beautiful flowers that are nurtured and allowed to unfold naturally from the bud.

Remember always to look for the beauty inside, and if at first you cannot see it then seek out and - if you are able to - nurture the potential that will become the fully flowering inner beauty shining out into the world.

Concerning Understanding - Chapter Nine

This is the Best Remembering

When you try to remember or bring something in to your conscious mind, it can be like searching for an item you know is somewhere nearby but you cannot find it. You realise you have stored details of its whereabouts in your sub-conscious mind for future reference; all you have to do is retrieve it.

However, at those times when you have stored it so safely and securely that it currently eludes, you this can prove difficult. It makes sense that if what you are seeking is important you will have stored it somewhere you felt it would be safe. When seeking an important item the problem is that you will probably have put it somewhere you believed it could not be found (accidentally or intentionally) by someone else. As a result you felt confident it would still be there when you next wished to access it. Unfortunately you managed to make it difficult for you to find also.

When you are eventually able to remember where the item is and you access it once again, whatever your reason for wishing to do so, you will know that this is such a good feeling, Yes? How frustrating then to find yourself searching for something and realising that you are not even sure what it is you are searching for. How can you possibly find it when you don't even know what it is? Perhaps you just have this powerful feeling that there is something you need to remember. But then not only are you unable to identify what you need to remember, you do not even know why you need to remember it.

This feeling I describe is not as unusual or illogical as you might think, even though it is not something you would tend to raise in everyday conversation. There can be several reasons for this. The first is that you might find it difficult to explain why you need to remember something so intangible; the other is that this is usually a profoundly personal feeling arising from the depths of your being.

When I shared with you my thoughts on the subject of searching, I referred to the simple searches you may well have carried out many times in your life. These are searches to remember the whereabouts of such mundane things as a garment to wear, needle and thread, or for your keys or your phone.

You will be aware from what I have already said that what I am describing here is *not* an attempt to remember the whereabouts of an item. It is the search for a remembering in and of itself; an effort to uncover some memory buried deep within you. This memory is so out of reach at the point you begin to try and recover it that you may feel it could be a memory of absolutely anything, and might be found absolutely anywhere in your store of memories. This may create in you a vague sense of unease, perhaps the kind of feeling you have when you sense you have forgotten to do something but cannot quite recall what it is you have forgotten.

This intangible elusive feeling of searching for a hidden memory is indeed a profound searching process. It is a stirring within you of the memory of your soul from which you were veiled at the time of your birth. This is the start of your conscious reconnection with me – your soul. It is the first sign that you are beginning to experience the memory of who you truly are.

This is the best remembering you can experience in this life. It is a glorious feeling of discovery and yet it is not discovery at all; it is simply a remembering of what you already know at the level of your soul about what we are here to experience together. You will find so many things that have been a puzzle or a mystery begin to make sense to you. A feeling of increased clarity is found and the inner calm I have already spoken of is achieved much more easily.

A realisation dawns that all of the striving and turmoil you often place upon yourself is unnecessary. You may realise the answers you seek will come to you if you simply allow them to, instead of putting up barriers of frustration and anxiety. When this process of remembering is triggered within you, there is often a tendency for your logical mind to step in and want to take over. It will wish to rationalise the feelings you are experiencing, to seek and find answers that make sense of it.

The "normal" thing that occurs to most human beings at a time like this is to begin looking around them and out into the wider world. This is like standing in a crowded place and checking out all of the people standing around you to the front and the side to reconnect with someone. When this is happening it can become frustrating because each person you check out is not the one you seek. Then eventually you realise they are standing right behind you. Your search has been in all of the wrong places, and you were widening your net of seeking rather than bringing it in closer to you.

Remembering is a gift, and you may think that gifts are always received from others. Often human beings feel the gifts they receive that cannot be explained logically are from angels. If this is happening for you at this or any other time, an important remembering is that your angelic gift is not from an angel outside of you, but from the angel within you.

Concerning Understanding - Chapter Ten

Reasons for Rejoicing

If you remove the first two letters from the word "rejoice", you are left with the first part of the word joy and the second part of the word voice. This describes well the meaning of the word. You will know from experience that when your heart is filled to capacity with joy there is an overwhelming desire to give voice to that joy. This is an act of rejoicing.

This life will always have its share of sadness, distress, and pain. However, in each and every life, no matter how rare or how swiftly fleeting, there will be a sense of joy. I have spoken of joy in my previous thoughts, and you will know that even in their darkest hour any individual will have in their memory at least one moment of this feeling.

Joy can be felt in many ways and for many reasons. It is usually experienced when something wonderful or happy occurs in your life. The discovery of a new relationship or friendship, receiving a gift that is exactly what you have always wanted; knowing you have achieved success in some way, or that you have finally got something good you thought you would never have. These are all things in life that are reasons to rejoice.

Now think of a time when you were experiencing a time

of such uncertainty or distress of some sort that you desperately wished for it all to be over with. Then suddenly you are released from your pain or agonising uncertainty. The feeling you experience at a time like this is often described as relief. However, if the distress or uncertainty was powerful then the relief will accordingly be powerful, and such times are often times of rejoicing. This kind of rejoicing is almost an inverted emotion, as it is about the removal of something unwanted from your life rather than the arrival of something you wanted.

When someone is so filled with joy that it overflows and pours out of them in an episode of rejoicing, it touches everyone around them. This often produces another kind of rejoicing namely rejoicing celebrated for another who has cause to rejoice.

There can be times in life when you feel like rejoicing but are aware that someone close to you is unhappy or in pain. Because of this you feel it would be insensitive to express your own joy. It is true there might be times when someone near to you is so very distressed, it would seem insensitive to rejoice in their presence. To do so might well highlight for them their own suffering and make it seem worse.

Still, if you were never to express your joy because someone else might not be as happy as you are, then you would in all likelihood never express your joy Such is life that there is always someone happy and someone else not too far away feeling sad or in pain.

You can only use your instincts or intuition in these matters, but it is well to remember, rejoicing is infectious and it can lift the spirits to see someone so happy that their joy overflows and becomes a state of rejoicing.

Think now of groups of people who have cause to rejoice, whether it is a crowd at a sports event cheering on their team and watching them succeed, or some major national or international event that is so positive it causes thousands upon thousands of people to rejoice. If you consider how much the energy in a room is lifted when just one person is rejoicing then imagine how significant an effect the rejoicing energy of thousands of people will have on the world around them.

Do not be afraid to express your joy, it is not childish or uncultured, it is honest and beautiful. When someone offers you something good, whether it is a material thing or a kindness, remember to express your joy and offer the energy of rejoicing on to them. It does not have to be enormous or world shattering, simply something that gives joy.

Be reminded also that you can help another or others to rejoice each and every day no matter how small the occasion that has given rise for rejoicing. Each experience of this kind increases the energy of rejoicing into in this world. So do your best as often as you possibly can to create reasons for rejoicing, however small the cause of your rejoicing is.

In the more affluent parts of the world there are many things that would once have been cause for rejoicing, and should perhaps still be so. A roof over your head, food in the cupboard, fresh clean water, a comfortable bed to sleep in and warm clothes to wear, are all things often taken for granted and not acknowledged as reasons to rejoice. Yet there are still many places in the world where rather than complaining when the rain clouds empty they will rejoice, and if their power supply is cut temporarily, they will rejoice when the supply of that power is restored.

To have the ability to rejoice in the smallest things fills the air around you with a delightful and uplifting energy for anyone who is in that sphere; how wonderful to be able to make others happy just by being happy and rejoicing in your happiness. So take the opportunity wherever possible to recognise those things worth rejoicing and share your rejoicing with others. You may find that it reminds those around you of things worthy of their rejoicing. If you can do this you will multiply this beautiful energy for the benefit of your fellow human beings.

It is an important lesson and one that will help me to progress along my path through this life with you, when you can find within your heart the ability to share without bitterness or envy, the rejoicing of others when your own heart is heavy or sad.

Concerning Understanding - Chapter Eleven

To Understand Humility

In looking at the meaning and practise of humility I wish first to speak of subservience, for both of these in action can give an impression of meekness and yet they are two different practises.

Subservience is usually seen between individuals who are generally considered to be of unequal importance. The subservient person will be the one who believes they are less important than the other and therefore there is a need for them to behave in a humble manner. Obedience and compliance are aspects of this behaviour, as is body language that clearly indicates this person considers they are inferior to the other.

There is also "false" subservience, which is when someone acts in a subservient way to create a false sense of importance in the other. This is usually carried out in order to fulfil some hidden agenda, for when subservience is offered there is a tendency to let down barriers, because there is no sense of threat from the seemingly subservient person in any way. The ego has been fed and they actually feel as important as the other person is allowing them to feel. This is not humility; it is not even true subservience, but pretence, and a means to an end.

True subservience is present when there is a genuine belief that you are in some way less than another person. This may relate to finance, culture, intellect or some other aspect of you both.

Subservience is by its very nature based in a form of fear. This is not the kind of fear you may first think of, such as the fear of some perceived threat or danger. It is simply a fear that you are not the equal of others. This form of fear comes from conditioning within society that places value on people for a number of reasons, none of which are based on the person having a right to be valued as a member of the human family.

Although compliance is sometimes described as humility, it is something else altogether. Humility is often mistakenly seen as meekness or compliance, but these things usually stem from feelings of inferiority or fear in the way genuine subservience is.

The humility I speak of here is not the kind of subservience that is often perceived as humility. While a person who behaves in a subservient way, that is to say submissive or meek toward others, may be described as *humble*, as I have already said subservience and humility are not one and the same.

While definitions of both subservience and humility will throw up the associated word "meek" that could be where the similarity ends. Where real subservience is based on a belief that another is superior to the self, humility is based on a belief that the other is neither superior nor inferior.

All individuals living on this planet are of equal value, no matter what role they play in life. This is a statement about the person not about their behaviour or the way they lead their lives. If I used the expression "he is only a humble road sweeper" most people would be able to relate to that, and will see someone performing this task as a lowly member of society. The mistake here is in describing what he does as being what he is.

Most people will know individuals in a lowly or *humble* position in society, who are kind, generous, respectful, hardworking, responsible and wise, or at the very least some of these aspects of character. They will also know individuals in exalted positions who are arrogant, cruel, insensitive, irresponsible, uncaring and unskilled in any way, or at the very least some of these aspects of character.

So you see exalted position or what is widely recognised as success, is often the result of having the good fortune to be in the right place at the right time, or having a particular talent that has created success of one kind or another. It does not indicate a superior human being, although the two can sometimes be found within the same person.

If you wish to understand humility it is first necessary to release your fears. These may be fears that you are not good enough, clever enough, rich enough or influential enough. They may be fears that what small security you have managed to accrue in life may be snatched away from you at any time, or that you have convinced the world you are more than you believe yourself to be. All of these fears influence your sense of value as a human being, and yet none of them are a true indicator of your value as a human being.

How you treat others, how you live your life, how honest and sincere you are, how kind and generous you are, how respectful and responsible you are, are all indicators of your value as a human being. So you see that no matter what your place in society is, this makes you of no more or less value as a human being.

To be polite or respectful is not subservience, to be considerate or tolerant is not subservience, nor is an unassuming manner subservience. Yet all of these are signs of humility. Those who lack humility are usually afraid to act with humility because they fear those qualities that come with humility may leave them vulnerable to being controlled or taken advantage of, or even of being considered lowly.

True humility comes from a place of peace and quiet confidence. It is a place that requires no puffing up of the chest or raising of the voice, no pushing or shoving to ensure you have the "best" position, or be "respected". The most important respect in this life is self-respect, and if you have that then humility will come automatically. Do not mistake feelings of self-importance for self-respect. Feelings of self-importance are usually a defence against a deep lack of self-respect. They have been put in place in the hope that if you act important, people will believe you are important. Thus you will believe you are worthy of self-respect. But this never works at a deeper level, for I am here in those deeper levels, and I know your every thought and emotion.

This does not mean because I know your deepest secrets that I do not respect you as a human being. It means that I do not require some sort of proof of your value as a human being. You are my human being and the vehicle with which I travel through this life. You are here so that I may have the experiences that will help me grow. I also know that some of those experiences will reduce your belief in yourself, or your respect for yourself, because you have not achieved what you hoped to achieve, or what someone else believed you should achieve.

So the story unfolds and human beings all across the planet acquire the belief they are less than they are, and abandon all of those things that would make them more. They continue to live with their fear, and therefore feel unable to act with humility in case it makes people believe they are humble and lowly.

When you open your heart to the world and allow yourself to see others for who they are deep down at the root of their being, not as the role they play in life, you will begin to understand that everyone is working from the same root source; everyone has within them a soul which they carry through this life. You will begin to understand that kindness and tolerance are what set your value as a human being, not arrogance or high status within society.

This is when you will find humility coming to you naturally, for you will have nothing to prove other than to prove who you are at that deeper level of your being with your practise of humility.

When you overcome your fear enough to practise humility, you are rising to higher levels of understanding than you have ever known. If you have no need to appear superior to another, this is when you have listened to me your soul and mastered humility, and with true humility comes great strength.

Concerning Understanding - Chapter Twelve

Another Kind of Renewal

Renewal is often seen as replacement of something you feel is no longer needed. You therefore dispose of the old and replace it with the new – simple, yes? This need so prevalent in modern society, to constantly replace material items you own, has been encouraged by those who wish to persuade you to continue buying more and more, not caring whether or not what you have is really in need of renewal. There are times when things wear out or break, or just become incompatible with other things you wish them to work with. When that is the case you have good reason for renewing with something more suitable, and more functional.

Unfortunately, developments in modern technology have shown that it is cheaper and often quicker or simpler to make things from some form of 'plastic'. Many of these 'plastic' items do not have a long life in terms of their usefulness. However, they do have a long life in terms of being non bio-degradable following their disposal when they are seen as no longer needed. Bio-degradation is nature's waste management and recycling system that breaks down anything natural and as a result keeps the planet clean and healthy.

Many of the man made materials being produced in the

world today cannot be dealt with by this natural process; and even the natural waste the human race produces is outstripping nature's ability to deal with it efficiently, and natural forms of renewal are fast becoming unsustainable.

Planet earth is becoming suffocated and poisoned by many of the plastic (and other) unnatural items presently in production and circulation in today's world; it is therefore vital for the human race to seriously consider when they are creating new materials how easily they can safely be disposed of (once they are no longer required or of use) so as not to harm this wonderful planet that is their home.

The vast hunger for renewal by human beings, in what is usually described as civilised society is creating an increasing problem, and while they believe they are getting rid of the old to make way for some kind of renewal, they are often simply moving things around. Eventually those things that are cast aside will come back to haunt the human race if they do not slow down their constant thirst for creating things that cannot be re-used, or safely disposed of.

In recent times there has been an increase in creating ways of recycling items no longer of use so that their component parts can be re-used to satisfy the materialism of today's world. However, while it is important for you and each and every other human being on the planet to be aware of what you accumulate and how planet friendly it is, this is just one type of renewal. It is one that requires some serious thinking about new ways of fulfilling the kind of constant thirst for renewal of material items, and what those material items need to be made of.

There is another kind of renewal I wish to speak of here, and that is human energy renewal. This really is a different kind of renewal and it is one that is continuing to take place in your life from the time you are born. This renewal takes place on a physical level where aspects of your physical being are undergoing cell renewal; as old cells die off new ones are created. This does not create piles of old unwanted cells for the process is all a part of nature and the natural flow.

You will see that I speak of human energy renewal and this is a more profound and less well-known process. You might have heard the expression "finding renewed energy", and this usually refers to someone having become physically exhausted and after resting for a while finding renewed energy to continue what they wish to do. This is also a naturally occurring form of renewal that does not create toxic waste for the planet to cope with.

Nevertheless, there is yet another kind of renewal taking place as you live your life and learn and grow. This is the constant renewal of your life energy that is vital in order for you to continue living. This is the kind of energy that is around you always and that you draw in naturally from the universe to sustain your healthy functioning. This renewal process is more complete, more thorough, and less wasteful.

There is an incalculable amount of energy the universe is made up of, some of it in solid material form that you see around you every day and, that as a physical being you are made of. When these physical parcels of energy have reached the end of their natural lifespan they die back into the earth, becoming a part of it, and in time they become nourishment for new physical natural life forms.

For this is how the universe has designed itself in the highest spirit of renewal, where nothing is wasted or destroyed; it is rejuvenated and given new life. This is the universe carrying out a level of recycling that those who care about the earth can only dream of.

Then there is the deeper, more spiritual renewal, a kind of renewal that can actually make you feel like a new person. As I have already mentioned, during the course of your life your physical body is the same one that is quietly maintaining its own natural form of renewal until it can do so no more. Spiritual renewal is a renewal of the essence of who you are; your character and emotions, your ability to love, give, care, and nurture. This is renewal of the process of your thoughts and feelings, not of your brain but of your mind.

In this form of renewal the mental and emotional energy that may have become weary or outdated, is returned to the source of its creation to be renewed, and you are filled with divine energy instantly ready for you to use.

You may wonder why spiritual energy should need to be renewed, or indeed why it can become outworn, outdated, or even wounded, but this is all a part of the path of the soul. Remember, I came here and incarnated within your physical aspect to complete my path through this life. I did so to gain experience from your life path as a human being. During the course of these various experiences, spiritual energy is there for you to draw upon to deal with the challenges you face and to help you overcome such challenges, so that you learn and grow from them rather than being overwhelmed.

It will therefore be of great value to you if you become aware of this process and are able to consciously draw to you new, fresh, spiritual energy to replace that which has become depleted and weary. For each time you consciously make your connection with the energies of the universe and call upon them for renewal of your spiritual energy, the old and tired energy will be returned to source for healing as the new energy fills your being.

If you knowingly accept your gift of new energy from the universe with gratitude for the renewal granted to you, and have the intention to release and renew, this is what will occur. So if you feel that your intangible spiritual energy, what is sometimes described as your spirit, is becoming weary, remember the universe has energy to spare., The amount of energy is not finite for it is in a constant process of circulation and renewal.

Remember too that this renewal is taking place in your life constantly, even when you are unaware of it. Ask yourself how much more powerful the process can be if you consciously participate in the miracle of renewal.

Concerning Understanding - Chapter Thirteen

Find Your Inner Counsellor

There will be times in life when you feel uncertain about what you should be doing next or how to deal with a situation. You may have a sense that somehow you have lost your direction or your connection with those people who matter to you or even that certain things are fading out of your life in spite of being important to you.

When this kind of situation becomes a part of your life experience it can relate to a number of different things. A friendship may become subject to conflict or misunderstanding. A relationship you believed was sound and stable may suddenly seem to be built on sand and drifting away from beneath your feet. Perhaps you have some confusion or some difficulty regarding whether to remain where you are or move home, or it may be your current job or even your whole career that is coming to a questionable stage.

Where something is significant in a person's life or has a feeling of being crucially important; and then what once seemed to be straightforward becomes confusing or contradictory, the help of a counsellor is often sought. There are many wise Counsellors in life who are trained to help in situations such as those I have mentioned. They actually work at being a good counsellor, and study the art of counselling. They work at it every day, and may build a career out of their counselling work.

There are also many people in this world who do not consider they are counsellors, who would not be described as counsellors, but who nevertheless are profoundly wise and offer good and valuable counsel to those who seek their advice. You may have a friend or friends who would fulfil the role of counsellor for you, if you reach a point in life where you feel the need to talk things through with someone else.

It is true to say that there are some professional counsellors who sadly lack the vital and innate skills needed in order to counsel others, in spite of having completed extensive training in their profession as a counsellor. On the other hand there are, as I have mentioned above, those who do not describe themselves as counsellors and do not counsel in a professional way; but who are excellent untrained counsellors with natural counselling skills.

If you reach a point where you believe a counsellor is what you need, ensure there is a rapport between you and your chosen counsellor. It is not even as simple as a counsellor being *good* at what they do or *bad* at what they do. For counselling to succeed there needs to be a subtle and yet powerful sense of connection and empathy that matches the vibration of the person they are counselling.

Compassion, empathy, and good sound common sense, are vital qualities to seek in a counsellor. Remember if you are seeking a counsellor to help you with some issue in your life, they are not there to tell you what to do or where to go. The most powerful role of a counsellor is simply to be there and be present as you find your own way to the answers you seek. For the truth of the matter is that the wisest and most profoundly powerful counsellor you can ever consult is your own inner wisdom. An external counsellor who excels at counselling will be someone who quietly helps you find that inner wisdom within you.

A good counsellor provides the quiet space away from the busy world around you, and the influence of others' opinions about what you should or should not do. In that quiet space you are able to consult your own deepest thoughts and emotions, without feeling any sense of guilt or fear about the outcome if you make this decision or that.

Consider then what is taking place when you consult a counsellor; you are retreating to a peaceful place away from outside noise and influence. As a result you are able to think clearly and without interruption or pressure, and you are able to be honest about how you feel and what you truly wish to do. You already have the answers to your questions. Even when you have many questions the answers are somewhere deep within you. A truly wise counsellor simply helps you look within to find those answers.

So when you feel you may be in need of counselling, remember to seek out a quiet space, listen carefully to the voice of your soul, and find your way past the surface whims that will draw your attention upon first asking.

When you consider answers that come to you in quiet contemplation you will know intuitively which of these are wisest. Have faith in this inner counsel that speaks to you when it has been sought in that truly peaceful and undisturbed state of tranquillity.

For the one who knows what is best in any situation of uncertainty or confusion is the wisdom of your own heart. I stress that this is not a recommendation to listen to the whims or passing fancies of others or even your own; it is to listen to the truth deep within you.

This is a counsellor of the highest order and if you allow yourself the space and quiet time to make your connection with it you will recognise its wisdom without uncertainty. This is when you find yourself saying "I know" and when asked how you know you cannot always explain.

But, the strength of that knowing is sufficient to clear away all doubt and uncertainty, when you find your inner counsellor.

Concerning Understanding - Chapter Fourteen

Passing Knowledge On

What do you perceive knowledge to be? Do you see it simply as information acquired or is it something more? You can gain knowledge throughout your life in many different ways. The most common of these is to acquire a basic understanding of how you function in human form, and your relationship to everyone and everything you come into contact with or experience.

This is knowledge you absorb moment by moment from the day you are born into this life. You will acquire much of this knowledge in a subconscious or automatic way, unaware that you are doing so. This is knowledge gained physically and emotionally, in addition to the mental form that is the most widely recognised way of increasing your knowledge on any given subject or aspect of life.

While academic or intellectual knowledge can be extremely valuable to you there are so many other kinds, which, rather than being intentionally studied for or worked at are gained through experience; through simply living your life.

If you begin by looking at your early life and are aware you had (or still have) what would generally be seen as "good parents" they will have given you the knowledge of how to be a good parent if you are blessed with children of your own.

If you move forward to the time when you attended school, you will recall this was a place dedicated to acquiring knowledge. Each day would be spent attending lessons, which are a very specific exercise in passing knowledge on. However, there will be many lessons from which you will have acquired knowledge, even though they were never included in your school curriculum. You will have learned how to interact with your fellow pupils and teachers, and how to manage time and be punctual for your lessons. You will have learned the reasons for discipline, and eventually the value of it. You will also have learned what to expect when you are undisciplined or rebellious and that if you disrespect others they will disrespect you in return.

In a paradoxical way when you fail to attend lessons, or fail to pay attention when knowledge is being offered to you in a lesson, you will still acquire knowledge. But, this will be an inverted form of knowledge, because it will give you an understanding of what you have missed and how it has placed you at a disadvantage to your fellow pupils on exam day, when you are required to show that you have in fact taken on board the knowledge you were offered.

We are speaking here of what is generally seen as a way of acquiring knowledge in this life. Every day that you live you are acquiring knowledge of one kind or another. Each experience is a form of knowledge gained. It may be the knowledge of how snow feels when it falls on you, or the knowledge of how warm you feel when in the sun for a period of time. Perhaps you will gain the knowledge that if you over indulge in a favourite food or treat, the result is not pleasure but pain. You may learn that if you put your hand into a fire it will be burned or if you jump from a great height you are unlikely to survive unscathed – if at all. Life is made up almost entirely of the acquisition of knowledge of one kind or another, much of it gained through experience.

When I discussed wisdom I clarified the difference between wisdom and knowledge. So perhaps what we should be asking here is what you should do with the knowledge you have gained. To return to my observation above, if you put your hand in a fire and it is burned you will have acquired the knowledge that fire burns. What you do with that knowledge is what can be of use to you; for if you avoid putting your hand into the fire again then you have turned your knowledge into wisdom.

I began by discussing the kind of knowledge most widely recognised as knowledge, and that is the academic or intellectual kind. This is because it is knowledge that is usually specialised, a kind of knowledge that is centred on a certain subject or aspect of life. As a result an in depth study of it will yield considerable knowledge on that subject. This has the benefit of helping you to understand much more fully the matter that has drawn your interest. You will therefore have the ability to be extremely good at anything related to that particular matter.

What is even better is that (if you study sufficiently) you will be able to then pass on to others the knowledge you have acquired. This has several points in its favour, one of these is that whenever knowledge is passed on from one person to another or from one generation to the next, the knowledge is preserved and will not be lost to the world.

The knowledge that exists in this world is part of a continuing process of growth, for amongst those who knowledge is passed on to there will always be those who explore that knowledge even further and as a result discover new knowledge not previously held. It is a profound mistake to assume at any time during the course of this life that you have all the knowledge you need and there is no more anyone can teach you. Knowledge can be acquired up to the time you draw your last breath in this body. You may ask of what use such knowledge would be if you are to die and take it to your grave? The answer to this is the physical aspect of you that goes to the grave to be returned to planet earth, is not the part of you that retains the knowledge.

I mentioned earlier that when the physical part of you can no longer function the body dies, but I, your soul, will return home together with your conscious aspect. This conscious aspect of you will be absorbed into me so we can continue the journey together. When the time is right, I as a soul will find a new physical human being into which I may incarnate to share the experiences of the life they live. The knowledge from all my previous incarnations, (including yours) will be preserved and carried forward, and so a part of you (a very essential part of you) will live on, and the knowledge you gained with that last breath will also be carried forward, together with all of the knowledge you gained in this lifetime.

Remember this and you may begin to realise the importance of knowledge and the acquiring of it in this life. Remember too that much of the knowledge you will gain as we walk the path of this life together, will be knowledge absorbed by you naturally from the experiences you have, and the interactions with the world around you and other beings you connect with. Much of this knowledge will equip us to travel our future life paths. However, do not forget my words on wisdom and the importance of turning your knowledge into wisdom, or what you might call a wise way of using the knowledge.

For the value of knowledge is not in the acquisition and retention of it but in the practical execution of it. There will be times this wise execution of your knowledge will enhance your life; at other times it will enhance the lives of others. If you are able to use your knowledge wisely enough to do both of these things you will have fulfilled your soul path with integrity and honour.

In Conclusion

You will see that the insights expressed in this book relate to many of your earthly life experiences, which, while you may not have realised it, are stepping stones on the path of your soul. Each one of these experiences contains a lesson that will move your soul along its chosen path, or indicate to you that you have made progress and reached another stage along the way.

While you may seek a spiritual advisor when you are searching for guidance in such matters, there are times when this is not practical or possible. The insights in this book are more powerful than might on first reading be apparent. They will be worth giving closer consideration to if you are seeking a deeper awareness of where you are on the path of your soul, and when dealing with the challenges you encounter along the way.

When you read these words you may have found yourself saying "I already knew that". This is of course true, for the insights offered here are not anything that is new to you, they are simply offered to remind you what you might have forgotten in the constant hubbub that surrounds the human condition.

This forgetfulness is in any event a part of the experience of your soul, and if you were always to remain totally aware of and connected to this wisdom at every point of your life, then there would be little for your soul to experience. You would simply remain calm, focussed, and totally filled with the wisdom of the universe; transcending all trauma, crisis, or confusion. In doing so you would have failed to participate in what your soul has come here to experience and learn from.

From the perspective of your soul you would know that all would be well, and that any problem you encounter along the way was simply a part of this human existence. You would understand further that at the end of this particular life your consciousness would return with your soul to the dimension from whence it came.

What you might describe as a human being, is from the perspective of this book the vehicle in which your soul completes its journey through life. However, in today's hectic world that deeper and more powerful level of your being can become buried under the daily demands made on you, and the seemingly endless need to conform to one standard or another in your every-day human life.

Opportunities to consider the issues that are deeply important to you, and to connect with that subtle level of your being which is always calm, clear, and focussed, are usually few and far between.

On those occasions when you make the time to *step off the roundabout of life* for a short while, and find yourself a quiet space in which to consider these issues, you may become aware that you have been looking at all the superficial factors you believe are relevant. However, as a result you may be missing what is really going on for you beneath the surface, and in doing so you will fail to make the connection between head and heart, body and soul. This is a vital connection if you are to be true to yourself and fairer to the significant others in your life.

It is my hope that this book will help you to look at yourself in a wider and deeper way, and as more than your tangible physical aspect. It is about the journey of your soul through life on earth, viewed through the experiences of your physicality that you are already aware of, but from the perspective of your soul.

It is also reminding you that your soul may well have journeyed through many previous lives and may yet journey through many more. This alone places many of those experiences that you may feel are overwhelming, into an entirely different perspective.

END

27226012R00241

Printed in Great Britain
by Amazon